THE PURITAN ETHIC IN UNITED STATES FOREIGN POLICY

Edited by
DAVID L. LARSON
University of New Hampshire

NEW PERSPECTIVES
IN
POLITICAL SCIENCE

D. VAN NOSTRAND COMPANY, INC.
PRINCETON, NEW JERSEY
TORONTO NEW YORK LONDON

D. VAN NOSTRAND COMPANY, INC.
120 Alexander St., Princeton, New Jersey
(*Principal Office*)
24 West 40 Street, New York 18, New York

D. VAN NOSTRAND COMPANY, LTD.
358, Kensington High Street, London, W.14, England

D. VAN NOSTRAND COMPANY (Canada), LTD.
25 Hollinger Road, Toronto 16, Canada

Publihed simultaneously in Canada by
D. VAN NOSTRAND COMPANY (Canada), LTD.

PRINTED IN THE UNITED STATES OF AMERICA

Contents

Part IV
THE PRACTICE

Notes on Contributors

DEAN ACHESON—"Ethics in International Relations Today" was an address delivered at Amherst College in December 1964. A graduate of both Yale and Harvard Law School and private secretary to Associate Justice Louis D. Brandeis, he entered the administration of Franklin D. Roosevelt as an assistant secretary of the Treasury and eventually rose to be Secretary of State from 1949 to 1953 under President Truman. He is now a senior partner of Covington and Burling, a Washington law firm with which he has been associated for over forty years. Among his publications are *A Democrat Looks at His Party, A Citizen Looks at Congress, Power and Diplomacy.*

EDWARD HALLETT CARR—"The Limitations of Realism" is from his book *The Twenty Years Crisis 1919-1939.* He is a former career officer in the British Foreign Service and is now a Fellow in Trinity College at Cambridge University. Among his more well known publications are: *Dostoyevsky, The Romantic Exiles, Karl Marx: A Study in Fanaticism, International Relations since the Peace Treaties, Michael Bakunin, Britain: A Study of Foreign Policy from Versailles to the Outbreak of the War, Conditions of Peace, Nationalism and After, The Soviet Impact on the Western World, Studies in Revolution, A History of Soviet Russia* (8 vols.), *German-Soviet Relations Between the Two World Wars 1919-1939, The New Society, What Is History?*

JOHN FOSTER DULLES—"Morals and Power" was an address to the National War College on June 16, 1953. A graduate of Princeton and George Washington University Law School, he was associated with the law firm of Sullivan and Cromwell from 1911 to 1949. The namesake and grandson of a former Secretary of State, he seemed motivated and marked for high office. In the bipartisan wave after World War II he held various responsible positions in the Department of State until 1953 when President Eisenhower named him Secretary of State, a post which he held until shortly before his death in 1959. Among his publications are *War, Peace and Change* and *War or Peace.*

J. WILLIAM FULBRIGHT—"Old Myths and New Realities" was delivered in the United States Senate on March 25, 1964. He is a former Rhodes Scholar and received his training in law which he taught for several years before he became president of the University of Arkansas. He was elected to Congress in 1943, has been a member of the Senate since 1945, and is now Chairman of the Committee on Foreign Relations. He has published three books: *Bridges East and West, Prospects for the West,* and *Old Myths and New Realities.*

LYNDON B. JOHNSON—"Pattern for Peace in Southeast Asia" was an address on April 7, 1965 at Johns Hopkins University. He was elected to Congress in 1937 and to the Senate in 1948. He became majority whip of the Senate in 1951 and majority leader in 1953. He was elected Vice President of the United States in 1960. Upon the assassination of President Kennedy in November 1963, he acceded to the Presidency. Among his publications are *My Hope for America* and *A Time for Action,* which are indicative of his idealism and pragmatism.

GEORGE F. KENNAN—"The Two Planes of International Reality" is from his book *Realities of American Foreign Policy*. He is a former career officer in the Foreign Service who wrote the famous article on containment in *Foreign Affairs* while he was still ambassador to the Soviet Union. Partially as a result of this article, Ambassador Kennan retired from the Foreign Service and became permanent professor in the Institute for Advanced Study at Princeton University. Among his better-known works are *American Diplomacy 1900-1950; Das Amerikanisch Russische Verhältnis; Russia Leaves the War; Decision to Intervene; Russia, the Atom and the West; Russia and the West Under Lenin and Stalin.*

JOHN F. KENNEDY—"Toward a Strategy of Peace" was a commencement address at American University, June 10, 1963. He was elected to Congress in 1947 and to the Senate in 1952. He was elected President in 1960. President Kennedy, as much as any president since Wilson, recognized the difficulties of the ideological problem presented by the "Puritan Ethic." He made some valiant efforts to inject greater realism in United States foreign policy before his untimely death. Among his publications are *Profiles in Courage, Why England Slept, A Nation of Immigrants, The Burden and the Glory, The Strategy of Peace.*

DAVID L. LARSON—"Objectivity, Propaganda, and the Puritan Ethic" is taken from an address delivered at the Naval War College. He graduated from Dartmouth College and received his graduate education at the Fletcher School of Law and Diplomacy, Tufts University, and has held positions at the Fletcher School, Tufts University, the Naval War College and is now associate professor of Political Science at the University of New Hampshire. His book, *The "Cuban Crisis" of 1962,* was published in 1964.

WALTER LIPPMANN—"The Eclipse of the Public Philosophy" is from his book *The Public Philosophy*. He is a nationally syndicated columnist and one of the deans of American journalism. He is one of the founders of *The New Republic* and an editor of the *United States in World Affairs* (*1931-33*) for the Council on Foreign Relations. Among Mr. Lippmann's better-known works are: *A Preface to Politics, The Stakes of Diplomacy, Public Opinion, The Method of Freedom, The New Imperative, The Good Society, Some Notes on War and Peace, U.S. Foreign Policy, The Cold War, The Public Philosophy, The Coming Test with Russia, Western Unity and the Common Market, The Essential Lippmann.*

HANS J. MORGENTHAU—"A Realist Theory of International Politics" is from his famous book *Politics Among Nations.* He is professor of Political Science and director of the Center for the Study of American Foreign and Military Policy at the University of Chicago. He is the author of numerous articles in the *American Political Science Review, The New York Times Magazine, Commentary* and other journals as well as several books including *Scientific Man vs. Power Politics, In Defense of the National Interest, Dilemmas of Politics,* and *The Purpose of American Politics.*

REINHOLD NIEBUHR—"The Morality of Nations" is from his book *Moral Man and Immoral Society.* He is one of the leading Protestant theologians of the twentieth century, professor emeritus of philosophy and religion at Union Theological Seminary, and research associate at the Institute of War and Peace Studies of Columbia University. Among his better-known works are: *Beyond Tragedy, The Children of Light and the Children of Darkness, Christian Realism and Political Problems, Faith and History, The Irony of American History, Man's Nature and His Communities, The Nature and Destiny of Man, The Structure of Nations and Empires, The World Crisis and American Responsibility.*

FRANKLIN D. ROOSEVELT—"The Arsenal of Democracy" was an address to a joint session of Congress on January 6, 1941 in support of the Lend-Lease Act. He was governor of New York and President of the United States from 1933 until his death in 1945. He had one of the most profound effects on United States foreign policies in that he successfully led the United States through World War II and into the United Nations. This, and the changing international power structure, brought the United States out of its isolationism of the late 1930's.

DEAN RUSK—"Some Fundamentals of American Policy" is from an address before the International Chamber of Commerce. He was a Rhodes Scholar, professor of government and dean at Mills College, and held various positions in the Department of State before he left to become president of the Rockefeller Foundation. In 1961 President Kennedy named him Secretary of State and he remained in that position under President Johnson.

KENNETH W. THOMPSON—"Judaeo-Christian Realism" is from his book on *Christian Ethics and the Dilemmas of Foreign Policy*. He is vice president of the Rockefeller Foundation in charge of the Social Sciences division. He is also the author of *Political Realism and the Crisis of World Politics* and the co-author of *Principles and Problems of International Politics, Man and Modern Society, Conflict and Cooperation Among Nations* and *Foreign Policies in a World of Change*. Dr. Thompson has also contributed numerous articles and reviews to the *American Political Science Review, World Politics, Review of Politics,* and the *Year Book of World Affairs*.

WOODROW WILSON—"A League for Peace" was an address before the United States Senate on January 22, 1917. He was a distinguished scholar and professor of government, jurisprudence and political economy, president of the American Political Science Association, president of Princeton University, and governor of New Jersey before becoming President of the United States. He was probably the closest embodiment of the "Puritan Ethic" and the personification of idealism in United States foreign policy. His greatest achievement was the Treaty of Paris, 1919, and his worst defeat was the Senate rejection of the Treaty and the League of Nations. He was also the author of a classical work on *Congressional Government*.

Introduction

ON DECEMBER 12, 1964 THE FOLLOWING EDITORIAL APPEARED IN *The New York Times* on "Morality and Realism" in response to a lecture (see Essay 8) delivered at Amherst College on December 9 by former Secretary of State Dean Acheson entitled "Ethics in International Relations Today":

> America's leading iconoclast, Dean Acheson, has addressed himself in his usual trenchant style to the subject of morality and ethics in American foreign policy. As might have been expected, he's agin' them—or appears to be, since he holds that no "Standards" exist for right and wrong in international relations.
>
> The crux of Mr. Acheson's argument is that it is "stupid"—almost "immoral"—for the United States to deny itself "the use and threat of force" to achieve its purposes. He points out that "our adversaries employ it, under handy excuses, whenever it seems useful."
>
> Unquestionably, many American involvements in foreign affairs have been soft-headed and many more have been injurious to the moral principles this country seeks to advance. But much of this misdirection is attributable to ambivalence in trying to wed expediency and morality—a marriage that usually serves neither.
>
> Moral restraints are a measure of realism, not of weakness, in a world dominated by nuclear weapons. Belligerence can be self-defeating if the rest of the world decides that the United States is reckless or ruthless in the use of its wealth and strength.

That such a partisan editorial could appear in such a respectable newspaper, is indicative of the confusion, ignorance and strength of the prevailing value system or ideology of the United States in regard to its international relations. However, criticism merely for the sake of criticism or as an end in itself, does not seem to be a particularly productive exercise unless some positive means of correcting the situation or some viable alternatives are offered. The inherent assumption in this approach is that there are usually causal and effectual relationships in human affairs. While it may be relatively easy to describe the effects or the manifestations of a situation, it is often quite difficult to ascertain the causes and even more difficult to assay a solution.

This collection of essays is offered as a critique, a commentary, and a possible remedy for some of the psychological or intellectual weaknesses of United States foreign policy. This is an admittedly ambitious exercise, but one in which we should all participate periodically if not continually. The focus of this symposium is the dilemma posed by the necessity for greater realism and the high content of idealism in United States foreign policy. The essays are representative rather than comprehensive and indicate the dimensions of the problem rather than a possible solution.

The documentary outline of the development and content of the "Puritan Ethic" are contained in the appendix and should provide a context within which to place the discussion. It should be noted, however, that the "Puritan Ethic," as I use the term, connotes some ideological and moral phenomena in United States foreign policy. It has some philosophical and historical content to be sure, but it is primarily designed to express the prevailing values and value system of what seems to be a majority of the American people in their view of the United States and its foreign policy. One of the more troublesome aspects of this value system is that compared to most other nation-states, particularly the Soviet Union, it is relatively inflexible.

The symposium is divided into four sections: the Problem, the Dialogue, the Debate, and the Practice. The section devoted to the problem attempts to identify and define the moral and ideological aspects of United States national policy. The section on the dialogue is limited to the theoretical aspects of the problem as seen by four eminent scholars and academicians. The section on the debate shifts to the institutional and governmental framework as seen by people from the legislative and executive branches of government. The last section covers the practice as viewed by the constitutional authority exercising its power and responsibility in protecting and projecting the national interests of the United States.

It would be tempting to write synoptic introductions to each essay, but this would probably be both unnecessary and presumptuous. The selections were made largely for their pertinency and clarity, and ought to stand on their own merits. Another reason for avoiding this editorial pitfall is the personal bias or prejudice of the editor. This bias is both the source of concern and the rationale for the symposium, and in all fairness to the reader ought to be set out.

The essence of my theory or approach to international relations is that there are few, if any, absolutes in the foreign policies of nation-states except possibly the continuity of conflict. This approach advocates the relativity of foreign policies not only to each other and the point of contention or concern, but also to time, place, circumstance, and the general context of international relations as a whole. This relativity also pertains to the national policy and power of each nation-state given the general absence of any effective rules of international law or international organization. As a result, the international community of nation-states is still largely as primitive and decentralized as it was back at the time of the Thirty Years' War. The Thirty Years' War witnessed the breakdown of a tenuous universalism in the Western world and the rise of nationalism based upon the newly emergent nation-state. Since that time each nation-state essentially has had to depend upon its own national power and policies to project its national interests and to protect its territorial integrity and political independence. This does not mean that international law and international organizations have had no beneficial effect. However, with nation-states maintaining the fiction of sovereign equality there has been little willingness to submit either to international law or to some form of supra-national organization. Unless and until some form of international government is formed with powers of legislation, adjudication, and enforcement adequate to govern the international society of nation-states, each nation-state is largely dependent upon its own power, resources and will to protect and project its national interests. If this is the case, then it would seem that the nation-state with the greatest power and the greatest responsibilities of world leadership ought to act upon more prudent principles and behave in a more realistic manner. Unless this is done reasonably soon, it is questionable if the United States will be able to maintain an effective foreign policy and help to develop some pragmatic alternative to anarchy and destruction.

We have outlived the old standards; we have burst,
like an overtight thong,
The ancient, outworn, Puritanic traditions of
Right and Wrong.

ROBERT W. SERVICE—"The Woman and the Angel," from *The Spell of the Yukon*

PART I

The Problem

1. Objectivity, Propaganda, and the Puritan Ethic*

by David L. Larson

AS AN OPENING PROPOSITION IN THIS DISCUSSION OF OBJECTIVITY, propaganda, and ideology in international relations, allow me to suggest that no one is objective when observing social phenomena. Everything we observe is distorted by the "mind's eye." The human mind directs the mind's eye to see what it wants to see. Everything we observe approximates reality according to our own preconceived notions, as well as our physical and mental well-being, and is not reality itself. Such devices as the camera, the computer, typing machines, and a variety of other mechanical devices reduce the interpretative and analytical aspects of observation and communication in the natural sciences to a manageable minimum. However, the social sciences are far different.

The social sciences deal with human phenomena and not physical phenomena *per se*. They include history, economics, philosophy, psychology, sociology, and politics, whereas the natural sciences include mathematics, physics, chemistry, botany, and biology. The humanities dealing with language, literature, music, and fine arts lie somewhere between social studies and natural sciences.

There have been some recent attempts to reduce the subjective aspects of the social studies and increase their objective aspects through the use of mass data, data processing, and statistics. The people practicing this art are called behavioralists. They believe that with large samples, good questions, and proper tabulation the behavior of people individually and collectively can be analyzed

* Lecture delivered at The Naval War College, Newport, Rhode Island, August 20, 1964.

and predicted. This may be so, but should not be translated into quasi-scientific laws as in the natural sciences. The behavioralist difficulty comes with the *human factor* or the subjective elements in the human equation. It is difficult, if not impossible, to predict human behavior with any assurance or finality, particularly if you assume that man is rational and possesses free will. Therefore, when dealing with human behavior we have to be particularly careful to be as objective as possible.

Objectivity then might be described as the attempt to collect, collate, evaluate, and interpret all the data relevant to a specific topic in the attempt to be as unbiased and unprejudiced as possible in approximating truth or reality. This is an extraordinarily complex process and requires considerable diligence and effort. As was suggested earlier, perfect objectivity and completeness is impossible. All we can reasonably expect of any person evaluating social phenomena is that he be as critical, as analytical, and as thorough as possible. As an old professor of mine was fond of saying, "Accept nothing and test everything." This is probably a good maxim to live by when seeking objectivity.

However, if after careful investigation there are some gaps in the analysis, it is perfectly acceptable to make some assumptions in the absence of positive information to the contrary. These assumptions may be stated in the forms of premises or hypotheses, but should be used with great discrimination and clearly stated as subjective determinations or value judgments. One reason to use assumptions is obviously to round out or complete a case. However, it naturally follows that the more assumptions made, the further the analysis is from reality and objectivity.

Objectivity is not only desirable in scholarship, but also is necessary to the average citizen in sorting out fact from fiction. Today's world has a large quantity of fact, but probably an even larger body of fiction. These fictions are particularly prevalent in the area of human behavior and especially politics. Every nation-state has its own system of values, interests and beliefs which tend to make it unique and distinct from every other nation-state. These value judgments are in a sense assumptions made by that particular society which provide some cohesive rationale for internal order as well as for external action. This is what we describe as an ideology.

Ideologies also have some other connotations which are worth mentioning by way of illustration to give some greater meaning and depth to the concept:

1. An ideology has been described as the cement which helps to hold a constitutional and institutional system together.
2. An ideology is sometimes used as a basis for the national interest in the positive sense and sometimes used as a rationalization of power or action(s) taken in the negative sense.
3. An ideology has also been described as giving purpose, meaning and direction to the national interest.

From these elaborations we can see that there is an apparently close relationship between an ideology and the national interest. This is a favorite argument of political scientists, as endless as the "chicken or egg" debate. We do not have time to analyze exhaustively the relationship of ideology to national interest, however intriguing that problem may be.

An ideology is a highly subjective collection of values, interests and beliefs, suited to the tastes and needs of a particular nation-state. If the ideology is firmly implanted and generally supported by the people there are usually few difficulties in maintaining this prevailing value system at home. However, as soon as an ideology is projected into another nation-state, it becomes propaganda. Propaganda, in this sense, is the attempt to spread a particular national ideology from one nation-state to another and in most instances around the world. The conviction that a particular nation-state has the ultimate truth embedded in its values, interests, and beliefs led to the phenomenon of "nationalistic universalism" described by Professor Hans Morgenthau. This, rather simply, is the projection of the national ideology around the world. We see this in the universal communism espoused by the Soviet Union and the universal constitutional democracy espoused by the United States. These are not the only national ideologies aiming at universal acceptance. Virtually every ideology has universal aspirations in order to rationalize and justify its acceptance in the nation-state.

It would be virtually impossible to catalog or describe all the national ideologies of the world. Suffice it to say that the ideology, both internally and externally, is usually the prerogative of the responsible authority. This is to say that Maoism is essentially what Mao says it is, Titoism is essentially what Tito says it is, Gaullism is essentially what de Gaulle says it is and so forth. Thus, in a totalitarian regime or a nation-state with a strong national consensus, it is relatively easy to define the national ideology. However, moving from the monolithic unity of the extreme right and left to the pluralism of the center, it is far more difficult to determine, much less define, the national ideology. This is acutely the case in a pluralistic society such as the United States, and is part of each great quadrennial debate.

However, one duty of the responsible citizen is to try to understand his own national ideology before evaluating others not only in the interests of objectivity but also of good citizenship. This is a most difficult task because to try to analyze one's own national character and ideology is somewhat like trying to psychoanalyze oneself. At best, auto-analysis is a highly subjective and a rather risky business, but one in which we should all engage at one time or another. Probably the clearest and most objective analyses of American national character, ideologies, and institutions are by outsiders such as: Alexis de Tocqueville (French—1834), James Bryce (British—1891), and Denis Brogan (British—1944).

American national character and ideology, like all national characters and ideologies, are largely products of historical traditions and contemporary experiences. The American historical tradition is rather long, going back through London, Paris, Geneva, Rome, Athens, and Jerusalem. The contemporary experience is short by the standards of history, and is usually traced to the primitive Calvinist movement which settled at Plymouth on Massachusetts Bay.

These primitive Calvinists, or fundamentalist Puritans, brought with them a unique system of government or "civill body politick." The Mayflower Compact was not quite the same as Locke's "original compact" or Rousseau's "social contract," which were developed much later, but certainly contained some of the principles of egalitarianism and popular sovereignty developed the following century. However, the most prevailing characteristic of the Puritan was his primitive fundamentalism. The will of God was to be found in the literal interpretation and application of the Bible. No clergy or ecclesiastical hierarchy was necessary to reveal the ultimate truth. It was the duty and responsibility of the Pilgrims to purify Christian practices and return to the "word of God" for the salvation of mankind, no matter how sinful it might be.

This Puritanism has helped to establish a rather strong tradition of fundamentalism in American national character, which is certainly still prevalent. This fundamentalism is in rather distinct contrast to the pragmatism of the British, the eclecticism of the Indian, the messianism of the Russian and the absolutism of the German. The original fundamentalism has long since been modified and enlarged, but it is still rather extraordinary to recall that in 1925 William Jennings Bryan and Clarence Darrow debated Biblical fundamentalism and Darwinian evolution.

The Puritan heritage, nonetheless, gave rise to a rather peculiar ideological phenomenon known as the "Puritan Ethic." This is a rather complex concept as it has evolved to the present, but in its simplest statement the essence seems to be that "Somehow, some way right will prevail over might." Particularly, if you place unbounding faith in the wisdom and will of God as revealed through the Scriptures, or "In God We Trust."

The foremost characteristic of the Puritan Ethic is a distrust of power—whatever the source and locus. Americans have traditionally been suspicious of the exercise of power whether personal, national, or international. This dislike of power may be traced to what they felt was the abuse of power and the conception of responsibility by both the ecclesiastical and secular authorities in England and on the Continent. It is also significant that the Plymouth Company was chartered and settled in the midst of the Reformation and Thirty Years War. The Mayflower Compact illustrates the dichotomy of the struggle between ecclesiastical and secular authority and the attempt to develop some third alternative where the Puritans "by these presents, solemnly and mutually, in the presence of God and of one another, covenant and combine ourselves together into a civill body politick, for our better ordering and preservation and furtherance of the ends aforesaid . . ." [1]

This distrust of uncontrolled power has led to several interesting manifestations. On the personal level it developed into a rather strong egalitarianism and rugged individualism. On the national level we see it woven into the Constitution of 1789 with its elaborate system of checks and balances, whereby none of the three major branches of government could be described as fully sovereign or absolute. Indeed, the essence of constitutional democracy seems to be the restraint and regulation of power. The more traditional concept of the head of state as the locus and source of sovereignty, based largely upon the divine right of kings and being unrestricted and absolute—is certainly not true of the President of the United States. Congress has the Constitutional power to lay and collect taxes, provide for the common defense, regulate commerce, support and maintain the Army and Navy as well as to make all laws. The Senate in particular expresses its advice and consent on treaties and appointments. Even with the rapid rise of executive initiative in foreign policy through such devices as the Executive Agreement to bypass the Senate, the President is still relatively restrained or restricted in his foreign policy, although he does exercise great powers. In fact, the broader statement might be made that American domestic policy and domestic politics exert an excessive influence on the direction and content of American foreign policy and the mix of international politics.

On the international level the characteristic American distrust and suspicion of power assumes even larger proportions. The basic dislike or misunderstanding of power and international politics by the American people has filled U.S. foreign policy, as Walter Lippmann says, with "stereotyped prejudices and sacred cows and wishful conceptions" and that the basic failure of American conceptual thinking on foreign policy is "to admit, to take as the premise of our thinking, the fact that rivalry and strife and conflict among states, communities and factions are the normal condition of mankind." [2]

The Puritan Ethic and American national character take the view that the struggle for power, prestige and prosperity are not the natural state of things and that war is somehow immoral, unjust, and illegal. Shortly after the emergence of the United States of America as a constitutional democracy of sorts in 1789, we can see the acceptance and espousal of international law as a means of resolving international conflicts through arbitration, adjudication, and mediation. In fact, this reliance on international law became one of the predominant characteristics of U.S. foreign policy down to World War I when dealing with stronger powers, but was not so much the case when dealing with weaker powers. The great American philosopher William James described this reliance on international law as a moral equivalent for war. Or again, "Somehow, some way right will prevail over might."

The outbreak of the French Revolution in 1789 evoked a response of considerable sympathy in the United States on ideological grounds as vindication of the American Revolution and verification of the rightness of the Puritan Ethic. However, when Great Britain began to take restrictive countermeasures against the French, the United States was placed in an awkward dilemma between the idealism of the ideology and the realism of the national interest. After considerable internal stress and some strain which resulted in Thomas Jefferson leaving as Secretary of State, the United States developed a new synthesis out of the conflict between the thesis of idealism and the antithesis of realism. This new policy was officially described as one of "neutrality" or "non-involvement." This approach had its roots in the Treaty Plan of 1784 and was also manifested in such declarations as "freedom of the seas," "neutral ships make neutral goods except for contraband of war," and so on. This was really more of an accommodation by an essentially weak commercial nation-state with the realities of international politics and an attempt to avoid being caught in the struggles of the Great Powers. On April 22, 1793 President Washington signed the Proclamation of Neutrality, which was both an internal measure to restrain Francophile sympathies and an external measure to reassure the British. This was indeed a difficult time for the United States, but as Professor Bemis points out, the secret of Washington's diplomacy was in the notion that Europe's distress became America's advantage. This was one of the bedrocks of United States foreign policy, with a few minor exceptions, down to World War I.

The prime manifestations of the United States desire to remain disengaged from European power struggles as well as to increase internal power and hegemony in the Western Hemisphere are Washington's Farewell Address and the Monroe Doctrine. A few excerpts in this connection are illustrative:

1. Washington's Farewell Address

> Observe good faith and justice toward all nations. Cultivate peace and harmony with all. Religion and morality enjoin this conduct. . . . The great rule of conduct in regard to foreign nations is, in extending our commercial relations to have as little political connection as possible. So far as we have already formed

> engagements let them be fulfilled with perfect good faith. Here let us stop. . . .
>
> Europe has a set of primary interests which to us have none or a very remote relation. Hence she must be engaged in frequent controversies, the causes of which are essentially foreign to our concerns. Hence, therefore, it must be unwise in us to implicate ourselves by artificial ties in the ordinary vicissitudes of her politics as the ordinary combinations and collisions of her friendships or enmities. . . .
>
> Our detached and distant situation invites and enables us to pursue a different course.[3]
>
> 2. Monroe Doctrine
>
> a. . . . That the American continents by the free and independent condition which they have assumed and maintain are henceforth not to be considered as subjects for future colonization by any European powers . . .
>
> b. In the wars of the European powers in matters relating to themselves we have never taken any part, nor does it comport with our policy to do so.
>
> c. With existing colonies or dependencies of any European power we have not interfered and shall not interfere.
>
> d. It is impossible that the allied powers should extend their political system to any portion of either continent without endangering our peace and happiness.[4]

In this connection it is difficult to escape the analogy between the "neutrality" and "non-involvement" of the United States in its first century and a quarter of diplomacy, and the contemporary "neutralism" and "non-alignment" of many Afro-Asian nations. Europe's distress and the *Pax Britannia* of the 19th century were certainly to America's advantage, and the bipolar power struggle of today with its "balance of terror" seems to have been to the advantage of the neutralists. The interesting paradox in this analogy is that the United States with its Puritan Ethic and moralistic condemnation of war, criticizes the latter-day "neutralists" and "non-aligners" as immoral.

This leads us into another major characteristic of the Puritan Ethic and American national character: moralism. As Cecil Crabb says, "Moralism is not the same as morality . . . Morality has to do with the substance of behavior. It is conduct in accordance with a pre-determined code of behavior, and throughout Christendom this refers to behavior sanctioned by the Christian faith. Moralism [in the political sense] is concerned with [the] appearances, with the concepts and language employed in foreign relations, with the symbols used, and with the way that ends and means are visualized and expressed publicly." [5] From this definition we can occasionally see the attempts of the United States to extend its value system based largely upon the Puritan Ethic to other civilizations and cultures with different and differing value systems. While moralistic behavior in the foreign policy of the United States may seem high-minded at home, it often seems high-handed abroad.

This moralistic attitude on the part of the United States has been expressed in several forms and slogans such as "Manifest Destiny," "no compromise with principle," "make the world safe for democracy," "self-determination," "atheistic communism," "unconditional surrender," "total victory," and "we will never commit aggression."

Manifest Destiny is a rationalization on the part of the United States for expanding across the continent and eventually across the Pacific Ocean. Americans made a clear distinction between what they called "expansionism" and crass, immoral, European "imperialism." It is rather interesting that the strongest condemnation of Manifest Destiny was expressed by Robert C. Winthrop, Congressman from Massachusetts, the home as it were, of the Puritan Ethic in the late 1840's. In his words Manifest Destiny was opening:

> . . . a new chapter in the law of nations or rather in the special laws of our own country, for I suppose the right of a manifest destiny to spread will not be admitted to exist in any other nation except the universal Yankee nation.[6]

The height of Manifest Destiny was reached in 1900 in the debate over whether to annex the Philippines. Senator Albert Beveridge from the good fundamentalist state of Indiana was the leading spokesman for annexation. His speech on Manifest Destiny is interesting from several standpoints: (a) the rationalization of imperialism, (b) the invocation of the Puritan Ethic, and (c) the messianic mission of the United States to save the world:

> Mr. President, the times call for candor. The Philippines are ours forever, territory belonging to the United States as the Constitution calls them. And just beyond the Philippines are China's

> illimitable markets. We will not retreat from either. We will not repudiate our duty in the archipelago. We will not abandon our opportunity in the Orient. We will not renounce our part in the mission of our race, trustee under God, of the civilization of the world. And we will move forward to our work, not howling our regrets like slaves whipped to their burdens, but with gratitude for a task worthy of our strength, and thanksgiving to Almighty God that He marked us as His chosen people, henceforth to lead in the regeneration of the world.[7]

Another aspect of moralism is the rather negative sounding phrase of "no compromise with principle." This is partially an outgrowth of Puritan fundamentalism with such corollaries as "right is right and wrong is wrong." This aspect of moralism and its relatively inflexible dicta has certain overtones of the Continental concept of compromise as capitulation, and not the Anglo-Saxon concept of compromise as a mutual bargain. Compromise has also acquired the connotation of "appeasement" in the fundamentalist lexicon of Puritanism. Appeasement in turn has acquired an intrinsically immoral connotation, and we can see some historical antecedents going back to the XYZ affair with France and the treaties with the Barbary Pirates. The cry then was, "Millions for defense, not a penny for tribute." The depth of appeasement was reached in 1938 at Munich. Although the United States was seized with a fit of pseudo-neutrality, it roundly condemned the dismemberment of Czechoslovakia as "immoral" and a "sell-out." The subsequent events leading to World War II seemed to confirm this conviction and became an important element in American national character.

Appeasement is really a rather good word in and of itself and literally means to bring a state of peace, to pacify, to calm—to win an enemy or opponent over by displaying a willingness to be just and fair. Appeasement then in the literal sense implies more of an attitude toward negotiation rather than the giving away of something. However, appeasement retains the connotations of capitulation and duplicity. These concepts have clearly become identified in the public mind with diplomacy as somehow immoral and associated with "secret deals" and "sell-outs." This Puritanical suspicion of diplomacy has traditionally been supported by the relative isolation of the United States and the lack of necessity to negotiate and compromise continually. This suspicion of diplomacy and diplomats was further heightened by nineteenth century practices of bribery and secret agreements. The leading example of this was the Secret Treaty of London in 1915 which essentially bought off Italy to come in on the side of the Allied and Associated Powers and caused a feeling of revulsion and guilt by association in the United States. The result, of course, was the first of President Wilson's Fourteen Points:

> Open covenants of peace, openly arrived at, after which there shall be no private international understandings of any kind, but diplomacy shall proceed always frankly and in the public view.[8]

It is rather interesting to see the Puritanical word "covenant" used here and again in the Covenant of the League of Nations. It was almost as though the United States were launched on a Great Crusade not only to "make the world safe for democracy" but also to spread the Puritan Ethic.

A fundamental tenet of the Puritan Ethic is the dignity and equality of all men. This derives from the concept that man is anthropomorphic and thereby somewhat divine, and that all men were equal before God. This rather naturally led to popular sovereignty, mass nationalism, and then self-determination. Almost half of Wilson's Fourteen Points were directly or indirectly associated with the concept of self-determination. Auto-determination may be somewhat of a fiction in practice, but to say that "when in the course of human events, it becomes necessary for one people to dissolve the political bonds which have connected them with another," has had no effect or impact on international relations, would probably be the understatement of the last two centuries.

The moralism of the United States has led to the fundamentalist espousal of principles, but has also led to the assumption of some rather unrealistic postures such as: unconditional surrender, total victory, no appeasement, and universal democracy. These postures have been encouraged by the self-delusions of omnipotence and omniscience. These delusions of power and truth are clearly rooted in the fundamentalist absolutism of the Puritan Ethic. Unfortunately these delusions have given rise to the general belief in "instantaneous foreign policy"—or "no sooner said than done." As

Denis Brogan, the astute British observer remarked, "The illusion of American omnipotence" has given rise to the belief that "any situation which distresses or endangers the United States can only exist because some Americans have been fools or knaves." Brogan goes on to say that Americans have yet to learn that "the world cannot be altered overnight by a speech or a platform." [9]

Another aspect of the Puritan Ethic and American national character is the peculiar phenomenon of isolationism. This isolationism, of course, was partially a conscious desire to be rid of Europe's religious, political, and economic troubles; but it was also partially derived from geographic separation and absorption in creating and expanding a new civilization. However, traditional American isolationism was not a retreat into itself, like Japan from 1604 to 1854, but was a cautious participation in the economic and political aspects of international politics *as its power permitted.* And therein lies the key. Again, except for the 1920's and 1930's, American isolationism was almost a direct function of its economic and political power: As power increased, "isolationism" decreased. However, at no time was the United States isolated from the rest of the world, economically, politically, or ideologically: the United States had the second largest commercial fleet in the world until 1862, it purchased Louisiana, enunciated the Monroe Doctrine, annexed Texas, fought Mexico, expanded across a continent, and acquired an empire—this could hardly be described as apolitical. Ideologically, the United States helped to finance and support virtually every nationalist revolution from Argentina to Cuba and from Greece to Norway. This was not exactly isolationism! The cry of isolation seems to be more an anguished rationalization for the lack of adequate or commensurate power, which was alien to the Puritan Ethic, rather than non-participation. On the contrary, a substantial case can be made for an activist, positive diplomacy on the part of the United States in the nineteenth century.

However, the myth of isolationism tended to give rise to the predominance of domestic policy over foreign policy. This was also fostered by the need for internal development and the creation of a new society. In 1839, John Louis O'Sullivan wrote an article entitled "The Great Nation of Futurity." A short excerpt from this selection is illustrative:

> Our national birth was the beginning of a new history, the formation and progress of an untried political system, which separates us from the past and connects us with the future only; so far as regards the entire development of the rights of man, in moral, political and national life, we may confidently assume that our country is destined to be the great nation of futurity.[10]

This passage also helps to illustrate further the messianic vision of the Puritan Ethic and the need to develop and secure the "New Society" at home before engaging in an active foreign policy. This sounds strangely reminiscent of the Stalin-Trotsky argument of 1923-24 as well as the statements of contemporary neutralists and the advocates of the "Great Society."

The last large ingredient of the Puritan Ethic is optimism and confidence. Optimism bred out of the concept that "somehow, some way right will prevail over might," and confidence in the innate and ultimate superiority of the American system and the American way of life. This optimism and confidence have never really been seriously challenged from without, although it was attacked from within during the Civil War. With the possible exception of the War of 1812, the United States has not fought a major international war on its national territory nor has it been defeated. This unparalleled success may be partially attributed to prudence, but it has also tended to increase the national confidence and create an aura of invincibility, to strengthen the feeling of omnipotence and the attitude of omniscience.

This optimism and confidence are also strengthened by the overwhelming success of the American economy, but has seemingly become somewhat distorted into a sense of superiority. However, this sense of superiority is somewhat modified by the traditional humanitarianism and philanthropic attitude of the American people, which is also part of the Puritan Ethic. Nonetheless, the residue remains.

The Puritan Ethic, then, is indeed a complex phenomenon with a "strange" admixture of a number of idealistic ingredients. Cecil Crabb probably has one of the most succinct statements on the Puritan Ethic in foreign policy as seen from abroad:

> To foreigners, Americans must resemble nothing so much as the sombre Puritan: motivated by high ideals, austere, (and) un-

> shakeable in his conviction that goodness will triumph in the end—but at the same time impatient with wrongdoing, sanctimonious and at times, insufferably self-righteous.[11]

The crux of the ideological problem confronting American foreign policy today seems to be that the United States has allowed itself to become intellectually isolated from the realities of international politics. As Dean Rusk has said, "We can no longer secure the blessings of liberty to ourselves and our posterity by isolating our nation, our continent, or our hemisphere from the rest of the world." [12] Exactly what is meant or implied by this proposition? This is difficult to describe in a few words and might better be defined by some related propositions.

First, it has been suggested that this intellectual isolation is a relatively new phenomenon. This would seem to be the case when one views the diplomatic history of the United States for the past one hundred and eighty years or so.[13] Up until the close of World War I, the United States took an active and vital interest in the the economic and political affairs of the world with a constant view toward furthering its own national interests. The tremendous territorial expansion is but one example, the constant pressure for freedom of the seas is another example, and, of course, the Monroe Doctrine is the classic example. The participation of the United States in World Wars I and II was really in defense of the national interest and the maintenance of some balance of power in Europe, and not so much an idealistic crusade to "make the world safe for democracy" or to "save democracy"—although participation was sold to the American people largely upon these bases.

After the failure of the Great Crusade to win the fruits of victory at Paris in 1919 or in Congress in 1920, the American people seemed to recoil psychologically from the brutality of the war and the Machiavellian machinations of Lloyd George, Clemenceau, and Orlando. Those Europeans were somehow immoral, ungrateful wretches and the United States should not have allowed them to "drag us into the war." The attempt to find a scapegoat and assess the moral and legal guilt for the war upon the Germans found expression in Article 231 of The Treaty of Versailles and after World War II in the Nuremberg and Tokyo War Crimes Trials.

The depths of the psychological withdrawal of the American people seemed to be manifested in the Smoot-Hawley Tariff of

1930, the Stimson Doctrine on the non-recognition of territory acquired by illegal means, and the investigation of the Nye Committee which sought to attach the blame for United States participation in World War I upon the financial and munitions industries. As the international situation steadily deteriorated in China, Ethiopia, Spain, Czechoslovakia, Austria and finally Poland and France—the United States attempted to divorce itself from the realities of international politics by passing a series of four meaningless neutrality acts and the establishment of "America First Committees." The American people were embroiled in what they thought was their own economic collapse and the vast majority could not quite comprehend what was going on overseas and did not really make an effort to understand. It took the dramatic blow struck at Pearl Harbor to jolt them back to reality, but typically the American people tended to overreact. As Hugh Gaitskell once said, "You Americans have the tendency to define things in terms of black or white and not in shades of gray." [14]

At the conclusion of World War II the United States emerged relatively unscathed and by far the most powerful nation in the world. While the cry was to "get the boys back home for Christmas" and return to some kind of normalcy, there was a great qualitative difference in the policy of involvement in world affairs and a commitment to world leadership than after World War I. This time the United States again became the prime sponsor of a great international organization, but with the advance support of Congress in the Fulbright and Connally Resolutions. The United Nations came into being to succeed the League of Nations as the guarantor of peace through the principle of collective security. The unanimity of the Five Great Powers in supporting the Charter was one of the fallacious assumptions of the system. The Soviet "veto" soon stalled any effective and decisive action on the part of the Security Council and the United Nations as a whole. The Soviet pressures in Greece, Turkey, Iran, Korea, and Western Europe were such that the United States had to find some solution outside the United Nations or retreat again into isolationism. The measure of increasing awareness of the responsibilities of power and world leadership can be found in several statesmanlike acts which were in distinct contrast to the 1920's and 1930's: the United Nations Refugee and Rehabilitation Administration, the British Loan, the

Azerbaijan Resolution, the Truman Doctrine, the Marshall Plan, the North Atlantic Treaty Organization, and of course the commitment in Korea. The realization that a Cold War was on with the concomitant realization that it must be met, *seemed* to be accepted by most Americans.

However, by the end of the Korean Conflict the American people seemingly had drifted slowly back into their world of unreality. It may be that the indecisiveness of the Korean Conflict was a factor, but it was more probably a complex of several other factors created by the ambiguities and tensions of the Cold War. When nations which receive large amounts of aid and assistance return little but ingratitude and the request for more, Americans tend to become confused. When other nations expropriate or nationalize American private property and assets abroad, concern becomes mixed with confusion. When nations turn left or stay in dead center after achieving independence, Americans become annoyed. When a cold war or a hot war cannot be won but just seems to drag on interminably, Americans become frustrated or indifferent. When a communist regime is set up ninety miles off the coast of Florida, virtual panic and trauma set in. When the world lives in an age of nuclear warfare, there seems to be an unwillingness or an inability to understand and comprehend the magnitude of the problem. Also, the complexities of a bipolar, tripolar, quadripolar, or polypolar world almost seem to be too much. Things just are not defined in black and white terms and the moral standards of the United Nations system are not being adhered to.

Second, this intellectual isolation is partially caused by the mental lethargy of the American people. Like their Anglo-Saxon cousins across the Atlantic, Americans are not particularly deep thinkers and do not try to fathom the inner motivations or causes of national action and behavior.[15] There is a tendency among Americans to take things at face value, or to be rather superficial in their attitudes and opinions. If they are fortunate, they can somehow muddle through with the support of extraordinary economic wealth and military power. However, unlike their British cousins who tend to keep both their eyes and feet on the ground, the average American tends to have his feet off the ground and his eyes on the stars, or possibly his head in the clouds. The American tends to look upward toward the utopian goal, rather than downward or straight ahead for reality.

Third, much of the present intellectual isolation from reality in foreign policy seems to belong more to the generation of the 1920's and 1930's, rather than to the generation of the 1950's and 1960's. It seems that most of the values and attitudes of the present elites and influences were formed during the interwar period. This is natural enough, but when these attitudes and values become relatively fixed and inflexible there are some unfortunate connotations in the formulation of contemporary foreign policy.

The Great Depression of the 1930's made an indelible impression upon the average American. He tended to look inward for solutions to his difficulties and we begin to see the development of trenchant nationalism with a touch of xenophobism. This interwar isolationism and psychological withdrawal from the realities of world politics seem to have carried over into the thinking and policies of today. There also seems to have been some transmission of these interwar attitudes and values to the postwar generation. This transmission seems to be manifested in relatively conservative political and economic views, which is somewhat paradoxical and difficult to describe. This neo-conservatism may be a part of the intellectual isolation, or an attempt to seize upon something relatively stable and secure in this amorphous world where there no longer seems to be total victory, total defeat, or total war—everything seems to be limited—which is all a bit uncertain and disturbing. Nothing is clear-cut and there are few if any absolutes. Everything seems to be relative.

Fourth, that this intellectual isolation is partially due to the lack of interest, education and experience in international relations. The lack of interest seems to stem from a failure to realize that domestic policy and foreign policy are inseparable parts of national policy which is designed to protect and project the whole national interest and not just a fragmentary portion. From this lack of interest or realization there seems to be a general absence of any deep motivation to educate oneself for understanding or careers in international relations. This attitude seems to have been mitigated somewhat by the experiences of the G.I.'s overseas in World War II and since by the Peace Corps and private business which have begun to realize the interdependence of the world and opportunities of comparative advantage in the diversification of land, labor, and capital.

Some enlightened members of the interwar generation and many of the postwar generation have seen the advantages of an internationalist viewpoint, but cultivation of an interest in, education for, and experience in international affairs takes a while, maybe a few generations. In this connection one is reminded of the story about an American tourist visiting an English estate and admiring the beautiful lawns. On the way out he asked the grounds-keeper, "How do you get such beautiful lawns?" The grounds-keeper thought a moment and then replied, "With six hundred years of tender loving care."

Fifth, it has been suggested that this intellectual isolation is partially due to the predominant economic and preponderant military power of the United States. There seem to be two major elements to this concept. First, with a gross national product (GNP) in 1963 of about $583,918 millions and total imports and exports of about $38,156 millions, the dependence of the United States on international trade was slightly more than 6½% of the GNP. While the commodities traded may have been of relative importance, the impact upon the national economy was of relative insignificance compared to the other leading industrial or agricultural nations of the world. And yet, in terms of total international trade, the United States is the largest importer and exporter, and therein lies the paradox. Secondly, the tremendous military power of the United States has not been used for the more traditional imperialist or nationalist ends. This is the first time in history when a preponderant military power has refrained from fully and effectively using its strength, which has tended to create a power vacuum in the conventional and unconventional sense. While nuclear power may have served the national interest in deterring or negating the possibility of mutual destruction, its application in situations less than a central war would not only be clumsy but also foolish. The one possible exception to this may have been the Cuban Crisis of 1962, which might readily justify the entire commitment. However, it might be worthwhile to expand the resources available and extend their application in the conventional and unconventional types of warfare at the lower end of the strategic spectrum.

Sixth, this intellectual isolation is partially due to the prevalence of domestic policy over foreign policy. This is a misconception because domestic policy is a function of foreign policy and *vice versa*. Or, domestic policy and foreign policy are part of the same continuum, and merely ways of looking at or approaching national policy. However, the emphasis on the domestic side of national policy is somewhat understandable. From earliest history, Americans were more concerned with making a living, protecting themselves and carving out new portions of the wilderness than they were with the machinations of international politics. When the seemingly limitless frontier began to close around 1890, Americans tended to take greater notice of foreign affairs, but the preoccupation with domestic affairs and the pursuit of material wealth from 1620 down to the present has fairly well established a pattern of thinking. This may be perfectly natural but not particularly rational since 1914 and especially since 1945. Although there is a great deal of talk about foreign policy, like the weather little more is done about it except in times of great international crisis. For example, there are some people who feel that the civil rights issue took precedence over South Vietnam in the national elections of 1964. This precedence may have been perfectly right morally and politically, but the apparent eclipse of the issues involved in South Vietnam was not. The distinctions between conserving the Union from within and preserving the Union from without seem rather elusive.

How many votes did South Vietnam represent in the national election of 1964? How many Congressmen and Senators were elected or re-elected on the basis of foreign policy issues? In 1965 Congress appropriated about $9 billion for a domestic agricultural subsidy and about $3 billion for a foreign (and domestic) political subsidy. Which did you hear more about? Again, lack of understanding, lack of self-interest, or lack of identification with all the issues which affect individual and collective well-being.

Seventh, this intellectual isolation is partially due to the dichotomy between internal pragmatism and external idealism. In terms of their own personal affairs, business, and politics, Americans tend to be quite pragmatic and seem to have a fairly high degree of toleration for corruption, crime, and incompetence—just so long as it does not directly affect them individually. However, when it comes to foreign affairs they tend to be rather idealistic and intolerant. An example of this was the calculated realism demonstrated by the Truman and Eisenhower administrations in coming to the economic, political, and military assistance of Yugoslavia after its expulsion from the Cominform and excommunication from the international communist movement in 1948.[16] This policy produced several tangible and some intangible benefits to the United States over a thirteen-year period until it was gradually repudiated by Congress between 1962 and 1963. Senator William Proxmire of Wisconsin and Congressman Wilbur Mills of Arkansas led the attack largely on the grounds that Yugoslavia was still under a communist oriented government and furthering the aims of international communism. The prohibitions on economic and military assistance to Yugoslavia along with the elimination of the most-favored-nation trading privilege, came at a time when relations between the United States and Cuba were almost at their worst. While this may have been understandable, it was somewhat illogical to relate or equate Yugoslavia with Cuba as an actual or potential threat to the United States. So calculated realism suffered at the hands of intolerant idealism and fundamentalism. This is part of the dichotomy of which George Kennan warns in his essay on "Two Planes of International Reality."

Eighth, that this intellectual isolation is partially due to the incredible affluence and independence of the American economy. The United States is the economic symbol and manifestation of the "good life." It sets the material standard of living for the world, communist, socialist, and capitalist alike. However, due to a peculiar set of circumstances the United States has been able to achieve a standard of living that would be virtually impossible to approach anywhere else in the world. This affluence has tended to foster the insulation and indifference of many Americans from the rest of the economic world, despite the experiences of the early 1930's. And yet, this very affluence is greatly dependent upon the supply of raw materials, manufactured goods, and finished products from all over the world. Nevertheless, the "have not nations" are quite envious of this prosperity and are desperately striving to achieve similar affluence. The paradox is that some of the newer nations are trying to achieve American affluence by Soviet means, while the Soviets are apparently trying to achieve the same affluence by American means.

Ninth, this intellectual isolation is partially due to the relative geographic isolation of the United States from the rest of the world. This was more true historically than it is today, but the habits of thought accumulated over three centuries tend to persist. The geographic position of the United States has certainly reduced contact and removed the necessity of direct confrontation with the realities of international politics. Except for some brief skirmishes in Washington and at New Orleans, the United States has not fought a major war on its own territory. Even though we now have thermonuclear intercontinental ballistic missiles only thirty minutes or less from Moscow to Chicago, this geographic insulation mentally persists and permeates the thinking of most people. Examples of this might be the failure of the United States to effect any positive civil defense program, or aggressively press for some degree of nuclear disarmament.

Tenth, this intellectual isolation is *primarily* due to the Puritan Ethic. Or, that "somehow, some way right will prevail over might." This may be a highly commendable attitude in interpersonal relations within a nation-state, but not for international relations in a society of nation-states. Within the nation-state the national and subsidiary governments have a monopoly on power, which enables them to legislate, adjudicate, and execute the laws. However, outside of the nation-state there is no monopoly on power and only a highly primitive form of international legislation, adjudication, and execution. Unless and until there is some form of adequate international government based upon the principle of collective security, there will be no legal or moral standards of international behavior. There is, as yet, no real form of international power, so each nation-state is largely dependent upon its own resources to protect its territorial integrity and political independence and to project its national interests. The Puritan Ethic as a standard of international morality is as strangely out of place in the struggle for power, prestige, and prosperity between and among nation-states as Woodrow Wilson was in Paris in 1919. The prevailing international ethic today seems to more accurately reflect Thomas

Hobbes and his doctrine that might makes right, rather than right makes might.

NOTES

1. Howard W. Preston, *Documents Illustrative of American History 1606-1863* (New York: G. P. Putnam's Sons, 1898), pp. 30-31.
2. Walter Lippmann, "The Rivalry of Nations," *Atlantic Monthly*, No. 181 (February, 1948), p. 18.
3. James D. Richardson, *A Compilation of the Messages and Papers of the Presidents* (Washington, D.C.: Government Printing Office, 1896), Vol. I, pp. 213-224.
4. U.S., Congress, American State Papers: *Documents, Legislative and Executive, of the Congress of the United States,* Selected and Edited under the Authority of Congress by Asbury Dickins, Secretary of the Senate, and James C. Allen, Clerk of the House of Representatives, Second Series, Volume V, Foreign Relations (Washington: Gales & Seaton, 1858), pp. 245-250.
5. Cecil V. Crabb, Jr., *American Foreign Policy in the Nuclear Age* (New York: Harper & Row, 1960), p. 32.
6. Hans Kohn, *American Nationalism* (New York: The Macmillan Company, 1957), p. 183.
7. Ruhl J. Bartlett, *The Record of American Diplomacy,* Fourth edition enlarged (New York: Alfred A. Knopf, 1964), p. 385.
8. U.S., Congress, *Congressional Record,* 65th Congress, Second Session, Vol. LVI, Part 1 (Washington: Government Printing Office, 1918), p. 680.
9. Denis W. Brogan, "The Illusion of American Omnipotence," *Harpers,* No. 205 (December, 1952), pp. 21-28.
10. Hans Kohn, *American Nationalism,* p. 152.
11. Cecil V. Crabb, Jr., *American Foreign Policy in the Nuclear Age,* p. 35.
12. Dean Rusk, announcement of The Atlantic Council of the United States for *The Atlantic Community Quarterly,* January, 1965.
13. For a good survey refer to: Ruhl J. Bartlett, *Policy and Power* (New York: Hill and Wang, 1964).
14. Hugh Gaitskell, "The Anglo-American Alliance," Lecture delivered at The Fletcher School of Law and Diplomacy, Tufts University, October 17, 1959.
15. Sir Harold Nicolson, "National Character and National Policy," Montague Burton International Relations Lecture, 1930, University College, Notingham, England, pp. 4-13.
16. David L. Larson, "The Foreign Policy of the United States Toward Yugoslavia: 1943-1963," unpublished thesis, The Fletcher School of Law and Diplomacy, Tufts University, Medford, Massachusetts.

2. The Two Planes of International Reality*

by George F. Kennan

THIS SERIES OF LECTURES REPRESENTS AN EFFORT TO RELATE contemporary problems of foreign affairs to certain of the more basic external realities among which our policy has to operate, and also to the internal nature and purposes of our own society. It is my hope that when this exercise is completed, I shall have succeeded in expressing to you something that might be called a personal philosophy of foreign policy.

When one talks of any sort of philosophy it is always hard to know from what point of the compass to approach it. But in the case of foreign policy we are aided by the fact that what we are talking about is a practical exercise—one of the functions of government—and something that has been going on for a long time. Our concepts and outlooks with relation to it represent, whether we are aware of it or not, the accumulation of a long historical experience. I may be misled here by a tendency to idealization of the American past, a sort of nostalgia to which I am afraid our generation is somewhat prone. But it does seem to me that early American statesmen had a better idea than our generation has—a clearer idea, at any rate—of what they were trying to do in the conduct of governmental affairs generally. And for this reason I sometimes find it useful, when contemporary problems seem too confusing, to look back and try to find out when it was, and in what manner, that thought and reality began to come apart, as they so obviously seem to have done in so many respects, and how far we must re-

* *Realities of American Foreign Policy* (Princeton, New Jersey: Princeton University Press, 1954), pp. 3-30. (Copyright by Princeton University Press. Reprinted by permission of the Princeton University Press.)

trace our steps if we are to put Humpty Dumpty together again.

So I am going to devote this evening to a sketchy historical introduction. I must ask your indulgence if this seems to be a somewhat leisurely and detached approach to burning problems I know you would all like to hear discussed. We will come to the burning ones, in time. And I can promise you that when we do, they will still be there waiting for us, and still burning brightly. None of them is likely to be solved in the interval.

So I suggest that we begin our reflections with a theoretical recognition which, it seems to me, is often lost sight of in American thought. It is simply this: that the conduct of foreign relations ought not to be conceived as a purpose in itself for a political society, and particularly a democratic society, but rather as one of the means by which some higher and more comprehensive purpose is pursued. By this I mean that a political society does not live to conduct foreign policy; it would be more correct to say that it conducts foreign policy in order to live. Surely, the essential and important thing in the life of our own state is not what we do with regard to other nations but what happens right here among us, on this American territory for which we are responsible. Our foreign policy, in short, is only a means to an end. And that end must consist in whatever we consider to be the general objects of American society.

What are these objects? Why do we maintain on this North American territory a political society, separate from political societies elsewhere, to which we attach so much affection and loyalty and pride? What purpose do we conceive that we are promoting by doing this: is it merely the routine purpose of assuring the preservation of order among the inhabitants of a given territory? Or is it something more?

I think it is something more. If we look closely at other sovereign entities in history as in our own time, I think we will see that each of them has had some over-all purpose, going beyond just the routine chores of government—some purpose to which the total of its political life was supposed to be dedicated and by which its existence as a separate political entity was supposed to be justified. This purpose may often have been crude and not too clearly formulated. It may in some instances have been more felt than expressed. It may at times have been repressed and temporarily forgotten under the stress of some great external danger. But I suspect it has always been there. Sometimes it has been the glorification of a dynasty and the promotion of its prestige and power. At other times, as in the case of some of the older and smaller European countries today, it has been the cultivation of a national identity and a national way of life. In the case of Nazi Germany it was the development of the military qualities of a people for their own sake, and the conquest and subjugation of other nations as a sort of exercise in the military virtues. Again, in the Soviet Union, it has been nominally the cultivation of a given social theory, and the facilitating of a supposed natural process by which a social order on that theory was to become a dominant throughout the world.

You see: there has been no uniformity, no generally accepted universal pattern. This was only natural. Had the objects of society not been, in each case, unique and specific ones, there would have been no rationale for the maintenance of a separate state at all. Wherever a unifying purpose *has* become dominant among a group of states, as in the case of the thirteen colonies, or where some conqueror has succeeded in making himself the dominant military and political reality in a wider area, there political unification has tended to follow, or the trappings of national sovereignty, if retained at all, have become meaningless, as in the case of the Soviet satellites.

What, then, is this over-all purpose in the case of our own country? What would you say we hoped to accomplish by maintaining a political society separate from that of other nations?

If we go back and consult the thinking of the founding fathers, who were after all the people who took responsibility for deciding that there should be such a country as the United States, we see that government was thought of by them as a means of protecting the individual in the exercise of certain rights—life, liberty, and the pursuit of happiness, as the Declaration of Independence put it—but also, most importantly, the right to hold property and to dispose over it. It was felt that these rights were ones with which men had been endowed by their Creator. It was regarded as natural and just and useful that men should be permitted to enjoy these rights. Many people felt that the English Crown was failing at that time to assure the enjoyment of them to the inhabitants of the

North American colonies. And in order that this enjoyment might be fully assured, our forefathers chose to extract themselves, as we all recall, from their previous state of subjection to the Crown of King George III, and to set up on their own as a nation.

You will note that under this theory the state was not conceived as being an end in itself. Nor was it to be the bearer of any concrete social program. So far as I can ascertain, our forefathers believed that such progress and improvement as might conceivably be brought about in the condition of human beings would be most apt to ensue if men were left as free as possible to pursue their own self-interest and happiness, each in his own way. The individual citizen was thought to be capable of a rational understanding of his own self-interest; by pursuing this interest, as he understood it, he would achieve certain things for himself and his family; and the sum total of all these little private achievements, constituting something that has often been called "the greatest good of the greatest number," would plainly serve the best interests of society at large.

It is clear that under this concept the fountains of human betterment were not believed to proceed directly from government. Progress was not considered to be a product of the exercise of political power by man over man. Political power, in fact, was regarded only as the guardian of the natural processes from which the blessings of civilization would flow. The role of government was to be mainly that of the benevolent watchdog.

I say "mainly." It is quite plain that this *laissez faire* concept could never be workable in its pure form. Government, even while acquitting itself of its watchdog function, could not afford to be only an impassive and detached spectator of the results. Inevitably, it had to accept a certain degree of responsibility for what was going on. Government consisted, after all, of people—citizens, like the rest of us—doing important things, exercising important responsibilities. The manner in which they exercised these responsibilities could not fail to affect the way in which the country would develop. In this way it came to be generally recognized at an early date that government did, to be sure, have a certain part to play in the shaping of the national destiny, but that this part was definitely a subordinate one.

With the course of time, this concept assumed the stature of established American doctrine. A half-century ago Woodrow Wilson taught, in the halls of this same institution, that "it should be the end of government to *assist in accomplishing the objects of organized society.*" [1] Note that he did not say that government was to monopolize the accomplishment of these objects. He did not say that government was even to have the leading part in their accomplishment. He was, in fact, quite emphatic in his belief that the state could not "be made a wise foster mother to every member of the family politic." [2] The hope of society still lay, as he saw it, "in an infinite individual variety, in the freest possible play of individual forces." [3]

Admittedly, there have been many changes in our lives, even just since Wilson's time. Circumstances have forced the Federal Government to play a much greater role in the determination of the development of our national life than Wilson envisaged when he wrote those words. In particular, government has come to have an importance in the shaping of financial and economic realities that makes it, whether it so wishes or not, the greatest single arbiter of our economic life—and particularly of what we might call the metabolism of our national economy.

But I would submit—and this is a vital question from the standpoint of foreign policy—that the basic condition of our society, a condition in which certain elementary processes are permitted to work themselves out and the objects of government remain primarily protective and subsidiary, has not been changed. Great and important areas in our lives still remain largely removed from government influence and subject overwelmingly to the laws of free, private competition. I am referring here above all to the great processes of technological change by which our lives are so importantly affected. Over their creation of new technology and particularly over the manner of its introduction into our lives, our government exercises little effective control. Such things as the automobile, the telephone, radio, and television were not planned or deliberately selected for their social implications. Yet from these developments there flow some of the most important forces shaping the nature of our society today and in the future, forces that determine how we should live, what our community relationships should be, what should be the relation between our personal lives and our work, and finally even the educational influences to which we and our children are to be subjected. With respect to all these forces, the law of *laissez faire* is still acknowledged basically to apply. If someone were to come along tomorrow, as perhaps someone will, with another invention no less devastating than these others in its effects on our personal lives, we would submit to it without a murmur. And we would do so because it has been, and continues to be, a basic object of our American society that this sort of development should be permitted to take place.

From such a view of the objects of American society it seems to me that certain logical conclusions flow with respect to foreign policy, and these are, as I see it, very much the conclusions at which the earliest American statesmen themselves arrived. For these early American statesmen the problem of foreign policy amounted simply to this: in the handling of our relations with other nations what could be done to promote the accomplishment of these particular objects?

The first and obvious answer was: that one ought to protect the physical intactness of our national life from any external military or political intrusion—in other words, that one ought to look to the national security—for only in the absence of hostile foreign interference could these processes, in the usefulness of which we believed, be given full freedom to operate.

Secondly, one could see to it that insofar as the activities of our citizens in pursuit of their private interests spilled over beyond our borders and into the outside world, the best possible arrangements were made to promote and to protect them. In this way our government soon found, and has retained to this day, a logical and important field of action in trying to see to it that Americans engaged in private activity of every sort abroad got the best help and protection we could give them. This has meant a great many things in terms of foreign affairs. It has meant commercial policy, commercial treaties, protection of American shipping, and a thousand other functions I will not bore you by trying to enumerate. These things still constitute today a large part of the work of our consular service abroad.

It is characteristic that in trying to protect Americans in their private activities in other countries our government has normally acted on the theory that this sort of activity was *ipso facto* conducive to the best interests of the nation. It has not, as a rule, attempted to examine each specific thing Americans were doing abroad, with a view to judging whether it was desirable from the standpoint of the national interest. This was entirely logical, because you will remember that the pursuit of individual private interest was accepted by the founding fathers as a good in itself, which the government was there to protect, and into the merits of which government had no need to inquire. Yet this is one of the assumptions we shall be obliged to question at a later point in these lectures.

It is important to recognize that these two functions, the assurance of the national security and the promotion of private American activity abroad, were all that really did flow directly and logically from the original objects of American society. If you accepted them, and them alone, as the valid points of departure in the conduct of our foreign affairs, you came up with a policy very modest and restrained. Its sights were leveled on fixed and limited objectives, involving only the protection of the vital processes of our life. There was not room in such a policy for international benevolence, for lofty pretensions, or for the assumption of any attitude either of moral superiority or moral inferiority to any other nation. Since under this concept the development of American society was essentially an experiment—a bet, if you will, on the likelihood that certain processes would bring beneficial results if permitted to work themselves out—there was no room in it for any messianic tendencies, or for any belief that we had ideological answers to everybody else's problems. We were not like the Russians: we did not come along bearing in our hands a patent medicine of social reform which we were prepared to recommend to all comers as the cure for every ailment. We simply had certain convictions relating to our own society. We were concerned that we should be permitted to work these convictions out. We were concerned that our foreign environment should be as favorable as possible to that process. We conducted our foreign affairs to this end. That was all.

On the other hand, this concept did not rule out a very alert and vigorous and imaginative attention to the real sources of our national security. Nowhere did it imply that we should not look carefully and coldly at the world beyond our borders, as George Washington obviously did, with a view to detecting possible sources of danger to ourselves and to acting smartly and incisively, if necessary, to forestall their development. There was nothing in it that said we should be ashamed to recognize the realities of power or to deal frankly with them in the interests of the survival and intactness of our national life.

On the contrary, American statesmen in the early part of the nineteenth century dealt very frankly and very confidently with power realities. They assumed, correctly, that the European powers would have no love for us, no great respect for the values of our system, little regard for the importance of our continued existence and prosperity as a separate state. They properly feared European intrigues in the New World. They worked vigorously to restrain the European powers in their territorial ambitions here. They proceeded with little compunction to extend our own sovereignty to the Pacific, as an alternative to the penetration of the western territories by European governments. They encouraged the severance generally of the political bonds between the people of this hemisphere and Europe, and they made our country the guarantor of the permanence of this separation, wherever it occurred. All of this involved power considerations. Yet none of it at the time was considered evil, or Machiavellian, or cynical. It was simply regarded as a response to the obvious and logical requirements of our situation.

Had we been able to keep these simple and basic purposes more clearly in mind, I think there might have been much less confusion among us as we moved into the problems of the twentieth century.

But unfortunately with the advance of the nineteenth century, the consciousness of the power factor in the scheme of our foreign relations seemed to pass gradually out of the American mind. This was perhaps only natural and inevitable. The triumph of the British at the end of the Napoleonic Wars put an end to the long period of unrest in Europe in which the infancy of our country had proceeded. It established for us that shield of British naval supremacy which was so effective that many of us came to forget its very existence. The rounding out of our own territory on this continent effectively brought to an end all question of any further serious territorial encroachment by Europeans in our own immediate neighborhood. Except for the brief interlude of Napoleon

III and his venture into Mexico at the time of the Civil War, there was no further major challenge to the validity of the Monroe Doctrine. All these things served to dull the consciousness of power relationships among our people.

And, as this consciousness faded from their minds, Americans seemed to lose their feeling for reality generally about foreign policy. A posture flowing strictly from the objects of our society, as originally conceived, ceased to satisfy them. Here, as in other respects, the romantic spirit seized them. They were, after all, the children of the Victorian age, susceptible in every way to a curious diffuseness and imprecision of outlook. They wanted their architecture gaudy, pretentious, unfunctional, overladen with ornament. And similarly, I am afraid, they wanted their statesmanship impressive, unfunctional, with the emphasis on outward appearance rather than on inner reality. A situation arose in which we Americans were no longer content just to *be* something. We were now concerned to *appear* as something—something lofty, something noble, something of universal significance. And it is characteristic of our national self-centeredness that it was primarily before ourselves—before the mirror of our own adolescent self-esteem—not before others, that we were most concerned to appear in this way.

So it was that American statesmen came to devote themselves increasingly to the cultivation of what I might call, for the sake of convenience, the American dream. It was a dream marked by a certain innocence, if you will. It was innocent of every conscious evil intent. But like all manifestations of innocence, it contained a goodly measure of ignorance (which is always less appealing). It was highly subjective. We were satisfied, by this time, with our own borders; and we found it pleasant to picture the outside world as one in which other peoples were similarly satisfied with theirs, or ought to be. With everyone thus satisfied, the main problem of world peace, as it appeared to us, was plainly the arrangement of a suitable framework of contractual engagements in which this happy *status quo,* the final fruit of human progress, could be sealed and perpetuated. If such a framework could be provided, then, it seemed, the ugly conflicts of international politics would cease to threaten world peace. Because then, you see, everything would have been foreseen: there would be a legal or contractual provision for everything. Problems could then be solved not with regard to the ugly political realities of the moment but strictly on the basis of general norms of state behavior, laid down and accepted in advance.

All that was needed was the framework, and this we Americans were eminently equipped to provide. Did we not have the unique and indispensable experience? Had not our Constitution played precisely this part in abolishing violence between the several states? Our national genius, our sense of decency, our feeling for compromise and the law, our frankness and honesty—had not these qualities succeeded in producing on this continent a society unparalleled for its lack of strain and violence and for its buoyant, confident outlook on the future of mankind? Of course, there had been this regrettable episode of the Civil War; but that was our own business, and that was over now. The march of progress had been resumed. There was no reason why the outside world, with our assistance, should not similarly compose itself to a life without violence. In this way we saw ourselves moving benevolently, helpfully, among the waiting peoples of the world, our experience now finally recognized as relevant to a wider sphere of humanity, our virtues no longer just the virtues of the American frontier but the virtues of the world at large.

I do not mean to ridicule this outlook or to deny that it contained many elements of real generosity, of courage, and perhaps—over the long term—even of insight. It was not wholly irrelevant to the world in which it was meant to operate, and is not wholly irrelevant to our world today. Wherever nations are fully reconciled to each other's existence and borders and status in the world, and wherever their relations are not seriously clouded by ulterior political involvements, there is room for such a framework of legal obligation, designed to prevent the minor disputes from becoming major ones.

But it was important to bear in mind at all times the natural limitations that surrounded the operation of these principles, and above all not to look to them as substitutes for diplomacy or as magic keys to world peace. Yet this was precisely what large parts of the American public and a number of prominent American statesmen did. And the result was that over the course of several decades American statesmanship was preoccupied, and the attention of the American public diverted, with the cultivation of projects largely utopian in nature and decidedly barren of practical results.

The most elaborate of these projects was the negotiation of an extensive framework of treaties of arbitration and conciliation. Now I would not like to be misunderstood. My point is not that there was no place for arbitration. There was. It was a useful and important device for the settlement of certain types of dispute, under certain specific conditions. But the tendency of many Americans was to glorify the arbitral principle beyond its capabilities, to push it to extremes, to hope for too much from it. The fault, like most of the faults of American statesmanship, was one of emphasis, not of concept or intent. And as a result of this misplaced emphasis the United States Government, during the period from the turn of the century to the 1930's signed and ratified a total of ninety-seven international agreements dealing with arbitration or conciliation, and negotiated a number of others which, for one reason or another, never took effect. Of the ninety-seven, seven were multilateral ones; the remainder, bilateral. The time, trouble, and correspondence that went into the negotiation of this great body of contractual material was stupendous. Yet so far as I can ascertain, only two of these treaties of conventions were ever invoked in any way. Only two disputes were actually arbitrated on the basis of any of these instruments; and there is no reason to suppose that these disputes would not have been arbitrated anyway, on the basis of special agreements, had the general treaties not existed. The other ninety-five treaties, including incidentally every single one negotiated by Secretaries of State Bryan, Kellogg, and Stimson, appear to have remained wholly barren of any practical result. Nor is there any evidence that this ant-like labor had the faintest effect on the development of the terrible wars and upheavals by which the first half of this century was marked.

A second line of utopian endeavor that preoccupied American statesmanship over long periods of time was the attempt to arrive at multilateral arrangements for disarmament, particularly among the great European powers. Our own most direct involvement was of course in the field of naval armaments, but we also took an active part in the general disarmament discussions that were carried on in Geneva under the auspices of the League of Nations during the decade from 1925 to 1935.

Now here, again, the goal was a worthy one. And if the effort, like that devoted to arbitration, again represented much wasted time and misplaced attention, the fault was certainly by no means exclusively ours. Other powers, notably the French and the British, were even more directly involved.

But the fact is that it had been pointed out by thoughtful people, many years before these discussions began, that armaments were a symptom rather than a cause, primarily the reflection of international differences, and only secondarily the source of them. I know of no sound reason why, even in 1925, anyone should have supposed that there was any likelihood that general disarmament could be brought about by multilateral agreement among a group of European powers whose mutual political differences and suspicions had been by no means resolved. The realities underlying the maintenance of national armaments generally were at that time no more difficult to perceive than they are today. More than once, these realities had been brought to the public by thoughtful writers.

Yet prodigious efforts were expended on these fruitless discussions at Geneva. The record of the deliberations seems to run something like 30,000 pages. Some 500 official documents, each the result of laborious deliberation and editing and re-editing, entered merely into the report presented by the Preparatory Commission to the Disarmament Conference itself; and this was only the beginning. And at the time this mountainous labor was in progress, Weimar Germany was disintegrating miserably into the illness of National-Socialism, and new political realities were being created which were soon to sweep all this labor from the scene of world history, as though it had never existed.

And let us not forget the Kellogg Pact: one of the strangest and most bizarre of the episodes of modern diplomacy. Here was an instance in which competing groups of well-meaning peace enthusiasts in our country succeeded in needling two harried Foreign Ministers, M. Briand and Mr. Kellogg, into an embarrassing involvement from which the latter could see no graceful exit except by pressing all the nations of the world into associating themselves with one of the most meaningless and futile of all international engagements. For months the two unhappy statesmen were obliged to duel publicly with each other to see who could appear most concerned for world peace without sacrificing anything real from the standpoint of national interest. Again, the effort that went into the negotiation was formidable. People were encouraged to place solemn hopes and expectations in the enterprise. Millions took it in dead seriousness. When the Treaty was signed, in the Hall of Clocks at the Quai d'Orsay, it was the greatest international ceremony of the inter-war period. Yet the final solution could not, as might have been foreseen, have been more sterile. When World War II came along, twelve years later, even the memory of the Pact of Paris was lost in the general shuffle.

The evil of these utopian enthusiasms was not only, or even primarily, the wasted time, the misplaced emphasis, the encouragement of false hopes. The evil lay primarily in the fact that these enthusiasms distracted our gaze from the real things that were happening. These preoccupations extended over a period that included the Spanish-American War and the First World War. Great events were in progress at all times. When the first batch of these arbitration treaties was being negotiated, the Russian fleet was steaming slowly around the coasts of Africa and Asia to its doom in Tsushima, in the Russian-Japanese War. When Elihu Root was busy with his quota of them in the years between 1907 and 1909, the Anglo-Russian Entente was being formed, the concert of the powers with relation to the Balkan problem was disintegrating, and tension was growing between England and Germany over the German naval construction program. Bryan applied himself to his arbitration and conciliation treaties on the very eve of the outbreak of the First World War; and the early months of hostilities found our diplomats in Europe still persistently plucking the sleeves of puzzled foreign ministers in the warring countries, trying to persuade them to give attention to these curiously irrelevant documents while the lights were going out all over Europe and the guns were already speaking in the most terrible and tragic of all wars.

I could give further examples of this sort, but I am sure that I do not need to. The connection is clear. The cultivation of these utopian schemes, flattering to our own image of ourselves, took place at the expense of our feeling for reality. And when the rude facts of the power conflict did finally intrude themselves directly upon us, in the form of the enemies against whom we were forced to fight in the two World Wars, we found it difficult to perceive the relation between them and the historical logic of our epoch, because we understood the latter so poorly. These enemies appeared to us in the aspect of monsters that had arisen from nowhere, as by some black magic. We deluded ourselves with the belief that if they could be in some way exorcized, like evil spirits, through the process of military defeat, then nothing would remain of them and our world would be restored to us as though they had never existed. It was hard for us to see that these enemies were the reflection of deeper causes which could be only partially alleviated, and might in some cases be actually aggravated, by the miseries of war and the abrupt imbalances of national power implicit in such things as total victory and unconditional surrender.

Only in this way could it have come about, I think, that during World War II so many Americans could have deceived themselves so seriously about the prospects for a peaceful world after the termination of hostilities and have been so little prepared for what actually proved to be the postwar reality. After all, the cultivation of this dream of a conflictless world, from which the evil spirits would have been exorcised and in which we Americans would be able to unfold, at last, our talents for peaceful organization, continued to preoccupy many of us right down through the period of hostilities and particularly during the months surrounding their conclusion. The only difference was that now multilateral organization had taken the place of arbitration or disarmament or what you will as the new password to world peace. By means of multilateral organization, preferably on a universal scale, we were now going to bring to the world a thousand blessings—everything from the I.T.O. Charter and the International Monetary Fund to U.N.E.S.C.O., all designed to bring into fruition in our time the sort of world we had dreamed about, all predicated on the belief that the dark cloud of violence and aggression that had cast its shadow over the world in the years between 1938 and 1945 was the product of the ill will of a few individuals and would disappear when those individuals were banished from the scene.

And it was precisely in the midst of this happy illusion that many

Americans became aware for the first time of the nature of what is now called the Russian threat. It is true: the Bolsheviks had been in power for more than two decades before World War II. But this had had no appreciable effect on our thinking about the place of power in international affairs. In the 'twenties the Moscow communists had appeared to polite Anglo-Saxon society chiefly as a group of extremely bad-mannered people—anarchists and extremists, bristling with beards and bombs, misguided, motivated by all the wrong principles, unlikely to remain in power for any length of time, sure to be punished in the end for their insolent recalcitrance. The fact of their survival of the crisis of collectivization and the first Five Year Plan in the early 'thirties, and the simultaneous passage of the western world through the ordeal of the economic depression—these things produced, to be sure, a certain change in the outlook of many Americans. The stability of Soviet power was now no longer seriously questioned. Skepticism yielded in many minds to a certain sneaking envy of the Soviet Government for its greater measure of control over the economic processes that were causing us so much trouble. F.D.R and others found charitable and comforting explanations for Soviet behavior. At bottom, they concluded, the Soviet leaders were no different from anybody else. If they sometimes behaved badly it was because people had not treated them properly, because the French and British and our own Republicans had snubbed them and offended them in the early years of their power and caused them to be over-sensitive and defensive. A little balm to wounded hearts, a little polite treatment, a little flattery in the form of admission to the councils of the Allies—this would fix everything.

In all of this, you see, there was still little appreciation of Soviet power as a threat to us in the geopolitical sense. On the contrary, throughout the years of the 'thirties there was a constant hope that the Soviet leaders could be lured into some sort of collaboration not only in the destruction of the evil apparition of Hitlerism but even in the construction of the brave new world for which Americans then hoped. Moscow played ably on these illusions with its policies of the 'thirties: its entry into the League of Nations, its talk of the indivisibility of peace, its sudden moral indignation over the totalitarian excesses of National-Socialism. To be sure, there was then the shock caused by the initial attitude of Moscow toward the Second World War—the Non-Aggression Pact, the partition of Poland, the attack on Finland, the cynical absorption of the Baltic countries. These things were irritating and disturbing to the western liberal mind. But they left no lasting imprint. When Pearl Harbor and its consequences suddenly swept all this aside and made us in effect the allies of Moscow in the struggle against Hitler, and when the great American capacity for enthusiasm and self-hypnosis applied itself to the building up of the image of Stalin's Russia as an earnest, upright partner in the quest for a world we could understand, then in a great many American minds the last doubts were removed. There was no longer any question about it: Russia was no problem from the standpoint of the power relationships of a future world. The only question was one of how we were to arrange that wonderful peacetime collaboration by means of which we two great continental nations, so similar in geography and resources, so similar—as many thought—in history and outlook, would walk hand in hand down the shining vistas of a peaceful international future.

It was against this background that many Americans suddenly became aware for the first time, of the horrible reality of the post-war world—of the fact that this earnest and upright partner was not there at all, and that in his place there was only another one of these great inexplicable monsters, more formidable this time than all the others, sitting astride the resources of half the world and the prostrate peoples of eastern Europe and China, sitting here and grinning inscrutably at us like some graven image, like something really out of this world: committed to the encompassing of our ruin, inaccessible to our words and reasoning, concerned only for our destruction. And now it suddenly occurred to many people what dangers could reside in the association of the dominant portion of the physical resources of Europe and Asia with a political power hostile to ourselves. There was suddenly brought home to people the truism that a combination of the physical resources and manpower of Russia and China with the technical skills and machine tools of Germany and eastern Europe might spell a military reality more powerful than anything that could be mobilized against it on its own territory from any other place in this world, and that this combination was well on the way to fruition. When people asked themselves how this situation could have come about, they were obliged to recognize that so far as the European area was concerned the events that had produced it were ones to which we Americans, intent on the destruction of Hitler, had given our blessing. And when they asked themselves what could now be done to remedy the situation, they were forced to recognize that any drastic remedy involved the most appalling difficulties and complications.

On top of this came the fearful realities of the atomic bomb, the long-distance bomber, and the guided missile. With the development of these weapons, the traditional bastions of our security—our geographic remoteness, our protecting oceans, the vastness of our territory, the strength of our economy—all these things seemed to crumble, one after the other, as in one of these apocalyptic movies where the walls of great cities slowly and ponderously disintegrate before your eyes. There loomed suddenly before people a world of power realities overwhelming, now, in their significance, a world in which the statistics of military force seemed to constitute the only terms in which external reality could be understood and expressed, the only language of international dealings. With their eyes riveted on Russia—fascinated, like a bird before a snake, with the incredible dilemmas of atomic power—many Americans now became wholly absorbed with power values, to a point where they were impatient of any discussion of international affairs that tried to take account of anything else, inclined to dismiss references to any other problems as frivolous and inconsequential, as a form of fiddling while Rome, the Rome of western civilization, burned before our eyes.

Yet through all of this the other world was still there, too—the more familiar world, the one that did not threaten us, did not wish our destruction. It had not ceased to exist just because the Russian problem had now become visible. There were still great portions of the globe inhabited by peoples who did not grin at us like some inscrutable, malevolent monster. There were still governments quite reconciled to our continued existence and prosperity. There were still people prepared to explore with us all sorts of ideas as to how the peaceful coexistence of nations could be rendered more fruitful, more stable, more beneficial to everyone. Along with all the nightmares of the postwar years, the needs of this other world continued to press themselves upon us, to compete for our attention, to constitute a demand on the resources of our foreign policy. This was, after all, a world to which our traditional approaches were at least still relevant, whether or not they were sound.

And because this was so, American political thought came to be affected, in the postwar era, by a sort of schizophrenia. It operated on two different planes, quite separate from each other and seemingly having nothing to do with each other. We found ourselves living in two different worlds: one world a sane and rational one, in which we felt comfortable, in which we were surrounded by people to whom we were accustomed and on whose reactions we could at least depend; and the other world a nightmarish one, where we were like a hunted beast, oblivious of everything but survival, straining every nerve and muscle in the effort to remain alive. In one of these worlds the old traditional concepts still applied, and we could still be guided, as it seemed, by the American dream. In the other, there was only the law of the jungle; and we even had to do violence to our own traditional principles—or many of us felt we did—to fit ourselves for the relentless struggle of which it was the theater.

Were these two worlds really wholly separate ones? Was there no way they could be brought into an integral and comprehensible relationship with one another? Was there no way in which unity and harmony could again be introduced into the concepts of American foreign policy?

These were the questions that pressed themselves upon Americans from the dual nature of their world environment as they faced it in the aftermath of World War II. They are the questions to which we shall address ourselves in the remaining lectures of this series.

NOTES

1. Woodrow Wilson, *The State: Elements of Historical and Practical Politics* (Boston, D. C. Heath and Co., 1898), p. 633.
2. *Ibid.,* p. 630.
3. *Ibid.,* p. 633.

3. The Eclipse of the Public Philosophy*

by Walter Lippmann

1. ON THE EFFICACY OF IDEAS

THERE ARE THOSE WHO WOULD SAY, USING THE WORDS OF PHILOSOPHERS to prove it, that it is the characteristic illusion of the tender-minded that they believe in philosophy. Those who can, do; those who cannot, teach and theorize. And being theorists by profession, they exaggerate the efficacy of ideas, which are mere airy nothings without mass or energy, the mere shadow of the existential world of substance and of force, of habits and desires, of machines and armies.

Yet the illusion, if it were one, is inordinately tenacious. It is impossible to remove it from the common sense in which we live and have our being. In the familiar daylight world we cannot act as if ideas had no consequences. The whole vast labor and passion of public life would be nonsense if we did not believe that it makes a difference what is done by parties, newspapers, books, broadcasts, schools and churches. All their effort would be irrelevant, indeed nonsense, like an argument about what Nebuchadnezzar should be served for tomorrow morning's breakfast.

The most thoroughgoing skeptic is unable, in practice, to make a clean sweep—to say that since ideas have no consequences there is no such thing as a good idea or a bad one, a true idea or a false one. For there is no escaping the indubitable fact of experience that we are often mistaken, and that it makes a difference to have been wrong.

* From *The Public Philosophy* by Walter Lippmann, by permission of Atlantic-Little, Brown and Co.

The chemistry of our bodies is never mistaken. The reaction of one chemical element to another chemical element is always correct, is never misled by misinformation, by untruth, and by illusion. The doctor can be mistaken about the chemistry of his patient, having failed to detect a substance which falsifies his diagnosis. But it is only the doctor who can be wrong; the chemical process cannot be.

Why do we make mistakes? Because an important part of human behavior is reaction to the pictures in their heads. Human behavior takes place in relation to a pseudo-environment—a representation which is not quite the same for any two individuals, of what they suppose to be—not what is—the reality of things.[1] This man-made, this cultural environment, which has its being in the minds of men, is interposed between man as a biological organism and the external reality. It is in this realm that ideas are efficacious. They are efficacious because men react to their ideas and images, to their pictures and notions of the world, treating these pictures as if they were the reality.

The airy nothings in the realm of essence are efficacious in the existential world when a man, believing it to be true or good, treats the idea as if it were the reality. In this way faith in an idea can quite literally remove a mountain. To be sure no man's idea can remove a mountain on the moon. But if the American people took it into their heads that life would not be worth living until Pike's Peak was in the suburbs of Chicago, they could move Pike's Peak. They could do it if they and their descendants were sufficiently devoted to the idea for a long enough time.

Nothing would happen to Pike's Peak if the idea of removing it were merely proclaimed and celebrated. The idea would have to become, like the idea of winning a war, the object and the focus of the nation's energies. Then the idea would operate in the minds of men who voted, who planned, who would engineer the undertaking, who would raise the money, would recruit the labor, would procure the equipment, and—shall we say—would suppress the mounting resistance of the objectors to the project.

Because ideas have the power to organize human behavior, their efficacy can be radical. They are indeed radical when, as the image of what a man should be, they govern the formation of his character and so imprint a lasting organization on his behavior.[2] Because the images of man are the designs of the molds in which characters are formed, they are of critical concern. What is the image of the good king, the good courtier, the good subject—of the good master and of the good slave—of the good citizen, the good soldier, the good politician, the good boss, the good workingman? The images matter very much. The ones which prevail will govern education. The ideas of what men should be like become efficacious in the existential world because, as they are imposed by the family, the school and the community, they cause men to "acquire the kind of character which makes them *want* to act in the way they *have* to act as members of the society or of a special class within it." They learn "to *desire* what, objectively it is necessary for them to do," and "*outer force* is . . . replaced by" the "*inner compulsion*" of their own characters.[3]

That there are limits to education in this sense, we cannot doubt. But we do not know where they are. There is, that is to say, no clear and certain boundary between character which is acquired and those more or less uneducable traits of human nature, evolved during the long ages and transmitted by inheritance. We are quite unable to predict with any certainty or precision how far the individual pupil is educable—or rather how far he is still educable by the time a particular educator gets hold of him, and after he has already acquired a character of sorts in his infancy.

Yet, however crude and clumsy our knowledge of the process, there is no doubt that a character is acquired by experience and education. Within limits that we have not measured, human nature is malleable. Can we doubt it when we remember that when Shakespeare was alive there were no Americans, that when Virgil was alive there were no Englishmen, and that when Homer was alive there were no Romans? Quite certainly, men have acquired the ways of thinking, feeling and acting which we recognize as their ethnic, national, class, and occupational characteristics. Comparatively speaking these characteristics are, moreover, recently acquired. Even within the brief span of historical time characters have been acquired and have been lost and have been replaced by other characters. This is what gives to man's history, despite his common humanity, its infinite variety.

Because human nature is, as Hocking puts it, "the most plastic part of the living world, the most adaptable, the most educable,"[4] it is also the most mal-adaptable and mis-educable. The cultural heritage which contains the whole structure and fabric of the good life is acquired. It may be rejected. It may be acquired badly. It may not be acquired at all. For we are not born with it. If it is not transmitted from one generation to the next, it may be lost, indeed forgotten through a dark age, until somewhere and somehow men rediscover it, and, exploring the world again, recreate it anew.

The acquired culture is not transmitted in our genes, and so the issue is always in doubt. The good life in the good society, though attainable, is never attained and possessed once and for all. So what has been attained will again be lost if the wisdom of the good life in a good society is not transmitted.

That is the central and critical condition of the Western society: that the democracies are ceasing to receive the traditions of civility in which the good society, the liberal, democratic way of life at its best, originated and developed. They are cut off from the public philosophy and the political arts which are needed to govern the liberal democratic society. They have not been initiated into its secrets, and they do not greatly care for as much of it as as they are prepared to understand.

In Toynbee's terrible phrase, they are proletarians who are "in" but are not "of" the society they dominate.

2. THE GREAT VACUUM

To speak of a public philosophy is, I am well aware, to raise dangerous questions, rather like opening Pandora's box.

Within the Western nations, as Father Murray has put it, there is a "plurality of incompatible faiths";[5] there is also a multitude of secularized and agnostic people. Since there is so little prospect of agreement, and such certainty of dissension, on the content of the public philosophy, it seems expedient not to raise the issues by talking about them. It is easier to follow the rule that each person's beliefs are private and that only overt conduct is a public matter.

One might say that this prudent rule reflects and registers the terms of settlement of the religious wars and of the long struggle against exclusive authority in the realm of the spirit by "thrones or dominations, or principalities of powers."

Freedom of religion and of thought and of speech were achieved by denying both to the state and to the established church a sovereign monopoly in the field of religion, philosophy, morals, science, learning, opinion, and conscience. The liberal constitutions, with their bills of rights, fixed the boundaries past which the sovereign—the King, the Parliament, the Congress, the voters—were forbidden to go.

Yet the men of the seventeenth and eighteenth centuries who established these great salutory rules would certainly have denied that a community could do without a general public philosophy. They were themselves the adherents of a public philosophy—of the doctrine of natural law, which held that there was law "above the ruler and the sovereign people . . . above the whole community of mortals." [6]

The traditions of civility spring from this principle, which was first worked out by the Stoics. As Ernest Barker says:

> The rational faculty of man was conceived as producing a common conception of law and order which possessed a universal validity. . . . This common conception included, as its three great notes, the three values of Liberty, Equality and the brotherhood or Fraternity of all mankind. This common conception, and its three great notes, have formed a European set of ideas for over two thousand years. It was a set of ideas which lived and moved in the Middle Ages; and St. Thomas Aquinas cherished the idea of a sovereign law of nature imprinted in the heart and nature of man, to which kings and legislators must everywhere bow. It was a set of ideas which lived and acted with an even greater animation from the days of the Reformation to those of the French Revolution . . . Spoken through the mouth of Locke, (they had justified) the English Revolution of 1688, and had recently served to inspire the American Revolution of 1776 . . . They were ideas of the proper conduct of states and governments in the area of internal affairs. They were ideas of the natural rights of man—of liberty, political and civic, with sovereignty residing essentially in the nation, and with free communication of thoughts and opinions; of equality before the law, and the equal repartition of public expenses among all the members of the public; of a general fraternity which tended in practice to be sadly restricted within the nation, but which could, on occasion, be extended by decree to protect all nations struggling for freedom.[7]

These traditions were expounded in the treatises of philosophers, were developed in the tracts of the publicists, were absorbed by the lawyers and applied in the courts. At times of great stress some of the endangered traditions were committed to writing, as in the Magna Carta and the Declaration of Independence. For the guidance of judges and lawyers, large portions were described—as in Lord Coke's examination of the common law. The public philosophy was in part expounded in the Bill of Rights of 1689. It was re-exacted in the first ten amendments of the Constitution of the United States. The largest part of the public philosophy was never explicitly stated. Being the wisdom of a great society over the generations, it can never be stated in any single document. But the traditions of civility permeated the peoples of the West and provided a standard of public and private action which promoted, facilitated, and protected the institutions of freedom and the growth of democracy.

The founders of our free institutions were themselves adherents of this public philosophy. When they insisted upon excluding the temporal power from the realm of the mind and the spirit; it was not that they had no public philosophy. It was because experience had taught them that as power corrupts, it corrupts the public philosophy. It was, therefore, a practical rule of politics that the government should not be given sovereignty and proprietorship over the public philosophy.

But as time went on, there fell out of fashion the public philosophy of the founders of Western institutions. The rule that the temporal power should be excluded from the realm of the mind and of the spirit was then subtly transformed. It became the rule that ideas and principles are private—with only subjective relevance and significance. Only when there is "a clear and present danger" to public order are the acts of speaking and publishing in the public domain. All the first and last things were removed from the public domain. All that has to do with what man is and should be, or how he should hold himself in the scheme of things, what are his rightful ends and the legitimate means, became private and subjective and publicly unaccountable. And so, the liberal democracies of the West became the first great society to treat as a private concern the formative beliefs that shape the character of its citizens.

This has brought about a radical change in the meaning of freedom. Originally it was founded on the postulate that there was a universal order on which all reasonable men were agreed: within that public agreement on the fundamentals and on the ultimates, it was safe to permit and it would be desirable to encourage, dissent, and dispute. But with the disappearance of the public philosophy —and of a consensus on the first and last things—there was opened up a great vacuum in the public mind, yawning to be filled.

As long as it worked, there was an obvious practical advantage in treating the struggle for the ultimate allegiance of men as not within the sphere of the public interest. It was a way of not having to open the Pandora's box of theological, moral, and ideological issues which divide the Western society. But in this century, when the hard decisions have had to be made, this rule of prudence has ceased to work. The expedient worked only as long as the general mass of the people were not seriously dissatisfied with things as they are. It was an expedient that looked towards reforms and improvement. But it assumed a society which was secure, progressive, expanding, and unchallenged. That is why it was only in the fine Victorian weather, before the storm clouds of the great wars began to gather, that the liberal democratic policy of public agnosticism and practical neutrality in ultimate issues was possible.

3. THE NEGLECT OF THE PUBLIC PHILOSOPHY

We come, then, to a crucial question. If the discussion of public philosophy has been, so to speak, tabled in the liberal democracies, can we assume that, though it is not being discussed, there is a public philosophy? Is there a body of positive principles and precepts which a good citizen cannot deny or ignore? I am writing this book in the conviction that there is. It is a conviction which I have acquired gradually, not so much from a theoretical education, but rather from the practical experience of seeing how hard it is for our generation to make democracy work. I believe that there is a public philosophy. Indeed there is such a thing as the public philosophy of civility. It does not have to be discovered or invented. It is known. But it does have to be revived and renewed.

The public philosophy is known as *natural law,* a name which, alas, causes great semantic confusion.[8] This philosophy is the premise of the institutions of the Western society, and they are, I believe, unworkable in communities that do not adhere to it. Except on the premises of this philosophy, it is impossible to reach intelligible and workable conceptions of popular election, majority rule, representative assemblies, free speech, loyalty, property, corporations, and voluntary associations. The founders of these institutions, which the recently enfranchised democracies have inherited, were all of them adherents of some one of the various schools of natural law.

In our time the institutions built upon the foundations of the public philosophy still stand. But they are used by a public who are not being taught, and no longer adhere to, the philosophy. Increasingly, the people are alienated from the inner principles of their institutions. The question is whether and how this alienation can be overcome, and the rupture of the traditions of civility repaired.

Needless to say I am not about to argue that the rupture can be repaired by a neo-classical or neo-medieval restoration, or by some kind of romantic return to feudalism, folk-dancing, and handicrafts. We cannot rub out the modern age, we cannot roll back the history that has made us what we are. We cannot start again as if there had been no advance of science, no spread of rationalism and secularism, no industrial revolution, no dissolution of the old habitual order of things, no sudden increase in the population. The poignant question is whether, and, if so, how modern men could make vital contact with the lost traditions of civility.

The appearance of things is quite obviously unpromising. There is radical novelty in our modern ways of life. The climate of feeling and the style of thought have changed radically. Modern men will first need to be convinced that the traditions of civility were not abandoned because they became antiquated. This is one of the roots of their unbelief, and there is no denying its depth. Since the public philosophy preceded the advance of modern science and the industrial revolution, how can it be expected to provide a positive doctrine which is directly and practically relevant to the age we live in?

It does, one must admit, look like that, and quite evidently the original principles and precepts do not now provide the specific rules and patterns of a way of life in the circumstances of this age. A rereading of the political classics from Aristotle to Burke will not give the answers to the immediate and concrete questions: to the burning issues of diplomacy, military defense, trade, taxes, prices, and wages. Nor have the classical books anything to say about repairing automobiles, treating poliomyelitis, or proceeding with nuclear fission. As handbooks for the busy man, wanting to know how to do this or that, they are now lamentably out of date. The language is archaic, the idiom is strange, the images are unfamiliar, the practical precepts are addressed to forgotten issues.

But this irrelevance and remoteness might be the dust which has settled during the long time when philosophers and scholars and popular educators have relegated the public philosophy to the attic, when they have treated it as no longer usable by modern and progressive men. It is a neglected philosophy. For several generations it has been exceptional and indeed eccentric to use this philosophy in the practical discussion of public policies.

Neglect might well explain its dilapidated condition. If this were the explanation, it would encourage us to explore the question of a renascence. Could modern men again make vital contact with the traditions of civility? At least once before something of the sort did happen. The traditions were articulated in the Graeco-Roman world, and submerged in the West by the decline and the fall of the Western empire. Later on they were revived and renovated and remade in a great flowering of discovery and enterprise and creativity. The revival of learning did not provide maps for Columbus to use in discovering America. But it did produce much human wisdom which helped Columbus and his contemporaries to discover themselves and their possibilities.

The ancient world, we may remind ourselves, was not destroyed because the traditions were false. They were submerged, neglected, lost. For the men adhering to them had become a dwindling minority who were overthrown and displaced by men who were alien to the traditions, having never been initiated and adopted into them. May it not be that while the historical circumstances are obviously so different, something like that is happening again?

4. THE UNIVERSAL LAWS OF THE RATIONAL ORDER

For over two thousand years, says Barker, European thought has been acted upon by the idea that the rational faculties of men can produce a common conception of law and order which possesses a universal validity. This conception was first formulated as a theory by Zeno and the Stoics. It was absorbed by the Roman lawyers, was adopted by the Christian fathers, was re-established and reworked by Saint Thomas Aquinas, and in a new formulation, after the Renaissance and Reformation, it provided the philosophy of the English Revolution of 1688 and of the American Revolution of 1776. The long life of this idea and, above all, the recurring revival of the idea in all ages, would seem to indicate that it reflects a wide and recurring human need—that it is involved with practical questions of policy in the face of recurring political problems.

That the idea is not mere moonshine and cobwebs is attested by history. Barker tells us that in 330 B.C., Alexander was planning the empire in which he would be equally lord of the Greeks and the Persians, in which both Greeks and Persians would be equally bound to perform military service, and would be encouraged to intermarry. This was a revolutionary idea. Aristotle, who was then teaching at the Lyceum, advised Alexander against a policy which would bring the two worlds—the Greek and the barbarian—into the same political system. Aristotle advised Alexander to deal with the Greeks as a leader and with the Persians as a master.

But Alexander rejected the advice, certainly for practical reasons, and perhaps also for idealistic reasons. He "acted in the spirit of the policy afterwards enunciated by Eratosthenes (an Alexandrian scholar of the next century) who, 'refusing to agree with men who divided mankind into Greeks and barbarians . . . declared that it was better to divide men simply into the good and bad.' "[9]

In adopting this policy, Alexander anticipated in action what Zeno and the Stoics were soon to be teaching—that, as Plutarch wrote long afterwards, "men should not live their lives in so many civic republics, separated from one another by different systems of justice; they should reckon *all* as their fellow citizens, and there should be one life and one order (*cosmos*), as it were of one flock on a common pasture, feeding in common under one joint law."[10]

We must here dwell specially on the fact that Alexander anticipated in action what Zeno and the Stoics were soon to be teaching. This shows that the idea of a rational order is not only an attractive and a sublime conception but that it is a necessary assumption in the government of large and heterogeneous states. Alexander came to it in spite of Aristotle's teaching to the contrary. His practical experience compelled him to see that in an empire which included the Persians as well as the Greeks there had to be a common law which was valid for both. To be valid for both the Greeks and the Persians, the law had in some significant degree to have their consent. The Persians could not be commanded and coerced.

As in fact the laws were promulgated to the Persians by Alexander, who was a Greek, it was necessary to convince the Persians that Alexander's laws reflected something that was higher than the will and the intentions of the Greeks, something that was binding on both the Greeks and the Persians. That something was the faculty of distinguishing by reason the good and the bad. For this faculty was not peculiar to the Greeks but was common to both Persians and Greeks.

Alexander had discovered empirically what Zeno was to formulate theoretically—that a large plural society cannot be governed without recognizing that, transcending its plural interests, there is a rational order with a superior common law. This common law is "natural" in the sense that it can be discovered by any rational mind, that it is not the willful and arbitrary positive command of the sovereign power.[11] This is the necessary assumption, without which it is impossible for different peoples with their competing interests to live together in peace and freedom within one community.

The Roman lawyers worked out what Alexander had anticipated and what the Stoics taught. By the time of Cicero there were, says Barker, three different bodies and conceptions of law.[12] The first, called *ius civile,* was applicable only to Roman citizens. The second was a body of commercial laws, known as the *ius gentium,* that were enforced by the Roman courts in all commercial cases: "a common law of contract throughout the empire." [13]

The *ius gentium* was meant to contain what was common and universal, separated from what was peculiar and local, in the laws of all states. And beyond this practical common law for commercial intercourse, the Roman jurists recognized that in theory there was also natural law, the *ius naturale,* which is "the law imposed on mankind by common human nature, that is, by reason in response to human needs and instincts." [14] This is not, says Barker, "a body of actual law, which can be enforced in actual courts"

. . . but "a way of looking at things—a spirit of 'humane interpretation' in the mind of the judge and the jurist—which may, and does, affect the law which is actually enforced, but does so without being actual law itself."

The idea of a universal rational order became substantial and effective in the Roman law. This was the law of a great society which did in fact bring peace and order to the Western world. The remembrance of the Roman peace is stamped indelibly on the consciousness of Western men. After the fall of the Roman Empire, the Roman law, which was practiced in some degree almost everywhere, and was taught everywhere, was recognized as "the law of an international civilization and relatively universal." [15]

With the beginning of the new age, after 1500, Roman law, as codified and digested in the *Corpus Juris* of Justinian, was regarded as the concrete expression of universal human reason. When the question came to be asked, says Barker, "What does this conception of Natural Law actually contain or include?" the answer tends to be, during the Middle Ages generally and down to the rise of a new school of Natural Law after 1500, "It contains or includes the *whole* of Roman law, which is, *as a whole,* both supremely reasonable and universally diffused, and is therefore natural." [16]

5. THE RUPTURE IN MODERN TIMES

The new school of natural law, which flourished from about 1500 to 1800, was a response to the pluralism of the modern age; to the rise of national states, to the schism of the Church, to the explorations and to the expansion of world commerce, to the advance of science and of secularism, to the progressive division and specialization of labor. As the diversity of belief, opinion and interest became greater, the need for common criterion and for common laws became more acute.

The new school of natural law was able to meet this need until the end of the eighteenth century. That was long enough to preside over the foundings of the British and the American constitutional orders, and of those which derive from them. But the school of natural law has not been able to cope with the pluralism of the later modern age—with the pluralism which has resulted from the industrial revolution and from the enfranchisement and the emancipation of the masses of the people.

In the simple and relatively homogeneous society of the eighteenth century natural law provided the principles of a free state. But then the mode of such thinking went out of fashion. In the nineteenth century little was done to remint the old ideas. They were regarded as obsolete and false, as hostile to the rise of democracy, and they were abandoned to the reactionaries. The great frame of reference to the rational order was missing. No body of specific principles and precepts was worked out in order to regulate international relations, nor to cope with the problems raised by the industrial revolution and the advance of science and technology.

Yet, in this pluralized and fragmenting society a public philosophy with common and binding principles was more necessary than it had ever been. The proof of the need is in the impulse to escape from freedom, which Erich Fromm has described so well.[17] It has been growing stronger as the emancipation of the masses of the people from authority has brought the dissolution of public, general, objective criteria of the true and the false, the right and the wrong. "I can assure you," wrote André Gide in 1928, "that the feeling of *freedom* can plunge the soul into a sort of anguish." [18]

"We know it from within, by a sort of immediate and personal experience," says Gilson, who was writing between the wars, that "Western culture was steadily following its process of dissolution." [19] Similarly, Spengler's famous book on *The Decline of the West* was first published in 1918 but it was written before the outbreak of the war.

But until the historic disasters of our own time, the loneliness and anxiety of modern men had been private, without public and overt political effect. As long as the public order still provided external security, their inner insecurity was still a personal and private and inward affair. Since the breakdown of public order during the First World War, there has been no security for multitudes and no ease of mind for anyone.

Observing the public disorder in which he himself had always lived, and knowing how the inner disorder provoked the impulse to escape from it, Hitler conceived his doctrine. He had the insight of genius into human weakness, and he wrote in *Mein Kampf* that the masses are "like a woman . . . who will submit to the strong man rather than dominate the weakling . . . the masses love the ruler rather than the suppliant, and inwardly they are far more satisfied by a doctrine which tolerates no rival than by the grant of liberal freedom; they often feel at a loss what to do with it, and even easily feel themselves deserted." [20]

The masses that Hitler was planning to dominate are the modern men who find in freedom from the constraints of the ancestral order an intolerable loss of guidance and of support. With Gide they are finding that the burden of freedom is too great an anxiety. The older structures of society are dissolving and they must make their way through a time of troubles. They have been taught to expect a steady progress towards a higher standard of life, and they have not been prepared to withstand the frustrations of a prolonged crisis in the outer world and the loneliness of their self-centered isolation.

They are the men who rise up against freedom, unable to cope with its insoluble difficulties and unable to endure the denial of communion in public and common truths. They have found no answer to their need and no remedy for their anguish in the principles and practice of freedom as they have known them in the liberal democracies of this century. There is a profound disorientation in their experience, a radical disconnection between the notions of their minds and the needs of their souls. They have become the "lonely crowd" [21] that Riesman has described. They are Durkheim's anomic mass.[22] They are Toynbee's proletarians who are "in" but not "of" the community they live in; for they have "no stake in that community beyond the fact of its physical existence." Their "true hallmark . . . is neither poverty nor humble birth but is the consciousness—and the resentment that this consciousness inspires—of being disinherited." [23] They are, as Karl Jaspers says, men dissolved into "an anonymous mass" because they are "without an authentic world, without provenance or roots," [24] without, that is to say, belief and faith that they can live by.

NOTES

1. Cf. my *Public Opinion,* Chapters I to X.

2. I am using the term "character" as Erich Fromm does, in his *Man for Himself* (1947), p. 49, meaning "the relatively permanent form in which human energy is canalized in the process of assimilation and socialization."

3. Erich Fromm, "Individual and Social Origin of Neurosis," *Amer-*

ican Sociological Review, Vol. 9 (1944), pp. 380-384. Reprinted in Clyde Kluckhohn and Henry Alexander Murray, *Personality in Nature, Society, and Culture* (1948), pp. 407, *et seq.*

4. William Ernest Hocking, *Human Nature and Its Remaking* (1923) p. 15.

5. John Courtney Murray, S.J., "The Problem of Pluralism in America," in *Thought* (Fordham University, Summer, 1954).

6. Cf. Otto von Gierke, *Political Theories of the Middle Age,* translated with an introduction by Frederick William Maitland (London, Cambridge University Press, 1927), pp. 73-87; and more especially note #256. Also cf. Leo Strauss, *Natural Right and History* (1953).

7. Sir Ernest Barker, *Traditions of Civility* (1948), pp. 10-12.

8. Cf. Mortimer Adler, "The Doctrine of Natural Law in Philosophy," *University of Notre Dame Natural Law Institute Proceedings,* Vol. I, pp. 65-84.

9. Ernest Barker, Introduction to his translation of *Aristotle's Politics* (1946), p. lix.

10. *Ibid.,* lix-lx. Cf. Saint Paul on the One Church, which was "neither Greek nor Jew. . . . Barbarian, Scythian, bond nor free."

11. Cf. Otto von Gierke, *Natural Law and the Theory of Society,* translated with an Introduction by Ernest Barker (1934), Vol. I, pp. 224-225.

12. *Ibid.,* p. xxxvi.

13. F. de Zulueta, "The Science of Law," in *The Legacy of Rome,* edited by Cyril Bailey (Oxford, Clarendon Press, 1928), p. 202.

14. *Ibid.,* p. 204.

15. *Ibid.,* p. 181.

16. Gierke, *op. cit.,* p. xxxix.

17. Erich Fromm, *Escape from Freedom.*

18. *The Journals of André Gide,* translated by Justin O'Brien (1947-51), Vol. III, 1928-1939, entry for Nov. 15, 1928, p. 26.

19. Etienne Gilson, *The Unity of Philosophical Experience* (1937), p. 271.

20. Adolf Hitler, *Mein Kampf* (1939), p. 56.

21. David Riesman, *The Lonely Crowd.*

22. Emile Durkheim, *Suicide.*

23. Arnold Toynbee, *A Study of History* (1951), Vol. I, p. 41; Vol. V, p. 63.

24. Karl Jaspers, *The Origin and Goal of History,* translated from the German edition of 1949 by Michael Bullock (London, Routledge and Kegan Paul, Ltd., 1953), pp. 127-128.

PART II

The Dialogue

4. A Realist Theory of International Politics*

by Hans J. Morgenthau

THIS BOOK PURPORTS TO PRESENT A THEORY OF INTERNATIONAL politics. The test by which such a theory must be judged is not *a priori* and abstract but empirical and pragmatic. The theory, in other words, must be judged not by some preconceived abstract principle or concept unrelated to reality, but by its purpose: to bring order and meaning to a mass of phenomena which without it would remain disconnected and unintelligible. It must meet a dual test, an empirical and a logical one: Do the facts as they actually are lend themselves to the interpretation the theory has put upon them, and do the conclusions at which the theory arrives follow with logical necessity from its premises? In short, is the theory consistent with the facts and within itself?

The issue this theory raises concerns the nature of all politics. The history of modern political thought is the story of a contest between two schools that differ fundamentally in their conceptions of the nature of man, society, and politics. One believes that a rational and moral political order, derived from universally valid abstract principles, can be achieved here and now. It assumes the essential goodness and infinite malleability of human nature, and blames the failure of the social order to measure up to the rational standards on lack of knowledge and understanding, obsolescent social institutions, or the depravity of certain isolated individuals or

* Reprinted by permission of the publisher from *Politics Among Nations,* Third Edition by Hans J. Morgenthau. Copyright, 1948, 1958, © 1960 by Alfred A. Knopf, Inc.

For a similar statement refer to Niccolo Machiavelli, *The Prince,* introduction by Christian Gauss (New York: The New American Library, 1952), pp. 84-94.

groups. It trusts in education, reform, and the sporadic use of force to remedy these defects.

The other school believes that the world, imperfect as it is from the rational point of view, is the result of forces inherent in human nature. To improve the world one must work with those forces, not against them. This being inherently a world of opposing interests and of conflict among them, moral principles can never be fully realized, but must at best be approximated through the ever temporary balancing of interests and the ever precarious settlement of conflicts. This school, then, sees in a system of checks and balances a universal principle for all pluralist societies. It appeals to historic precedent rather than to abstract principles, and aims at the realization of the lesser evil rather than of the absolute good.

This theoretical concern with human nature as it actually is, and with the historic processes as they actually take place, has earned for the theory presented here the name of realism. What are the tenets of political realism? No systematic exposition of the philosophy of political realism can be attempted here; it will suffice to single out six fundamental principles, which have frequently been misunderstood.

SIX PRINCIPLES OF POLITICAL REALISM

1. Political Realism believes that politics, like society in general, is governed by objective laws that have their roots in human nature. In order to improve society it is first necessary to understand the laws by which society lives. The operation of these laws being impervious to our preferences, men will challenge them only at the risk of failure.

Realism, believing as it does in the objectivity of the laws of politics, must also believe in the possibility of developing a rational theory that reflects, however imperfectly and one-sidedly, these objective laws. It believes also, then, in the possibility of distinguishing in politics between truth and opinion—between what is true objectively and rationally, supported by evidence and illuminated by reason, and what is only a subjective judgment, divorced from the facts as they are and informed by prejudice and wishful thinking.

Human nature, in which the laws of politics have their roots, has not changed since the classical philosophies of China, India, and Greece endeavored to discover these laws. Hence, novelty is not necessarily a virtue in political theory, nor is old age a defect. The fact that a theory of politics, if there be such a theory, has never been heard of before tends to create a presumption against, rather than in favor of, its soundness. Conversely, the fact that a theory of politics was developed hundreds or even thousands of years ago—as was the theory of the balance of power—does not create a presumption that it must be outmoded and obsolete. A theory of politics must be subjected to the dual test of reason and experience. To dismiss such a theory because it had its flowering in centuries past is to present not a rational argument, but a modernistic prejudice that takes for granted the superiority of the present over the past. To dispose of the rival of such a theory as a "fashion" or "fad" is tantamount to assuming that in matters political we can have opinions but no truths.

For realism, theory consists in ascertaining facts and giving them meaning through reason. It assumes that the character of a foreign policy can be ascertained only through the examination of the political acts performed and of the foreseeable consequences of these acts. Thus, we can find out what statesmen have actually done, and from the foreseeable consequences of their acts we can surmise what their objectives might have been.

Yet examination of the facts is not enough. To give meaning to the factual raw material of foreign policy, we must approach political reality with a kind of rational outline, a map that suggests to us the possible meanings of foreign policy. In other words, we put ourselves in the position of a statesman who must meet a certain problem of foreign policy under certain circumstances, and we ask ourselves what the rational alternatives are from which a statesman may choose who must meet this problem under these circumstances (presuming always that he acts in a rational manner), and which of these rational alternatives this particular statesman, acting under these circumstances, is likely to choose. It is the testing of this rational hypothesis against the actual facts and their consequences that gives meaning to the facts of international politics and makes a theory of politics possible.

2. The main signpost that helps political realism to find its way through the landscape of international politics is the concept of interest defined in terms of power. This concept provides the link

between reason trying to understand international politics and the facts to be understood. It sets politics as an autonomous sphere of action and understanding apart from other spheres, such as economics (understood in terms of interest defined as wealth), ethics, aesthetics, or religion. Without such a concept a theory of politics, international or domestic, would be altogether impossible, for without it we could not distinguish between political and non-political facts, nor could we bring at least a measure of systematic order to the political sphere.

We assume that statesmen think and act in terms of interest defined as power, and the evidence of history bears that assumption out. That assumption allows us to retrace and anticipate, as it were, the steps a statesman—past, present, or future—has taken or will take on the political scene. We look over his shoulder when he writes his dispatches; we listen in on his conversation with other statesmen; we read and anticipate his very thoughts. Thinking in terms of interest defined as power, we think as he does, and as disinterested observers we understand his thoughts and actions perhaps better than he, the actor on the political scene, does himself.

The concept of interest defined as power imposes intellectual discipline upon the observer, infuses rational order into the subject matter of politics, and thus makes the theoretical understanding of politics possible. On the side of the actor, it provides for rational discipline in action and creates that astounding continuity in foreign policy which makes American, British, or Russian foreign policy appear as an intelligible, rational continuum, by and large consistent within itself, regardless of the different motives, preferences, and intellectual and moral qualities of successive statesmen. A realist theory of international politics, then, will guard against two popular fallacies: the concern with motives and the concern with ideological preferences.

To search for the clue to foreign policy exclusively in the motives of statesmen is both futile and deceptive. It is futile because motives are the most illusive of psychological data, distorted as they are, frequently beyond recognition, by the interests and emotions of actor and observer alike. Do we really know what our own motives are? And what do we know of the motives of others?

Yet even if we had access to the real motives of statesmen, that knowledge would help us little in understanding foreign policies, and might well lead us astray. It is true that the knowledge of the statesman's motives may give us one among many clues as to what the direction of his foreign policy might be. It cannot give us, however, the one clue by which to predict his foreign policies. History shows no exact and necessary correlation between the quality of motives and the quality of foreign policy. This is true in both moral and political terms.

We cannot conclude from the good intentions of a statesman that his foreign policies will be either morally praiseworthy or politically successful. Judging his motives, we can say that he will not intentionally pursue policies that are morally wrong, but we can say nothing about the probability of their success. If we want to know the moral and political qualities of his actions, we must know them, not his motives. How often have statesmen been motivated by the desire to improve the world, and ended by making it worse? And how often have they sought one goal, and ended by achieving something they neither expected nor desired?

Neville Chamberlain's politics of appeasement were, as far as we can judge, inspired by good motives; he was probably less motivated by considerations of personal power than were many other British prime ministers, and he sought to preserve peace and to assure the happiness of all concerned. Yet his policies helped to make the Second World War inevitable, and to bring untold miseries to millions of men. Sir Winston Churchill's motives, on the other hand, have been much less universal in scope and much more narrowly directed toward personal and national power, yet the foreign policies that sprang from these inferior motives were certainly superior in moral and political quality to those pursued by his predecessor. Judged by his motives, Robespierre was one of the most virtuous men who ever lived. Yet it was the utopian radicalism of that very virtue that made him kill those less virtuous than himself, brought him to the scaffold, and destroyed the revolution of which he was a leader.

Good motives give assurance against deliberately bad policies; they inspire. What it is important to know, if one wants to understand foreign policy, is not primarily the motives of a statesman, but his intellectual ability to comprehend the essentials of foreign policy, as well as his political ability to translate what he has comprehended into successful political action. It follows that while ethics in the abstract judges the moral qualities of motives, political theory must judge the political qualities of intellect, will, and action.

A realist theory of international politics will also avoid the other popular fallacy of equating the foreign policies of a statesman with his philosophic or political sympathies, and of deducing the former from the latter. Statesmen, especially under contemporary conditions, may well make a habit of presenting their foreign policies in terms of their philosophic and political sympathies in order to gain popular support for them. Yet they will distinguish with Lincoln between their "*official* duty," which is to think and act in terms of the national interest, and their "*personal* wish," which is to see their own moral values and political principles realized throughout the world. Political realism does not require, nor does it condone, indifference to political ideals and moral principles, but it requires indeed a sharp distinction between the desirable and the possible—between what is desirable everywhere and at all times and what is possible under the concrete circumstances of time and place.

It stands to reason that not all foreign policies have always followed so rational, objective, and unemotional a course. The contingent elements of personality, prejudice, and subjective preference, and of all the weaknesses of intellect and will which flesh is heir to, are bound to deflect foreign policies from their rational course. Especially where foreign policy is conducted under the conditions of democratic control, the need to marshal popular emotions to the support of foreign policy cannot fail to impair the rationality of foreign policy itself. Yet a theory of foreign policy which aims at rationality must for the time being, as it were, abstract from these irrational elements and seek to paint a picture of foreign policy which presents the rational essence to be found in experience, without the contingent deviations from rationality which are also found in experience.

The difference between international politics as it actually is and a rational theory derived from it is like the difference between a photograph and a painted portrait. The photograph shows everything that can be seen by the naked eye; the painted portrait does not show everything that can be seen by the naked eye, but it shows, or at least seeks to show, one thing that the naked eye cannot see: the human essence of the person portrayed.

Political realism contains not only a theoretical but also a normative element. It knows that political reality is replete with contingencies and points to the typical influences they exert upon foreign policy. Yet it shares with all social theory the need for the sake of theoretical understanding, to stress the rational elements of political reality; for it is these rational elements that make reality intelligible for theory. Political realism presents the theoretical construct of a rational foreign policy which experience can never completely achieve.

At the same time political realism considers a rational foreign policy to be good foreign policy; for only a rational foreign policy minimizes risks and maximizes benefits and, hence, complies both with the moral precept of prudence and the political requirement of success. Political realism wants the photographic picture of the political world to resemble as much as possible its painted portrait. Aware of the inevitable gap between good—that is, rational—foreign policy and foreign policy as it actually is, political realism maintains not only that theory must focus upon the rational elements of political reality, but also that foreign policy ought to be rational in view of its own moral and practical purposes.

Hence, it is no argument against the theory here presented that actual foreign policy does not or cannot live up to it. That argument misunderstands the intention of this book, which is to present not an indiscriminate description of political reality, but a rational theory of international politics. Far from being invalidated by the fact that, for instance, a perfect balance of power policy will scarcely be found in reality, it assumes that reality, being deficient in this respect, must be understood and evaluated as an approximation to an ideal system of balance of power.

3. Realism does not endow its key concept of interest defined as power with a meaning that is fixed once and for all. The idea of interest is indeed of the essence of politics and is unaffected by the circumstances of time and place. Thucydides' statement, born of the experiences of ancient Greece, that "identity of interest is the surest of bonds whether between states or individuals" was taken up in the nineteenth century by Lord Salisbury's remark that "the

only bond of union that endures" among nations is "the absence of all clashing interests." It was erected into a general principle of government by George Washington:

> A small knowledge of human nature will convince us, that with far the greatest part of mankind, interest is the governing principle; and that almost every man is more or less, under its influence. Motives of public virtue may for a time, or in particular instances, actuate men to the observance of a conduct purely disinterested; but they are not of themselves sufficient to produce a persevering conformity to the refined dictates and obligations of social duty. Few men are capable of making a continual sacrifice of all views of private interest, or advantage, to the common good. It is vain to exclaim against the depravity of human nature on this account; the fact is so, the experience of every age and nation has proved it and we must in a great measure, change the constitution of man, before we can make it otherwise. No institution, not built on the presumptive truth of these maxims can succeed.[1]

It was echoed and enlarged upon in our century by Max Weber's observation:

> Interests (material and ideal), not ideas, dominate directly the actions of men. Yet the "images of the world" created by these ideas have very often served as switches determining the tracks on which the dynamism of interests kept actions moving.[2]

Yet the kind of interest determining political action in a particular period of history depends upon the political and cultural context within which foreign policy is formulated. The goals that might be pursued by nations in their foreign policy can run the whole gamut of objectives any nation has ever pursued or might possibly pursue.

The same observations apply to the concept of power. Its content and the manner of its use are determined by the political and cultural environment. Power may comprise anything that establishes and maintains the control of man over man. Thus power covers all social relationships which serve that end, from physical violence to the most subtle psychological ties by which one mind controls another. Power covers the domination of man by man, both when it is disciplined by moral ends and controlled by constitutional safeguards, as in Western democracies, and when it is that untamed and barbaric force which finds its laws in nothing but its own strength and its sole justification in its aggrandizement.

Political realism does not assume that the contemporary conditions under which foreign policy operates, with their extreme instability and the ever present threat of large-scale violence, cannot be changed. The balance of power, for instance, is indeed a perennial element of all pluralistic societies, as the authors of *The Federalist* papers well knew; yet it is capable of operating, as it does in the United States, under the conditions of relative stability and peaceful conflict. If the factors that have given rise to these conditions can be duplicated on the international scene, similar conditions of stability and peace will then prevail there, as they have over long stretches of history among certain nations.

What is true of the general character of international relations is also true of the nation state as the ultimate point of reference of contemporary foreign policy. While the realist indeed believes that interest is the perennial standard by which political action must be judged and directed, the contemporary connection between interest and the national state is a product of history, and is therefore bound to disappear in the course of history. Nothing in the realist position militates against the assumption that the present division of the political world into nation states will be replaced by larger units of a quite different character, more in keeping with the technical potentialities and the moral requirements of the contemporary world.

The realist parts company with other schools of thought before the all-important question of how the contemporary world is to be transformed. The realist is persuaded that this transformation can be achieved only through the workmanlike manipulation of the perennial forces that have shaped the past as they will the future. The realist cannot be persuaded that we can bring about that transformation by confronting a political reality that has its own laws with an abstract ideal that refuses to take those laws into account.

4. Political realism is aware of the moral significance of political action. It is also aware of the ineluctable tension between the moral command and the requirements of successful political action. And it is unwilling to gloss over and obliterate that tension and thus to obfuscate both the moral and the political issue by

making it appear as though the stark facts of politics were morally more satisfying than they actually are and the moral law less exacting than it actually is.

Realism maintains that universal moral principles cannot be applied to the actions of states in their abstract universal formulation, but that they must be filtered through the concrete circumstances of time and place. The individual may say for himself: "*Fiat justitia, pereat mundus* (Let justice be done, even if the world perish)," but the state has no right to say so in the name of those who are in its care. Both individual and state must judge political action by universal moral principles, such as that of liberty. Yet while the individual has a moral right to sacrifice himself in defense of such a moral principle, the state has no right to let its moral disapprobation of the infringement of liberty get in the way of successful political action, itself inspired by the moral principle of national survival. There can be no political morality without prudence; that is, without consideration of the political consequences of seemingly moral action. Realism, then, considers prudence—the weighing of the consequences of alternative political actions—to be the supreme virtue in politics. Ethics in the abstract judges action by its conformity with the moral law; political ethics judges action by its political consequences. Classical and medieval philosophy knew this and so did Lincoln when he said:

> I do the very best I know how, the very best I can, and I mean to keep doing so until the end. If the end brings me out all right, what is said against me won't amount to anything. If the end brings me out wrong, ten angels swearing I was right would make no difference.

5. Political realism refuses to identify the moral aspirations of a particular nation with the moral laws that govern the universe. As it distinguishes between truth and opinion, so it distinguishes between truth and idolatry. All nations are tempted—and few have been able to resist the temptation for long—to clothe their own particular aspirations and actions in the moral purposes of the universe. To know that nations are subject to the moral law is one thing, while to pretend to know with certainty what is good and evil in the relations among nations is quite another. There is a world of difference between the belief that all nations stand under

the judgment of God, inscrutable to the human mind, and the blasphemous conviction that God is always on one's side and that what one wills oneself cannot fail to be willed by God also.

The lighthearted equation between a particular nationalism and the counsels of Providence is morally indefensible, for it is that very sin of pride against which the Greek tragedians and the Biblical prophets have warned rulers and ruled. That equation is also politically pernicious, for it is liable to engender the distortion in judgment which, in the blindness of crusading frenzy, destroys nations and civilizations—in the name of moral principle, ideal, or God himself.

On the other hand, it is exactly the concept of interest defined in terms of power that saves us from both that moral excess and that political folly. For if we look at all nations, our own included, as political entities pursuing their respective interests defined in terms of power, we are able to do justice to all of them. And we are able to do justice to all of them in a dual sense: We are able to judge other nations as we judge our own and, having judged them in this fashion, we are then capable of pursuing policies that respect the interests of other nations, while protecting and promoting those of our own. Moderation in policy cannot fail to reflect the moderation of moral judgment.

6. The difference, then, between political realism and other schools of thought is real and it is profound. However much the theory of political realism may have been misunderstood and misinterpreted, there is no gainsaying its distinctive intellectual and moral attitude to matters political.

Intellectually, the political realist maintains the autonomy of the political sphere, as the economist, the lawyer, the moralist maintain theirs. He thinks in terms of interest defined as power, as the economist thinks in terms of interest defined as wealth; the lawyer, of the conformity of action with legal rules; the moralist, of the conformity of action with moral principles. The economist asks: "How does this policy affect the wealth of society, or a segment of it?" The lawyer asks: "Is this policy in accord with the rules of law?" The moralist asks: "Is this policy in accord with moral principles?" And the political realist asks: "How does this policy affect the power of the nation?" (Or of the federal government, of Congress, of the party, of agriculture, as the case may be.)

The political realist is not unaware of the existence and relevance of standards of thought other than political ones. As political realist, he cannot but subordinate these other standards to those of politics. And he parts company with other schools when they impose standards of thought appropriate to other spheres upon the political sphere. It is here that political realism takes issue with the "legalistic-moralistic approach" to international politics. That this issue is not, as has been contended, a mere figment of the imagination, but goes to the very core of the controversy, can be shown from many historical examples. Three will suffice to make the point.[3]

In 1939 the Soviet Union attacked Finland. This action confronted France and Great Britain with two issues, one legal, the other political. Did that action violate the Covenant of the League of Nations and, if it did, what countermeasures should France and Great Britain take? The legal question could easily be answered in the affirmative, for obviously the Soviet Union had done what was prohibited by the Covenant. The answer to the political question depended, first, upon the manner in which the Russian action affected the interests of France and Great Britain; second, upon the existing distribution of power between France and Great Britain, on the one hand, and the Soviet Union and other potentially hostile nations, especially Germany, on the other; and, third, upon the influence that the countermeasures were likely to have upon the interests of France and Great Britain and the future distribution of power. France and Great Britain, as the leading members of the League of Nations, saw to it that the Soviet Union was expelled from the League, and they were prevented from joining Finland in the war against the Soviet Union only by Sweden's refusal to allow their troops to pass through Swedish territory on their way to Finland. If this refusal by Sweden had not saved them, France and Great Britain would shortly have found themselves at war with the Soviet Union and Germany at the same time.

The policy of France and Great Britain was a classic example of legalism in that they allowed the answer to the legal question, legitimate within its sphere, to determine their political actions. Instead of asking both questions, that of law and that of power, they asked only the question of law; and the answer they received could have no bearing on the issue that their very existence might have depended upon.

The second example illustrates the "moralistic approach" to international politics. It concerns the international status of the Communist government of China. The rise of that government confronted the Western world with two issues, one moral, the other political. Were the nature and policies of that government in accord with the moral principles of the Western world? Should the Western world deal with such a government? The answer to the first question could not fail to be in the negative. Yet it did not follow with necessity that the answer to the second question should also be in the negative. The standard of thought applied to the first—the moral—question was simply to test the nature and the policies of the Communist government of China by the principles of Western morality. On the other hand, the second—the political—question had to be subjected to the complicated test of the interests involved and the power available on either side, and of the bearing of one or the other course of action upon these interests and power. The application of this test could well have led to the conclusion that it would be wiser not to deal with the Communist government of China. To arrive at this conclusion by neglecting this test altogether and answering the political question in terms of the moral issue was indeed a classic example of the "moralistic approach" to international politics.

The third case illustrates strikingly the contrast between realism and the legalistic-moralistic approach to foreign policy. Great Britain, as one of the guarantors of the neutrality of Belgium, went to war with Germany in August 1914 because Germany had violated the neutrality of Belgium. The British action could be justified either in realistic or legalistic-moralistic terms. That is to say, one could argue realistically that for centuries it had been axiomatic for British foreign policy to prevent the control of the Low Countries by a hostile power. It was then not so much the violation of Belgium's neutrality per se as the hostile intentions of the violator which provided the rationale for British intervention. If the violator had been another nation but Germany, Great Britain might well have refrained from intervening. This is the position taken by Sir Edward Grey, British Foreign Secretary during that period. Under Secretary for Foreign Affairs Hardinge remarked to him in 1908: "If France violated Belgian neutrality in a war against Germany, it is doubtful whether England or Russia would move a finger to maintain Belgian neutrality, while if the neutrality of Belgium was violated by Germany, it is probable that the converse would be the case." Whereupon Sir Edward Grey replied: "This is to the point." Yet one could also take the legalistic and moralistic position that the violation of Belgium's neutrality per se, because of its legal and moral defects and regardless of the interests at stake and of the identity of the violator, justified British and, for that matter, American intervention. This was the position which Theodore Roosevelt took in his letter to Sir Edward Grey of January 22, 1915:

> To me the crux of the situation has been Belgium. If England or France had acted toward Belgium as Germany has acted I should have opposed them, exactly as I now oppose Germany. I have emphatically approved your action as a model for what should be done by those who believe that treaties should be observed in good faith and that there is such a thing as international morality. I take this position as an American who is no more an Englishman than he is a German, who endeavors loyally to serve the interests of his own country, but who also endeavors to do what he can for justice and decency as regards mankind at large, and who therefore feels obliged to judge all other nations by their conduct on any given occasion.

This realist defense of the autonomy of the political sphere against its subversion by other modes of thought does not imply disregard for the existence and importance of these other modes of thought. It rather implies that each should be assigned its proper sphere and function. Political realism is based upon a pluralistic conception of human nature. Real man is a composite of "economic man," "political man," "moral man," "religious man," etc. A man who was nothing but "political man" would be a beast, for he would be completely lacking in moral restraints. A man who was nothing but "moral man" would be a fool, for he would be completely lacking in prudence. A man who was nothing but "religious man" would be a saint, for he would be completely lacking in worldly desires.

Recognizing that these different facets of human nature exist, political realism also recognizes that in order to understand one of them one has to deal with it on its own terms. That is to say, if I want to understand "religious man," I must for the time being abstract from the other aspects of human nature and deal with its religious aspect as if it were the only one. Furthermore, I must apply to the religious sphere the standards of thought appropriate to it, always remaining aware of the existence of other standards and their actual influence upon the religious qualities of man. What is true of this facet of human nature is true of all the others. No modern economist, for instance, would conceive of his science and its relations to other sciences of man in any other way. It is exactly through such a process of emancipation from other standards of thought, and the development of one appropriate to its subject matter, that economics has developed as an autonomous theory of the economic activities of man. To contribute to a similar development in the field of politics is indeed the purpose of political realism.

It is in the nature of things that a theory of politics which is based upon such principles will not meet with unanimous approval—nor does, for that matter, such a foreign policy. For theory and policy alike run counter to two trends in our culture which are not able to reconcile themselves to the assumptions and results of a rational, objective theory of politics. One of these trends disparages the role of power in society on grounds that stem from the experience and philosophy of the nineteenth century; we shall address ourselves to this tendency later in greater detail.[4] The other trend, opposed to the realist theory and practice of politics, stems from the very relationship that exists, and must exist, between the human mind and the political sphere. For reasons that we shall discuss later[5] the human mind in its day-by-day operations cannot bear to look the truth of politics straight in the face. It must disguise, distort, belittle, and embellish the truth—the more so, the more the individual is involved actively in the processes of politics, and particularly in those of international politics. For only by deceiving himself about the nature of politics and the role he plays on the political scene is man able to live contentedly as a political animal with himself and his fellow men.

Thus it is inevitable that a theory which tries to understand international politics as it actually is and as it ought to be in view of its intrinsic nature, rather than as people would like to see it, must overcome a psychological resistance that most other branches of learning need not face. A book devoted to the theoretical understanding of international politics therefore requires a special explanation and justification.

NOTES

1. *The Writings of George Washington,* edited by John C. Fitzpatrick (Washington: United States Printing Office, 1931-44), Vol. X, p. 363.
2. Marianne Weber, *Max Weber* (Tuebingen: J. C. B. Mohr, 1926), pp. 347-8.
3. See other examples discussed in Hans J. Morgenthau, "Another 'Great Debate': The National Interest of the United States," *The American Political Science Review,* XLVI (December 1952), pp. 979ff. See also Hans J. Morgenthau, *Dilemmas of Politics* (Chicago: University of Chicago Press, 1958), pp. 54ff.
4. Morgenthau, *Politics Among Nations,* p. 31ff
5. *Ibid.,* p. 86ff.

5. The Morality of Nations*

by Reinhold Niebuhr

THE DIFFERENCE BETWEEN THE ATTITUDES OF INDIVIDUALS AND those of groups has been frequently alluded to, the thesis being that group relations can never be as ethical as those which characterize individual relations. In dealing with the problem of social justice, it may be found that the relation of economic classes within a state is more important than international relations. But from the standpoint of analyzing the ethics of group behavior, it is feasible to study the ethical attitude of nations first; because the modern nation is the human group of strongest social cohesion, of most undisputed central authority and of most clearly defined membership. The church may have challenged its pre-eminence in the Middle Ages, and the economic class may compete with it for the loyalty of men in our own day; yet it remains, as it has been since the seventeenth century, the most absolute of all human associations.

Nations are territorial societies, the cohesive power of which is supplied by the sentiment of nationality and the authority of the state. The fact that state and nation are not synonymous and that states frequently incorporate several nationalities, indicates that the authority of government is the ultimate force of national cohesion. The fact that state and nation are roughly synonymous proves that, without the sentiment of nationality with its common language and traditions, the authority of government is usually unable to maintain national unity. The unity of Scotland and England within a single British state and the failure to maintain the same unity between England and Ireland, suggest both the possibilities and the limitations of transcending nationality in the formation of states. For our purposes we may think of state and nation as interchangeable terms, since our interest is in the moral attitudes of nations which have the apparatus of a state at their disposal, and through it are able to consolidate their social power and define their political attitudes and policies.

The selfishness of nations is proverbial. It was a dictum of George Washington that nations were not to be trusted beyond their own interest. "No state," declares a German author, "has ever entered a treaty for any other reason than self interest," and adds: "A statesman who has any other motive would deserve to be hung." [1] "In every part of the world," said Professor Edward Dicey, "where British interests are at stake, I am in favor of advancing these interests even at the cost of war. The only qualification I admit is that the country we desire to annex or take under our protection should be calculated to confer a tangible advantage upon the British Empire." [2] National ambitions are not always avowed as honestly as this, as we shall see later, but that is a fair statement of the actual facts, which need hardly to be elaborated for any student of history.

What is the basis and reason for the selfishness of nations? If we begin with what is least important or least distinctive of national attitudes, it must be noted that nations do not have direct contact with other national communities, with which they must form some kind of international community. They know the problems of other peoples only indirectly and at second hand. Since both sympathy and justice depend to a large degree upon the perception of need, which makes sympathy flow, and upon the understanding of competing interests, which must be resolved, it is obvious that human communities have greater difficulty than individuals in achieving ethical relationships. While rapid means of communication have increased the breadth of knowledge about world affairs among citizens of various nations, and the general advance of education has ostensibly promoted the capacity to think rationally and justly upon the inevitable conflicts of interest between nations, there is nevertheless little hope of arriving at a perceptible increase of international morality through the growth of intelligence and the perfection of means of communication. The development of international commerce, the increased economic interdependence among the nations, and the whole apparatus of a technological civilization, increase the problems and issues between nations much more rapidly than the intelligence to solve them can be created. The silk trade between America and Japan did not give American citizens an appreciation of the real feelings of the Japanese toward the American Exclusion Act. Co-operation between America and the Allies during the war did not help American citizens to recognize, and deal sympathetically with, the issues of inter-allied debts and reparations; nor were the Allies able to do justice to either themselves or their fallen foe in settling the problem of reparations. Such is the social ignorance of peoples, that, far from doing justice to a foe or neighbor, they are as yet unable to conserve their own interests wisely. Since their ultimate interests are always protected best, by at least a measure of fairness toward their neighbors, the desire to gain an immediate selfish advantage always imperils their ultimate interests.[3] If they recognize this fact, they usually recognize it too late. Thus France, after years of intransigence, has finally accepted a sensible reparations settlement. Significantly and tragically, the settlement is almost synchronous with the victory of an extreme nationalism in Germany, which her unrelenting policies begot. America pursued a selfish and foolhardly tariff policy until it, together with other imbecilities in international life, contributed to the ruin of prosperity in the whole world. Britain, though her people are politically more intelligent than those of any modern nation, did not yield in Ireland in time to prevent the formation of a virus which is still poisoning Anglo-Irish relations. And while the American Civil War taught her a lesson, which she applied in preserving her colonial empire, there is as yet no proof that she will be wise enough to admit India into partnership, before the vehemence of Indian reaction to British Imperialism will make partnership upon even a minimum basis impossible. So runs the sad story of the social ignorance of nations.

There is always, in every nation, a body of citizens more intelligent than the average, who see the issues between their own and other nations more clearly than the ignorant patriot, and more disinterestedly than the dominant classes who seek special advantages in international relations. The size of this group varies in different nations. Although it may at times place a check upon the more extreme types of national self-seeking, it is usually not powerful enough to affect national attitudes in a crisis. The British liberals could not prevent the Boer War; American economists have recently inveighed against a suicidal tariff policy in vain, and German liberals were unable to check the aggressive policy of imperial Germany. Sometimes the humanitarian impulses and the sentiment of justice, developed in these groups, serve the policy of official governments and seem to affect their actions. Thus, the agitation of E. D. Morel against the atrocities in the Belgian Congo was supported by the British Government as long as it desired, for other reasons, to bring political pressure upon the Belgian King. Once this purpose was satisfied the British Cabinet dropped Mr. Morel's campaign as quickly as it had espoused it.[4] It is of course possible that the rational interest in international justice may become, on occasion, so widespread and influential that it will affect the diplomacy of states. But this is not usual. In other words the mind, which places a restraint upon impulses in individual life, exists only in a very inchoate form in the nation. It is, moreover, much more remote from the will of the nation than in private individuals; for the government expresses the national will, and that will is moved by the emotions of the populace and the prudential self-interest of dominant economic classes. Theoretically it is possible to have a national electorate so intelligent, that the popular impulses and the ulterior interests of special groups are brought under the control of a national mind. But practically the rational understanding of political issues remains such a minimum force that national unity of action can be achieved only upon such projects as are either initiated by the self-interest of the dominant groups, in control of the government, or supported by the popular emotions and hysterias which from time to time run through a nation. In other words the nation is a corporate unity, held together much more by force and emotion, than by mind. Since there can be no ethical action without self-criticism, and no self-criticism without the rational capacity of self-transcendence, it is natural that national attitudes can hardly approximate the ethical. Even those tendencies toward self-criticism in a nation which do express themselves are usually thwarted by the governing classes and by a certain instinct for unity in society itself. For self-criticism is a kind of inner disunity, which the feeble mind of a nation finds difficulty in distinguishing from dangerous forms of inner conflict. So nations crucify their moral rebels with their criminals upon the same Golgotha, not being able to distinguish between the moral idealism which surpasses, and the antisocial conduct which falls below that moral mediocrity, on the level of which every society unifies its life. While critical loyalty toward a community is not impossible, it is not easily achieved. It is therefore probably inevitable that every society should regard criticism as a proof of a want of loyalty. This lack of criticism as Tyrrell the Catholic modernist observed, makes the social will more egotistic than the individual will. "So far as society has a self," he wrote, "it must be self-assertive, proud, self-complacent and egotistical." [5]

The necessity of using force in the establishment of unity in a national community, and the inevitable selfish exploitation of the instruments of coercion by the groups who wield them, adds to the selfishness of nations. This factor in national life has been previously discussed and may need no further elaboration. It may be well to add that it ought not to be impossible to reduce this source of national selfishness. When governing groups are deprived of their special economic privileges, their interests will be more nearly in harmony with the interests of the total national society. At present the economic overlords of a nation have special interests in the profits of international trade, the exploitation of weaker peoples and in the acquisition of raw materials and markets, all of which are only remotely relevant to the welfare of the whole people. They are relevant at all only because, under the present organization of society, the economic life of a whole nation is bound up with the private enterprises of individuals. Furthermore the unequal distribution of wealth under the present economic system concentrates wealth which cannot be invested, and produces goods which cannot be absorbed, in the nation itself. The whole nation is therefore called upon to protect the investments and the markets which the economic overlords are forced to seek in other nations. If a socialist commonwealth should succeed in divorcing privilege from power, it would thereby materially reduce the selfishness of nations, though it is probably romantic to hope, as most socialists do, that all causes of international friction would be abolished. Wars were waged before the modern capitalistic social order existed, and they may continue after it is abolished.

The greed of the capitalistic classes has sharpened, but not created, the imperialism of nations. If, as Bertrand Russell prophesies,[6] some form of oligarchy, whether capitalistic or communistic, be inevitable in a technological age, because of the inability of the general public to maintain social control over the experts who are in charge of the intricate processes of economics and politics, the communistic oligarch would seem to be preferable in the long run to the capitalistic one. His power would be purely political and no special economic interests would tempt him to pursue economic policies at variane with the national interest. He might nevertheless have private ambitions and dreams of grandeur which would tempt him to sacrifice a nation to them. Since he would control the organs of propaganda, as do the capitalistic overlords, he might very well manufacture the popular emotion, required for the support of his enterprise.

The social ignorance of the private citizen of the nation has thus far been assumed. It may be reasonable to hope that the general level of intelligence will greatly increase in the next decades and centuries and that growing social intelligence will modify national attitudes. It is doubtful whether it will ever increase sufficiently to eliminate all the moral hazards of international relations. There is an ethical paradox in patriotism which defies every but the most astute and sophisticated analysis. The paradox is that patriotism transmutes individual unselfishness into national egotism. Loyalty to the nation is a high form of altruism when compared with lesser loyalties and more parochial interest. It therefore becomes the vehicle of all the altruistic impulses and expresses itself, on occasion, with such fervor that the critical attitude of the individual toward the nation and its enterprises is almost completely destroyed. The unqualified character of this devotion is the very basis of the nation's power and of the freedom to use the power without moral restraint. Thus, the unselfishness of individual makes for the selfishness of nations. That is why the hope of solving the larger social problems of mankind, merely by extending the social sympathies of individuals, is so vain. Altruistic passion is sluiced into the reservoirs of nationalism with great ease, and is made to flow beyond them with great difficulty. What lies beyond the nation, the community of mankind, is too vague to inspire devotion. The lesser communities within the nation, religious, economic, racial and cultural, have equal difficulty in competing with the nation for the loyalty of its citizens. The church was able to do so when it had the prestige of a universality it no longer possesses. Future developments may make the class rather than the nation the community of primary loyalty. But for the present the nation is still supreme. It not only possesses a police power, which other communities lack, but it is able to avail itself of the most potent and vivid symbols to impress its claims upon the consciousness of the individual. Since it is impossible to become conscious of a large social group without adequate symbolism this factor is extremely important. The nation possesses in its organs of government, in the panoply and ritual of the state, in the impressive display of its fighting services, and, very frequently, in the splendors of a royal house, the symbols of unity and greatness, which inspire awe and reverence in the citizen. Furthermore, the love and pious attachment of a man to his countryside, to familiar scenes, sights, and experiences, around which the memories of youth have cast a halo of sanctity, all this flows into the sentiment of patriotism; for a simple imagination transmutes the universal beneficences of nature into symbols of the peculiar blessings which a benevolent nation bestows upon its citizens. Thus the sentiment of patriotism achieves a potency in the modern soul, so unqualified, that the nation is given *carte blanche* to use the power, compounded of the devotion of individuals, for any purpose it desires. Thus, to choose an example among hundreds, Mr. Lloyd George during the famous Agadir Crisis in 1911 in which a European war became imminent because marauding nations would not allow a new robber to touch their spoils in Africa, could declare in his Mansion House speech: "If a situation were to be forced upon us in which peace could only be preserved by the surrender of the great and beneficent position Britain has won by centuries of heroism and achievement, by allowing Britain to be treated, when her interests were vitally affected, as if she were no account in the cabinet of nations, then I say emphatically that peace at that price would be a humiliation intolerable for a great country like ours to endure." [7] The very sensitive "honor" of nations can always be appeased by the blood of its citizens and no national ambition seems too base or petty to claim and to receive the support of a majority of its patriots.

Unquestionably there is an alloy of projected self-interest in patriotic altruism. The man in the street, with his lust for power and prestige thwarted by his own limitations and the necessities of social life, projects his *ego* upon his nation and indulges his anarchic lusts vicariously. So the nation is at one and the same time a check upon, and a final vent for, the expression of individual egoism. Sometimes it is economic interest, and sometimes mere vanity, which thus expresses itself in the individual patriot. Writing of his friend Winston Churchill, Wilfrid Scawen Blunt said: "Like most of them, it is the vanity of empire that affects him more than the supposed profits or the necessities of trade, which he repudiates." [8] The cultural imperialism which disavows economic advantages, but gains a selfish satisfaction in the aggrandizement of a national culture through imperialistic power, may reveal itself in the most refined and generous souls. Men like Ruskin and Tennyson were not free from it, and it is not absent even from religious missionary enterprises. Paul Pfeffer reports that some Russians hope not only to bestow their form of government upon the whole world but expect that Russian will become the universal language.[9] While economic advantages of national aggression usually accrue to privileged economic groups rather than to a total population, there are nevertheless possibilities of gain in imperialism for the average citizen; and he does fail to count upon them. A modern British writer on India declares: "It has been computed that every fifth man in Great Britain is dependent, either directly or indirectly, on our Indian connection for livelihood. That being so it passes comprehension of most thinking people why so little account has been taken of the dangerous forces which are every day gathering in India to destroy our trade and commerce." [10] Such a frank statement admits the motive of national egoism which is usually obscured by English, as by other imperialists with the pious insistence that nothing but concern for peace and order in India prompts Englishmen to bear their arduous burdens there.

A combination of unselfishness and vicarious selfishness in the individual thus gives a tremendous force to national egoism, which neither religious nor rational idealism can ever completely check. The idealists, whose patriotism has been qualified by more universal loyalties must always remain a minority group. In the past they have not been strong enough to affect the actions of nations and have had to content themselves with a policy of dissociation from the nation in times of crisis, when national ambitions were in sharpest conflict with their moral ideals. Whether conscientious pacifism on the part of two per cent of a national population could actually prevent future wars, as Professor Einstein maintains, is a question which cannot be answered affirmatively with any great degree of certainty. It is much more likely that the power of modern nationalism will remain essentially unchecked, until class loyalty offers it effective competition.

Perhaps the most significant moral characteristic of a nation is its hypocrisy. We have noted that self-deception and hypocrisy is an unvarying element in the moral life of all human beings. It is the tribute which morality pays to immorality; or rather the device by which the lesser self gains the consent of the larger self to indulge in impulses and ventures which the rational self can approve only when they are disguised. One can never be quite certain whether the disguise is meant only for the eye of the external observer or whether, as may be usually the case, it deceives the self. Naturally this defect in individuals becomes more apparent in the less moral life of nations. Yet it might be supposed that nations, of whom so much less is expected, would not be under the necessity of making moral pretensions for their actions. There was probably a time when they were under no such necessity. Their hypocrisy is both a tribute to the growing rationality of man and a proof of the ease with which rational demands may be circumvented.

The dishonesty of nations is a necessity of political policy if the nation is to gain the full benefit of its double claim upon the loyalty and devotion of the individual, as his own special and unique community and as a community which embodies universal values and ideals. The two claims, the one touching the individual's emotions and the other appealing to his mind, are incompatible with each other, and can be resolved only through dishonesty. This is particularly evident in war-time. Nations do not really arrive at full self-consciousness until they stand in vivid, usually bellicose, juxtaposition to other nations. The social reality, comprehended in the existence of a nation, is too large to make a vivid impression upon the imagination of the citizen. He vaguely identifies it with his own little community and fireside and usually accepts the mythos which attributes personality to his national group. But the impression is not so vivid as to arouse him to any particular fervor of devotion. This fervor is the unique product of the times of crisis, when his nation is in conflict with other nations. It springs from the new vividness with which the reality and the unity of his nation's discreet existence is comprehended. In other words, it is just in the moments when the nation is engaged in aggression or defense (and it is always able to interpret the former in terms of the latter) that the reality of the nation's existence becomes so sharply outlined as to arouse the citizen to the most passionate and uncritical devotion toward it. But at such a time the nation's claim to uniqueness also comes in sharpest conflict with the generally accepted impression that the nation is the incarnation of universal values. This conflict can be resolved only by deception. In the imagination of the simple patriot the nation is not a society but Society. Though its values are relative they appear, from his naive perspective, to be absolute. The religious instinct for the absolute is no less potent in patriotic religion than in any other. The nation is always endowed with an aura of the sacred, which is one reason why religions, which claim universality, are so easily captured and tamed by national sentiment, religion and patriotism merging in the process. The spirit of the nationally established churches and the cult of "Christentum and Deutschtum" of pre-war Germany are interesting examples. The best means of harmonizing the claim to universality with the unique and relative life of the nation, as revealed in moments of crisis, is to claim general and universally valid objectives for the nation. It is alleged to be fighting for civilization and for culture; and the whole enterprise of humanity is supposedly involved in its struggles. In the life of the simple citizen this hypocrisy exists as a naive and unstudied self-deception. The politician practices it consciously (though he may become the victim of his own arts), in order to secure the highest devotion from the citizen for his enterprises. The men of culture give themselves to it with less conscious design than the statesmen because their own inner necessities demand the deceptions, even more than do those of the simple citizens. The religious or the rational culture to which they are devoted helps them to realize that moral values must be universal, if they are to be real; and they cannot therefore give themselves to national aspirations, unless they clothe them in the attributes of universality. A few of them recognize the impossibility of such a procedure. Among most, the force of reason operates only to give the hysterias of war and the imbecilities of national politics more plausible excuses than an average man is capable of inventing. So they become the worst liars of wartime. "England," declared Professor Adolf Harnack, most eminent of German war-period theologians, "cuts the dyke which has preserved western Europe and its civilisation from the encroaching desert of Russia and Pan-Slavism. We must hold out for we must defend the work of fifteen hundred years for Europe and for England itself." [11] The great philosopher, Rudolf Eucken was even more unequivocal in identifying his nation's cause with ultimate values. "In this sense," he said, "we have a right to say that we form the soul of humanity and that the destruction of German nature would rob world history of its deepest meaning." [12] M. Paul Sabatier could declare, "No doubt we are fighting for ourselves but we are fighting, too, for all peoples. The France of today is fighting religiously . . . We all feel that our sorrows continue and fulfill those of the innocent victim of Calvary." [13] The literature of the war period teems with similar examples of the self-deception of intellectuals. There is always the possibility that some of it was prompted by dishonest truckling to the hysteria of the populace and the pressure of governments. But most of it was not as dishonest as that.

Hardly any war of history has been the occasion of more hypocrisy and sentimentality than the Spanish-American War. Yet as intelligent a man as Walter Hines Page could extract the following pious moral from it: "May there not come such a chance in Mexico—to clean out the bandits, yellow fever, malaria, hookworm—all to make the country healthful, safe for life and investment and for orderly self-government, at last? What we did in Cuba might thus be made the beginning of a new epoch in history, conquest for the sole benefit of the conquered, worked out by a sanitary reformation. The new sanitation will reclaim all tropical lands; but the work must first be done by military power—probably from the outside. May not the existing military power of Europe conceivably be diverted to this use? . . . And the tropics cry out for sanitation."[14] Perhaps it is rather significant that the American idea of a universal value should express itself in terms of sanitation.

The Spanish-American War offers some of the most striking illustrations of the hypocrisy of governments as well as of the self-deception of intellectuals. The hypocrisy was probably excessive, because a youthful and politically immature nation tried to harmonize the anti-imperialistic innocency of its childhood with the imperial impulses of its awkward youth. It was just beginning to feel and to test its strength and was both proud and ashamed of what it felt. President McKinley's various state papers and addresses are a perfect mine for the cynic. In a message to Congress before the outbreak of hostilities, he declared: "If it shall hereafter appear to be a duty imposed by our obligations to ourselves, to civilization and humanity to intervene with force it shall be done without fault on our part and only because the necessity for such action will be so clear as to command the support and the approval of the civilized world." He added: "I speak not of forcible annexation for that cannot be thought of. That by our code of morals would be criminal aggression."[15]

When the amiable President was finally pushed into the war by our passionate patriots, though Spain yielded to all of our demands, he answered a "pressing appeal to the feelings of humanity and moderation in the President and people of the United States" from the powers of Europe which sought to avert war by conciliation, by expressing the hope "that equal appreciation will be shown for our own earnest efforts and unselfish endeavors to fulfill a duty to humanity by ending a situation, the indefinite prolongation of which has become insufferable."[16] The war was launched on a wave of patriotic sentimentality in which both the religious idealists and the humanitarians went into ecstasies over our heroic defense of the Cuban people, forgetting that many American statesmen, beginning with the anti-imperialist Thomas Jefferson, had regarded the Spanish hold upon so proximate an island as Cuba as ultimately untenable. The actual annexation of Cuba was prevented only by the fact that the Teller Amendment, disavowing such an aim, was slipped unobserved into the Senate resolution which authorized hostilities.[17]

Since no promises were made in regard to the Philippines, the hypocrisy of a nation could express itself most unrestrainedly in the policies dealing with them. Though the little junta, of which Theodore Roosevelt and Senator Lodge were the leaders, had carefully planned the campaign of war so that the Philippines would become ours, the fiction that the fortunes of war had made us the unwilling recipients and custodians of the Philippine Islands was quickly fabricated and exists to this day. We decided to keep the Philippines against their will at the conclusion of a war ostensibly begun to free the Cubans. The President charged the peace commission which was to negotiate the peace treaty with Spain that it "should be as scrupulous and magnanimous in the concluding settlement as the nation had been just and humane in the original action." Since we constantly increased our demands during the session of the peace conference, the Spaniards must have gained a curious impression of the meaning of magnanimity. In regard to the Philippines the President charged the commissioners: The march of events rules and overrules human action. We cannot be unmindful that without any design on our part the war has brought us new responsibilities and duties which we must meet and discharge as becomes a great nation on whose growth and career from the beginning the Ruler of Nations has plainly written the high command and pledge of civilisation." [18] When after a great deal of negotiation among the commissioners and much debate between imperialists and anti-imperialists in America it was finally decided to ask for all of the Philippines, Secretary Hay wrote to the commissioners: "You are instructed to insist on the cession of the whole of the Philippines . . . The questions of duty and humanity appeal to the President so strongly that he can find no appropriate answer but the one he has marked out." [19] There were American citizens, of course, who saw through all of this hypocrisy. "Why," declared Mr. Moorfield Storey, one of the great liberal spirits of that day, "should Cuba with 1,600,000 people have a right to freedom and self-government and the 8,000,000 people who dwell in the Philippines be denied the same right?" [20] But these critics were not strong enough to prevail against the will-to-power of a vigorous young nation. The instructions to the army, after Spain finally ceded the islands and the peace treaty was signed, complete the chapter in hypocrisy with an almost perfect touch of dishonesty: "It will be the duty of the commander of the forces of occupation to announce and proclaim in the most public manner possible that we have come not as invaders or as conquerors but as friends." [21]

Later Mr. McKinley explained to a group of clergymen just how he arrived at his decision on American policy: "I walked the floor of the White house night after night until midnight; and I am not ashamed to tell you gentlemen that I went on my knees and prayed to Almighty God for light and guidance more than one night. And one night it came to me this way—that there was nothing left for us to do but to take them all, and to educate the Filipinos, and uplift and civilize and Christianize them, and by God's grace do the very best we could by them, as our fellowmen for whom Christ also died. And then I went to bed and went to sleep and slept soundly." [22]

America has not been altogether disobedient to Mr. McKinley's heavenly vision, for it has done a rather creditable job of education and sanitation in the islands. Nevertheless a modern observer of western imperialism in the orient, Nathaniel Peffer, gives a truer estimate than Mr. McKinley of the real motives of imperialism when he observes cynically: "Much might be said of their fitness for self-government, but why? What does it matter? The Filipinos will seize the government and proclaim themselves independent tomorrow if they had the power. And if and when they have the power, they will, whether fit for self-government or not. And were they as politically wise as Solons, the American Government would not give them their independence now, nor a hundred years from now, if American interests were to lose thereby." [23] Mr. Peffer's observations have received very recent verification by the fact that a new sentiment in favor of Philippine independence is prompted by the desire of American sugar interests to place Philippine sugar outside of the American tariff wall.

Mr. McKinley's hypocrisies were a little more than usually naive. But they could be fairly well matched in the history of other statesmen and nations. Mr. Gladstone was as pious and upright a statesman as Mr. McKinley, and probably more intelligent. He was, as McKinley, anti-imperialist by conviction. When the occupation of Egypt was forced upon him, he was anxious to preserve the guise, and perhaps even the reality, of his anti-imperial policy. He declared "Of all things in the world, that (permanent occupation) is the thing we are not going to do." The army was to be withdrawn "as soon as the state of the country and the organization of the proper means for the maintenance of the khedive's authority will admit of it." This pledge, said Gladstone, was a sacred pledge. It had "earned for us the confidence of Europe during the course of this difficult and delicate operation, and which, if one pledge can be more sacred than another, special sacredness in this case binds us to fulfill." [24] Nevertheless Gladstone did not fulfill it, and it has not been fulfilled since. The failure to do so is now proudly exhibited by Englishmen as an example of the British genius for "muddling through." At an earlier date when Kitchener was conquering the Sudan and came into conflict with the French General Marchand at Fashoda, Lord Rosebery declared in an address "I hope that this incident will be pacifically settled but it must be understood that there can be no compromise of the rights of Egypt." [25] The height of national hypocrisy was probably reached in the Preamble of the Treaty of the Holy Alliance in which the reactionary intentions of Russia, Prussia and Austria in forming the alliance are introduced in words reeking with dishonest religious unction: "Their Majesties solemly declare . . . their unshakable resolution . . . to take as their sole rule the precepts of holy Religion, precepts of righteousness, Christian love and peace . . . Consequently their Majesties have agreed, conformable to the words of Holy Writ which command all men to regard one another as brethren, to remain united by the bonds of a true and indissoluble brotherhood, and to help one another like fellow countrymen in all conditions and all cases. Towards their peoples and their armies they will behave as fathers to their families and they will guide them in the same spirit of brotherliness as that which inspires themselves. . . . The three allied sovereigns feel themselves but the pleni-potentiaries of Providence for the government of the three branches of the same family . . . All powers that solemnly subscribe to these principles will be received into this Holy Alliance." This document is particularly interesting because its sentiments betray the hand of that mystic sentimentalist, Czar Alexander of Russia, but the man who engineered the political deals which it is supposed to sanctify was the cynic and realist, Metternich. Somewhat in the same fashion the realities of the Treaty of Versailles were dictated by Clemenceau, while Wilson supplied the garnish of sentiment and idealism. No nation has ever made a frank avowal of its real imperial motives. It always claims to be primarily concerned with the peace and prosperity of the people whom it subjugates. In the Treaty of 1907 in which Russia and England partitioned Persia, the two nations promised to "respect the integrity and independence of Persia" and claimed to be "sincerely desiring the preservation of order throughout the country." [26] When Spain and France divided Morocco they joined in a statement in which they professed themselves "firmly attached to the integrity of the Moorish Empire under the sovereignty of the Sultan." [27] Most of the treaties by which the European nations have divided the spoils of empire are textbooks in hypocrisy. One can never be sure how much they are meant to fool the outside world, how much they are meant for the deception of their own deluded nationals, and how much they are meant to heal a moral breach in the inner life of statesmen, who find themselves torn between the necessities of statecraft and the sometimes sensitive promptings of an individual conscience. In men like McKinley, Gladstone, Woodrow Wilson, Herbert Asquith and Sir Edward Grey and Bethmann-Hollweg the latter element is quite important.

Our imperialistic policy in Latin-America and the Caribbean, which, as every historian knows, differs from the imperialism of European nations only in that it is slightly less military and more obviously commercial (though of course we are always ready to use our naval power when the occasion warrants), was given the halo of moral sanctity by Secretary Hughes in an address in 1924: "We are aiming not to exploit but to aid; not to subvert, but to help in laying the foundations for a sound, stable and independent government. Our interest does not lie in controlling foreign peoples. . . . Our interest is in having prosperous, peaceful and law abiding neighbors." [28] Such sentiments have been repeated innumerable times by American statesmen, in spite of the fact that every impartial history clearly records the economic motives which prompt our policies in our relation to our southern neighbors. The various messages of President Coolidge in which he dealt with the difficult problems of post-war readjustment were, almost without exception, marvellous examples of sanctimonious hypocrisy. Europe was constantly assured, for instance, that our only interest in post-war debt settlements was to preserve the sanctity of covenants and to prevent European nations from falling into slovenly business habits.

Moralists who have observed and animadverted upon the hypocrisy of nations have usually assumed that a more perfect social intelligence, which could penetrate and analyze these evasions and deceptions, would make them ultimately impossible. But here again they are counting on moral and rational resources which will never be available. What was not possible in 1914-1918, when the world was submerged in dishonesties and hypocrisies (the Treaty of Versailles, with its pledge of disarmament and the self-righteous moral conviction of the vanquished by the victors, being the crowning example), will hardly become possible in a decade or in a century, or in many centuries. Nations will always find it more difficult than individuals to behold the beam that is in their own eye while they observe the mote that is in their brother's eye; and individuals find it difficult enough. A perennial weakness of the moral life in individuals is simply raised to the nth degree in national life. Let a nation be accused of hypocrisy and it shrinks back in pious horror at the charge. When President Wilson addressed a peace communication to the belligerent powers in 1916 and with delicate irony, "took the liberty of calling attention to the fact that the objects which the statesmen of the belligerents on both sides have in mind in this war are virtually the same as stated to their own people and to the world," Lord Northcliffe reported that everybody in England was "mad as hell," that Lord Robert Cecil was "deeply hurt," and that the King actually broke down in pain over the suggestion.[29] In 1927 Senator Hiram Johnson, stung by European strictures of American hypocrisy and greed, declared "In all their long sordid international careers of blood and conquest, these nations that call America Shylock and swine, that sneer at our pretensions and deride our acts, have never done an idealistic, altruistic or unselfish international deed. Ever their cry has been for more land and new peoples and . . . where sinister diplomacy has failed blood and iron have subdued the weak and helpless. . . . Whatever our faults, and they are mostly internal, the United States is the only nation on earth that in its international relations has ever displayed either idealism or altruism. . . . The United States has written an international policy in deeds of generosity and mercy and written indelibly thus the answer to Europe's gibes and jeers." [30] It would be interesting to add that the author of these remarks was particularly active in passing the Japanese Exclusion Act.

Perhaps the best that can be expected of nations is that they should justify their hypocrisies by a slight measure of real international achievement, and learn how to do justice to wider interests than their own, while they pursue their own. England, which has frequently been accused by continental nations of mastering the arts of national self-righteousness with particular skill, may have accomplished this, partly because there is actually a measure of genuine humanitarian interest in British policy. The Italian statesman, Count Sforza, has recently paid a witty and deserved tribute to the British art in politics. They have, he declares, "a precious gift bestowed by divine grace upon the British people: The simultaneous action in those islands, when a great British interest is at stake, of statesmen and diplomats coolly working to obtain some concrete political advantage and on the other side, and without previous base secret understanding clergymen and writers eloquently busy showing the highest moral reasons for supporting the diplomatic action which is going on in Downing Street. Such was the case in the Belgian Congo. Belgian rule had been in force there for years; but at a certain moment gold was discovered in the Katanga, the Congolese province nearest to the British South African possessions; and the bishops and other pious persons started at once a violent press campaign to stigmatise the Belgian atrocities against the Negroes. What is astonishing and really imperial is that those bishops and other pious persons were inspired by the most perfect Christian good faith, and that nobody was pulling the wires behind them." [31] Another foreign critic and observer of English life, Wilhelm Dibelius, believes that there is justification for the moral pretensions of Britain: "England," he declares, "is the solitary power with a national programme, which while egotistic through and through, at the same time promises to the world as a whole, something which the world passionately desires, order, progress and eternal peace. . . . None of them (the other powers) have as yet succeeded in setting up, against the British ideal, an ideal of their own, national and international at the same time, as the British." [32] What Britain has achieved, if we are to take Doctor Dibelius' word for it, is probably the best that can be expected of any nation. It is questionable whether her achievement is great enough to make the attainment of international justice, without conflict, possible. Of that India is an example. In spite of the solid achievement of Britain in India, her imperialism there has been covered with the cant and hypocrisy which all nations affect; and it is obvious that India will gain a full partnership in the British Empire only as she is able to exert some kind of force against British imperialism.

If it is true that the nations are too selfish and morally too obtuse and self-righteous to make the attainment of international justice without the use of force possible, the question arises whether there is a possibility of escape from the endless round of force avenging ancient wrongs and creating new ones, of victorious Germany creating a vindictive France and victorious France poisoning Germany with a sense of outraged justice. The morality of nations is such that, if there be a way out, it is not as easy as the moralists of both the pre-war and post-war period have assumed.

Obviously one method of making force morally redemptive is to place it in the hands of a community, which transcends the conflicts of interest between individual nations and has an impartial perspective upon them. That method resolves many conflicts within national communities, and the organization of the League of Nations is ostensibly the extension of that principle to international life. But if powerful classes in national societies corrupt the impartiality of national courts, it may be taken for granted that a community of nations, in which very powerful and very weak nations are bound together, has even less hope of achieving impartiality. Furthermore the prestige of the international community is not great enough, and it does not sufficiently qualify the will-to-power of individual nations, to achieve a communal spirit sufficiently unified, to discipline recalcitrant nations. Thus Japan was able to violate her covenants in her conquest of Manchuria, because she shrewdly assumed that the seeming solidarity of the League of Nations was not real, and that it only thinly veiled without restraining the peculiar policies of various great powers, which she would be able to tempt and exploit. Her assumption proved correct, and she was able to win the quasi-support of France and to weaken the British support of League policies. Her success in breaking her covenants with impunity has thrown the weakness of our inchoate society of nations into vivid light. This weakness, also revealed in the failure of the recent Disarmament Conference and the abortive character of all efforts to resolve the anarchy of national tariffs, justifies the pessimistic conclusion that there is not yet a political force capable of bringing effective social restraint upon the self-will of nations, at least not upon the powerful nations. Even if it should be possible to maintain peace on the basis of the international *status quo,* there is no evidence that an unjust peace can be adjusted by pacific means. A society of nations has not really proved itself until it is able to grant justice to those who have been worsted in battle without requiring them to engage in new wars to redress their wrongs.

Since the class character of national governments is a primary, though not the only cause of their greed, present international anarchy may continue until the fear of catastrophe amends, or catastrophe itself destroys, the present social system and builds more co-operative national societies. There may not be enough intelligence in modern society to prevent catastrophe. There is certainly not enough intelligence to prompt our generation to a voluntary reorganization of society, unless the fear of imminent catastrophe quickens the tempo of social change.

The sharpening of class antagonisms within each modern industrial nation is increasingly destroying national unity and imperilling international comity as well. It may be that the constant growth of economic inequality and social injustice in our industrial civilization will force the nations into a final conflict, which is bound to end in their destruction. The disintegration of a national loyalty through class antagonism has proceeded so far in the more advanced nations, that they can hardly dare to permit the logic inherent in the present situation to take its course. Conditions in these nations, particularly in Germany where the forces and factors which operate in modern civilization may be seen in clearest outline, reveal what desperate devices are necessary for the preservation of even a semblence of national unity and how these very devices seem to make for an international conflict in which the last semblance of that unity will be destroyed. If the possibilities and perils of the contemporary situation are to be fully understood it will be necessary to study the class antagonism within the nations carefully and estimate their importance for the future of civilization.

NOTES

1. Johannes Haller, *The Aera Buelow.*
2. Quoted by Kirby Page, *National Defense,* p. 67.
3. Sometimes even the most realistic statesmen overestimate the nation's ability, wisely to prefer ultimate to immediate interests. Thus, Dr. Carl Melchior, German diplomat, thought it advisable in 1921 to accept an impossible reparations burden because "We can get through the first two or three years with the aid of foreign loans. By the end of that time foreign nations will have realised that these large payments can only be made by huge German exports and these exports will ruin the trade in England and America so that creditors themselves will come to us to request modification." Quoted by Lord D'Abernon, *An Ambassador of Peace,* Vol. I, p. 194. It required eleven years rather than two or three for the nations to realize what Dr. Melchior predicted, and even then, they did not act voluntarily.
4. See Wilhelm Dibelius, *England,* p. 106.
5. Quoted by Harold Laski, *Authority in the Modern State,* p. 274.
6. See Bertrand Russell, *The Scientific Outlook,* Chap. XI.
7. Quoted by G. Lowes Dickinson, *International Anarchy,* p. 34.
8. Quoted by Kirby Page, *National Defense,* p. 28.
9. Cf. Paul Pfeffer, *Seven Years in Soviet Russia.*
10. Geoffrey Tyson, *Danger in India.*
11. Quoted by Kirby Page, *National Defense,* p. 148.
12. *Ibid.,* p. 149.
13. *Ibid.,* p. 152. Mr. Page has gathered innumerable similar examples in Chapter IX of his book.
14. Quoted by Parker Moon, *Imperialism and World Politics,* p. 422.
15. Quoted by Walter Millis, *The Martial Spirit,* p. 90.
16. *Ibid.,* p. 136.
17. *Ibid.,* p. 143.
18. *Ibid.,* p. 374.
19. *Ibid.,* p. 387.
20. *Ibid.,* p. 254.
21. *Ibid.,* p. 396.
22. *Ibid.,* p. 384.
23. Nathaniel Peffer, *The White Man's Dilemma,* p. 228.
24. Parker Moon, *Imperialism and World Politics,* p. 228.
25. *Ibid.,* p. 153.
26. *Ibid.,* p. 279.
27. *Ibid.,* p. 201.

28. *Ibid.*, p. 407.

29. Charles and Mary Beard, *Rise of American Civilization,* Bk. II, p. 629.

30. Quoted by Kirby Page, *National Defense,* p. 196.

31. Count Carlo Sforza, *European Dictatorship,* p. 178.

32. Wilhelm Dibelius, *England,* p. 109.

6. The Limitations of Realism*

by Edward Hallett Carr

THE EXPOSURE BY REALIST CRITICISM OF THE HOLLOWNESS OF the utopian edifice is the first task of the political thinker. It is only when the sham has been demolished that there can be any hope of raising a more solid structure in its place. But we cannot ultimately find a resting place in pure realism; for realism, though logically overwhelming, does not provide us with the springs of action which are necessary even to the pursuit of thought. Indeed, realism itself, if we attack it with its own weapons, often turns out in practice to be just as much conditioned as any other mode of thought. In politics, the belief that certain facts are unalterable or certain trends irresistible commonly reflects a lack of desire or lack of interest to change or resist them. The impossibility of being a consistent and thorough-going realist is one of the most certain and most curious lessons of political science. Consistent realism excludes four things which appear to be essential ingredients of all effective political thinking: a finite goal, an emotional appeal, a right of moral judgment, and a ground for action.

The conception of politics as an infinite process seems in the long run uncongenial or incomprehensible to the human mind. Every political thinker who wishes to make an appeal to his contemporaries is consciously led to posit a finite goal. Treitschke declared that the "terrible thing" about Machiavelli's teaching was "not the immorality of the methods he recommends, but the lack of content of the state, which exists only in order to exist."[1] In fact, Machiavelli is not so consistent. His realism breaks down in the

* *The Twenty Years' Crisis, 1919-1939,* Second Edition (London: Macmillan & Co., Ltd., 1962), pp. 89-101. (Copyright by Macmillan and Company Limited. Reprinted by permission of Macmillan and Company Limited, St. Martin's Press, Inc., and the Macmillan Company of Canada Limited.)

last chapter of *The Prince,* which is entitled "An Exhortation to free Italy from the Barbarians"—a goal whose necessity could be deduced from no realist premise. Marx, having dissolved human thought and action into the relativism of the dialectic postulates the absolute goal of a classless society where the dialectic no longer operates—that one far-off event towards which, in true Victorian fashion, he believed the whole creation to be moving. The realist thus ends by negating his own postulate and assuming an ultimate reality outside the historical process. Engels was one of the first to level this charge against Hegel. "The whole dogmatic content of the Hegelian system is declared to be absolute truth in contradiction to his dialectical method, which dissolves all dogmatism." [2] But Marx lays himself open to precisely the same criticism when he brings the process of dialectical materialism to an end with the victory of the proletariat. Thus utopianism penetrates the citadel of realism; and to envisage a continuing, but not infinite, process towards a finite goal is shown to be a condition of political thought. The greater the emotional stress, the nearer and more concrete is the goal. The first world war was rendered tolerable by the belief that it was the last of wars. Woodrow Wilson's moral authority was built up on the conviction, shared by himself, that he possessed the key to a just, comprehensive and final settlement of the political ills of mankind. It is noteworthy that almost all religions agree in postulating an ultimate state of complete blessedness.

The finite goal, assuming the character of an apocalytic vision, thereby acquires an emotional, irrational appeal which realism itself cannot justify or explain. Everyone knows Marx's famous prediction of the future classless paradise:

> When work ceases to be merely a means of life and becomes the first living need; when, with the all-round development of the individual, productive forces also develop, and all the sources of collective wealth flow in free abundance—then only will it be possible to transcend completely the narrow horizon of *bourgeois* right, and society can inscribe on its banner: From each according to his capacities to each according to his needs.[3]

Sorel proclaimed the necessity of a "myth" to make revolutionary teaching effective; and Soviet Russia has exploited for this purpose the myth, first of world revolution, and more recently of the "socialist fatherland." There is much to be said for Professor Laski's view that "communism has made its way by its idealism, and not by its realism, by its spiritual promise, not by its materialistic prospects." [4] A modern theologian has analyzed the situation with almost cynical clearsightedness:

> Without the ultrarational hopes and passions of religion, no society will have the courage to conquer despair and attempt the impossible; for the vision of a just society is an impossible one, which can be approximated only by those who do not regard it as impossible. The truest visions of religion are illusions which may be partly realised by being resolutely believed.[5]

And this again closely echoes a passage in *Mein Kampf* in which Hitler contrasts the "programme-maker" with the politician:

> His (i.e., the programme-maker's) significance lies almost wholly in the future, and he is often what one means by the word "*weltfremd*" (Unpractical, utopian). For if the art of the politician is really the art of the possible, then the programme-maker belongs to those of whom it is said that they please the gods only if they ask and demand from them the impossible.[6]

Credo quia impossibile becomes a category of political thinking.

Consistent realism, as has already been noted, involves acceptance of the whole historical process and precludes moral judgments on it. As we have seen, men are generally prepared to accept the judgment of history on the past, praising success and condemning failure. This test is also widely applied to contemporary politics. Such institutions as the League of Nations, or the Soviet or Fascist regimes, are to a considerable extent judged by their capacity to achieve what they profess to achieve; and the legitimacy of this test is implicitly admitted by their own propaganda, which constantly seeks to exaggerate their successes and minimize their failures. Yet it is clear that mankind as a whole is not prepared to accept this rational test as a universally valid basis of political judgment. The belief that whatever succeeds is right, and has only to be understood to be approved, must, if consistently held, empty thought of purpose, and thereby sterilize and ultimately destroy it. Nor do those whose philosophy appears to exclude the possibility of moral judgments in fact refrain from pronouncing them. Frederick the Great, having explained that treaties should be observed for the reason that "one can trick only once," goes on to call the breaking of treaties "a bad and knavish policy," though there is nothing in his thesis to justify the moral epithet.[7] Marx, whose philosophy appeared to demonstrate that capitalists could only act in a certain way, spends many pages—some of the most effective in *Capital*—in denouncing the wickedness of capitalists for behaving in precisely that way. The necessity, recognized by all politicians, both in domestic and in international affairs, for cloaking interests in a guise of moral principles is in itself a symptom of the inadequacy of realism. Every age claims the right to create its own values, and to pass judgments in the light of them; and even if it uses realist weapons to dissolve other values, it still believes in the absolute character of its own. It refuses to accept the implication of realism that the word "ought" is meaningless.

Most of all, consistent realism breaks down because it fails to provide any ground for purposive or meaningful action. If the sequence of cause and effect is sufficiently rigid to permit of the "scientific prediction" of events, if our thought is irrevocably conditioned by our status and our interests, then both action and thought become devoid of purpose. If, as Schopenhauer maintains, "the true philosophy of history consists of the insight that, throughout the jumble of all these ceaseless changes, we have ever before our eyes the same unchanging being, pursuing the same course today, yesterday and forever," [8] then passive contemplation is all that remains to the individual. Such a conclusion is plainly repugnant to the most deep-seated belief of man about himself. That human affairs can be directed and modified by human action and human thought is a postulate so fundamental that its rejection seems scarcely compatible with existence as a human being. Nor is it in fact rejected by those realists who have left their mark on history. Machiavelli, when he exhorted his compatriots to be good Italians, clearly assumed that they were free to follow or ignore his advice. Marx, by birth and training a *bourgeois,* believed himself free to think and act like a proletarian, and regarded it as his mission to persuade others, whom he assumed to be equally free, to think and act likewise. Lenin, who wrote of the imminence of world revolution as a "scientific prediction," admitted elsewhere that "no situations exist from which there is absolutely no way out." [9] In moments of crisis, Lenin appealed to his followers in terms which might equally well have been used by so thorough-going a believer in the power of the human will as Mussolini or by any other leader of any period: "At the decisive moment and in the decisive place, you *must prove* the stronger, you must *be victorious*." [10] Every realist, whatever his professions, is ultimately compelled to believe not only that there is something which man ought to think and do, but that there is something which he can think and do, and that his thought and action are neither mechanical nor meaningless.

We return therefore to the conclusion that any sound political thought must be based on elements of both utopia and reality. Where utopianism has become a hollow and intolerable sham, which serves merely as a disguise for the interests of the privileged, the realist performs an indispensable service in unmasking it. But pure realism can offer nothing but a naked struggle for power which makes any kind of international society impossible. Having demolished the current utopia with the weapons of realism, we still need to build a new utopia of our own, which will one day fall to the same weapons. The human will will continue to seek an escape from the logical consequences of realism in the vision of an international order which, as soon as it crystallizes itself into concrete political form, becomes tainted with self-interest and hypocrisy, and must once more be attacked with the instruments of realism.

Here, then, is the complexity, the fascination and the tragedy of all political life. Politics are made up of two elements—utopia and reality—belonging to two different planes which can never meet. There is no greater barrier to clear political thinking than failure to distinguish between ideals, which are utopia, and institutions, which are reality. The communist who set communism against democracy was usually thinking of communism as a pure ideal of equality and brotherhood, and of democracy as an institution which existed in Great Britain, France or the United States and which exhibited the vested interests, the inequalities and the oppression inherent in all political institutions. The democrat who made the same comparison was in fact comparing an ideal pattern of democracy laid up in heaven with communism as an institution existing in Soviet Russia with its class-divisons, its heresy-hunts and its concentration camps. The comparison, made in each case between an ideal and an institution, is irrelevant and makes no sense. The ideal, once it is embodied in an institution, ceases to be an ideal and becomes the expression of a selfish interest, which must be destroyed in the name of a new ideal. This constant interaction of irreconcilable forces is the stuff of politics. Every political situation contains mutually incompatible elements of utopia and reality, of morality and power.

This point will emerge more clearly from the analysis of the nature of politics which we have now to undertake.

Man has always lived in groups. The smallest kind of human group, the family, has clearly been necessary for the maintenance of the species. But so far as is known, men have always from the most primitive times formed semi-permanent groups larger than the single family; and one of the functions of such a group has been to regulate relations between its members. Politics deals with the behavior of men in such organized permanent or semi-permanent groups. All attempts to deduce the nature of society from the supposed behavior of man in isolation are purely theoretical, since there is no reason to assume that such a man ever existed. Aristotle laid the foundation of all sound thinking about politics when he declared that man was by nature a political animal.

Man in society reacts to his fellow men in two opposite ways. Sometimes he displays egoism, or the will to assert himself at the expense of others. At other times he displays sociability, or the desire to co-operate with others, to enter into reciprocal relations of good-will and friendship with them, and even to subordinate himself to them. In every society, these two qualities can be seen at work. No society can exist unless a substantial proportion of its members exhibits in some degree the desire for co-operation and mutual good-will. But in every society some sanction is required to produce the measure of solidarity requisite for its maintenance; and this sanction is applied by a controlling group or individual acting in the name of the society. Membership of most societies is voluntary, and the only ultimate sanction which can be applied is expulsion. But the peculiarity of political society, which in the modern world takes the form of the state, is that membership is compulsory. The state, like other societies, must be based on some sense of common interests and obligations among its members. But coercion is regularly exercised by a governing group to enforce loyalty and obedience; and this coercion inevitably means that the governors control the governed and "exploit" them for their own purposes.[11]

The dual character of political society is therefore strongly marked. Professor Laski tells us that "every state is built upon the consciences of men." [12] On the other hand, anthropology, as well as much recent history, teaches that "war seems to be the main agency in producing the state";[13] and Professor Laski himself, in another passage, declares that "our civilization is held together by fear rather than by good-will." [14] There is no contradiction between these apparently opposite views. When Tom Paine, in the *Rights of Man,* tries to confront Burke with the dilemma that "governments arise either *out* of the people or *over* the people," the answer is that they do both. Coercion and conscience, enmity and good-will, self-assertion and self-subordination, are present in every political society. The state is built up out of these two conflicting aspects of human nature. Utopia and reality, the ideal and the institution, morality and power, are from the outset inextricably blended in it. In the making of the United States, as a modern American writer has said, "Hamilton stood for strength, wealth and power, Jefferson for the American dream"; and both the power and the dream were necessary ingredients.[15]

If this be correct, we can draw one important conclusion. The utopian who dreams that it is possible to eliminate self-assertion from politics and to base a political system on morality alone is just as wide of the mark as the realist who believes that altruism is an illusion and that all political action is based on self-seeking. These errors have both left their mark on popular terminology. The phrase "power politics" is often used in an invidious sense, as if the element of power or self-assertion in politics were something abnormal and susceptible of elimination, from a healthy political life. Conversely, there is a disposition, even among some writers who are not strictly speaking realists, to treat politics as the science of power and self-assertion and exclude from it by definition actions inspired by the moral consciousness. Professor Catlin describes the *homo politicus* as one who "seeks to bring into conformity with his own will the wills of others, so that he may the better attain his own ends." [16] Such terminological implications are misleading. Politics cannot be divorced from power. But the *homo politicus* who pursues nothing but power is as unreal a myth as the *homo economicus* who pursues nothing but gain. Political action must be based on a co-ordination of morality and power.

This truth is of practical as well as theoretical importance. It is as fatal in politics to ignore power as it is to ignore morality. The fate of China in the nineteenth century is an illustration of what happens to a country which is content to believe in the moral superiority of its own civilization and to despise the ways of power. The Liberal Government of Great Britain nearly came to grief in the spring of 1914 because it sought to pursue an Irish policy based on moral authority unsupported (or rather, directly opposed) by effective military power. In Germany, the Frankfort Assembly of 1848 is the classic example of the impotence of ideas divorced from power; and the Weimar Republic broke down because many of the policies it pursued—in fact, nearly all of them except its opposition to the communists—were unsupported, or actively opposed, by effective military power.[17] The utopian, who believes that democracy is not based on force, refuses to look these unwelcome facts in the face.

On the other hand, the realist, who believes that, if you look after the power, the moral authority will look after itself, is equally in error. The most recent form of this doctrine is embodied in the much-quoted phrase: "The function of force is to give moral ideas time to take root." Internationally, this argument was used in 1919 by those who, unable to defend the Versailles Treaty on moral grounds, maintained that this initial act of power would pave the way for subsequent moral appeasement. Experience has done little to confirm this comfortable belief. The same fallacy is implicit in the once popular view that the aim of British policy should be "to rebuild the League of Nations, to make it capable of holding a political aggressor in restraint by armed power, and thereafter to labour faithfully for the mitigation of just and real grievances." [18] Once the enemy has been crushed or the "aggressor" restrained by force, the "thereafter" fails to arrive. The illusion that priority can be given to power and that morality will follow, is just as dangerous as the illusion that priority can be given to moral authority and that power will follow.

Before proceeding, however, to consider the respective roles of power and morality in politics, we must take some note of the views of those who, though far from being realists, identify politics with power and believe that moral concepts must be altogether excluded from its scope. There is, according to this view, an essential antinomy between politics and morality; and the moral man as such will therefore have nothing to do with politics. This thesis has many attractions, and reappears at different periods of history and in different contexts. It takes at least three forms.

(i) Its simplest form is the doctrine of non-resistance. The moral man recognizes the existence of political power as an evil, but regards the use of power to resist power as a still greater evil. This is the basis of such doctrines of non-resistance as those of Jesus or of Gandhi, or of modern pacifism. It amounts, in brief, to a boycott of politics.

(ii) The second form of the antithesis between politics and morality is anarchism. The state, as the principal organ of political power, is "the most flagrant, most cynical and most complete negation of humanity." [19] The anarchist will use power to overthrow the state. This revolutionary power is, however, not thought of as political power, but as the spontaneous revolt of the outraged individual conscience. It does not seek to create a new political society to take the place of the old one, but a moral society from which power, and consequently politics, are completely eliminated. "The principles of the Sermon on the Mount," an English divine recently remarked, would mean "sudden death to civilised society." [20] The anarchist sets out to destroy "civilised society" in the name of the Sermon on the Mount.

(iii) A third school of thought starts from the same premise of the essential antithesis between morality and politics, but arrives at a totally different conclusion. The injunction of Jesus to "render unto Caesar the things that are Caesar's, and unto God the things that are God's," implies the coexistence of two separate spheres: the political and the moral. But the moral man is under an obligation to assist—or at any rate not to obstruct—the politician in the discharge of his non-moral functions. "Let every soul be subject to the higher powers. The powers that be are ordained of God." We thus recognize politics as necessary but non-moral. This tradition, which remained dormant throughout the Middle Ages, when the ecclesiastical and the secular authority was theoretically one, was revived by Luther in order to effect his compromise between reformed church and state. Luther "turned on the peasants of his day in holy horror when they attempted to transmute the 'spiritual' kingdom into an 'earthy' one by suggesting that the principles of the gospel had social significance." [21] The division of functions between Caesar and God is implicit in the very conception of an "established" church. But the tradition has been more persistent and more effective in Lutheran Germany than anywhere else. "We do not consult Jesus," wrote a German liberal nineteenth-century pastor, "when we are concerned with things which belong to the domain of the construction of the state and political economy";[22] and Bernhardi declared that "Christian morality is personal and social, and in its nature cannot be political." [23] The same attitude is inherent in the modern theology of Karl Barth, which insists that political and social evils are the necessary product of man's sinful nature and that human effort to eradicate them is therefore futile; and the doctrine that Christian morality has nothing to do with politics is vigorously upheld by the Nazi regime. This view is basically different from that of the realist who makes morality a function of politics. But in the field of politics it tends to become indistinguishable from realism.

The theory of the divorce between the spheres of politics and morality is superficially attractive, if only because it evades the insoluble problem of finding a moral justification for the use of force.[24] But it is not ultimately satisfying. Both non-resistance and anarchism are counsels of despair, which appear to find widespread acceptance only where men feel hopeless of achieving anything by political action; and the attempt to keep God and Caesar in watertight compartments runs too much athwart the deep-seated desire of the human mind to reduce its view of the world to some kind of moral order. We are not in the long run satisfied to believe that what is politically good is morally bad;[25] and since we can neither moralize power nor expel power from politics, we are faced with a dilemma which cannot be completely resolved. The planes of utopia and of reality never coincide. The ideal cannot be institutionalized, nor the institution idealized. "Politics," writes Dr. Niebuhr, "will, to the end of history, be an area where conscience and power meet, where the ethical and coercive factors of human life will interpenetrate and work out their tentative and uneasy compromises." [26] The compromises, like solutions of other human problems, will remain uneasy and tentative. But it is an essential part of any compromise that both factors shall be taken into account.

We have now therefore to analyze the part played in international politics by these two cardinal factors: power and morality.

NOTES

1. Treitschke, *Aufsatze,* iv, p. 428.
2. Engels, *Ludwig Feuerbach* (Engl. transl.), p. 23.
3. Marx and Engels, *Works* (Russian ed.), xv, p. 275.
4. Laski, *Communism,* p. 250.
5. R. Niebuhr, *Moral Man and Immoral Society,* p. 81.
6. Hitler, *Mein Kampf,* p. 231.
7. *Anti-Machiavel,* p. 248.
8. Schopenhauer, *Welt als Wille und Vorstellung,* ii, ch. 38.
9. Lenin, *Works* (2nd Russian ed.), xxv, p. 340.
10. Lenin, *Collected Works* (Engl. transl.), xxi, pt. i, p. 68.
11. "Everywhere do I perceive a certain conspiracy of the rich men seeking their own advantage under the name and pretext of the commonwealth" (More, *Utopia*). "The exploitation of one part of society by another is common to all past centuries" (*Communist Manifesto*).
12. *A Defence of Liberty against Tyrants* (*Vindiciae contra Tyrannos*), ed. Laski, Introd. p. 55.
13. Linton, *The Study of Man,* p. 240.
14. Laski, *A Grammar of Politics,* p. 20.
15. J. Truslow Adams, *The Epic of America,* p. 112. The idea that the state has a moral foundation in the consent of its citizens as well as a power foundation was propounded by Locke and Rousseau and popularized by the American and French revolutions. Two recent expressions of the idea may be quoted. The Czecho-Slovak declaration of independence of October 18, 1918, described Austria-Hungary as "a state which has no justification for its existence, and which, since it refuses to accept the fundamental basis of modern world-organisation (i.e. self-determination), is only an artificial and unmoral construction." In February 1938, Hitler told Schuschnigg, the then Austrian Chancellor, that "a regime lacking every kind of legality and which in reality ruled only by force, must in the long run come into continually increasing conflict with public opinion" (speech in the Reichstag of March 17, 1938). Hitler maintained that the two pillars of the state are "force" and "popularity" (*Mein Kampf,* p. 579).
16. Catlin, *The Science and Method of Politics,* p. 309.
17. It is significant that the word *Realpolitik* was coined in the once famous treatise of von Rochau, *Grundsatze der Realpolitik* published in 1853, which was largely inspired by the lessons of Frankfort.

The inspiration which Hitler's *Realpolitik* has derived from the lessons of the Weimar Republic is obvious.

18. Winston Churchill, *Arms and the Covenant,* p. 368. The argument that power is a necessary motive force for the remedy of "just" grievances is further developed on pp. 209-216.

19. Bakunin, *Euvres,* i, p. 150; cf. vi, p. 17: "If there is a devil in all human history, it is this principle of command and authority."

20. The Dean of St. Paul's, quoted in a leading article in *The Times,* August 2, 1937.

21. R. Niebuhr, *Moral Man and Immoral Society,* p. 77.

22. Quoted in W. F. Bruck, *Social and Economic History of Germany,* p. 65.

23. Bernhardi, *Germany and the Next War* (Engl. transl.), p. 29.

24. "Force in the right place," as Mr. Maxton once said in the House of Commons, is a meaningless conception, "because the right place for me is exactly where I want to use it, and for him also, and for everyone else" (House of Commons, November 7, 1933: *Official Record,* col. 130). Force in politics is always the instrument of some kind of group interest.

25. Acton was fond of saying that "great men are almost always bad men," and quotes Walpole's dictum that "no great country was ever saved by good men" (*History of Freedom,* p. 219). Rosebery showed more acuteness when he remarked that "there is one question which English people ask about great men: Was he 'a good man'?" (*Napoleon: The Last Phase,* p. 364).

26. R. Niebuhr, *Moral Man and Immoral Society,* p. 4.

7. Judaeo-Christian Realism: The Cold War and the Search For Relevant Norms*

by Kenneth W. Thompson

> There have accumulated around the Christian tradition various forms of worldly wisdom which condense the experience of centuries and have come to stand as part of our European heritage.—HERBERT BUTTERFIELD

WITH THE PRESENT SUBJECT I COME TO THE HEART OF THE PROBlem of ethics and foreign policy. For men and states, the search for justice and morality, whether in Augustine or in Plato or with contemporary writers, is a bewildering, frustrating, and uncertain task. Perhaps for this reason modern man is disposed to set it aside for more limited and manageable types of inquiry. Why not assume, in economics for instance, the model of an "economic man" who can be analyzed and appraised as if man's one goal was the maximization of profit? Or, alternatively, in things political, the assumption that all men seek power appears for many writers to be a more orderly and rational measure of political behavior. In the era of vastness and complexity through which civilization is presently dog-paddling, the insistence that we exclude the ethical and religious component appears virtually overpowering. I suggest we consider five attempts to come to terms with the relevance of ethical norms in three areas in which the problem is particularly acute.

* Thompson, Kenneth W., *Christian Ethics and the Dilemmas of Foreign Policy* (Durham, N.C.: Duke University Press, 1959), pp. 93-113. (Copyright by the Duke University Press. Reprinted by permission of the Duke University Press.)

1. THE PROBLEM OF RELEVANT NORMS IN ECONOMICS, HISTORY, AND DIPLOMACY

Even those students of economic and political life who concede that religion has some contribution to make are profoundly impressed with the difficulties. For example, John Maurice Clark, a contributor to the economic studies of the National Council of Churches, writes:

> Religion starts with values so pure that they are likely to seem inapplicable in any political and economic life except one for which an earthy humanity is not yet ready. And if one tries to carry out some of these values in the world of politics, business, or trade unions, one faces the necessity of marginal adjustments between values of different sorts. But because these values have been presented as absolutes, not subject to compromise, the individual finds himself convicted of inevitable sin, no matter how selfless his motives and how clear his understanding, because, forsooth, he is acting like economic man and weighing marginal increments of different kinds of values against one another.[1]

Professor Clark, therefore, maintains that only a marriage of technical competence and religious insight can yield a meaningful ethic for economics. Only someone who grasps both economic realities and the character of norms will have a contribution to make.

The controversy over morality in general and the moral evaluation of social action in particular also rages among students of contemporary history. Geoffrey Barraclough in his Stevenson Inaugural Lecture delivered at Chatham House on October 8, 1957, chose to discuss "History, Morals, and Politics." [2] He observed that not many years ago historians seemed to agree that their function was "to describe and explain, not to pronounce verdicts." The historian was not a judge but a detective who left any moral conclusions to his readers and their imaginations. With our recent unhappy experiences of unspeakably brutal tyrannies, totalitarian persecution, slave labor and concentration camps, this climate of opinion has noticeably shifted. In the words of Professor Barraclough's predecessor, Arnold J. Toynbee: "A historian is bound to make moral judgments on the human acts he is recording. . . . he could avoid making moral judgments only by closing his mind to the meaning of the story." [3] However, in the interests of clarity, Barraclough in his Inaugural insists that Mr. Toynbee's attitude must be subjected to critical scrutiny.

He asks, first of all, what of moral judgments in the field of private morality? Does it really add to the story to denounce in explicit terms the "wicked" and "evil" private lives of monarchs like Henry II or Emperor Charles the Great, or "the savage crimes" of Cromwell? When one condemns Charles the Great and Cromwell for their wickedness, what have we gained? "Are we supposed to strip off their title to greatness, like the decorations from a cashiered officer? Are we to do a subtraction sum from their major, admitted, positive achievements, and precisely how do we strike the balance?" Barraclough maintains that the question of moral judgment is more complicated than it is fashionable to admit. The gist of his argument is stated in these words:

> I would not suggest that the moral issue is irrelevant, and certainly nothing should be suppressed; but it is only one issue among many, and I cannot easily believe it is the most important of those with which historians have to deal. For the historian is concerned, after all, mainly with consequences; and though the consequences of Cromwell's massacres in Ireland were an enduring legacy of Anglo-Irish animosity, the consequences of Charlemagne's massacres in Saxony were, curiously enough, the opposite; the Saxons were soon the most loyal supporters of the Frankish monarchy. In some ways, it almost seems, our moral judgments raise more problems than they solve; for, though it would be pleasant to think that nemesis always overtakes the evil-doer, if we are really honest, we shall have to ask whether, politically, evil does not sometimes pay. . . . In fact, whether we like it or not, (there are) two standards of morality, public or private. No one will suppose (this problem) . . . can be solved by the simple device of declaring that it does "violence to the basic notions of our morality." Of course it does: precisely that is "the problem of morality in history and politics." [4]

Professor Barraclough multiplies present-day examples to illustrate the complexity of moral judgment. President Nasser of Egypt is said by many in the West to have broken engagements freely entered into with British representatives. But "can we expect the Eastern peoples to share without question our attitude toward the inviolability of treaties . . . between a weak Eastern and a strong Western power?" "Furthermore, although it is easy to argue that in changed circumstances, a treaty freely negotiated should not be repudiated, but should be altered . . . by negotiation . . . this is more easily said than done. Instances do not come readily to mind, at least in cases where major political interests and national prestige are involved." [5] Insistence upon the inviolability of treaties is almost necessarily advantageous to those whom historians describe as "the beneficiaries of the status quo." Professor Barraclough concludes: "The brutal fact is that few young peoples would have secured their independence and their power to guide their own destiny if they had not broken through the network of public law constructed by the beneficiaries of the status quo to stabilize a position favorable to themselves; and few historians will be found to condemn them out of hand for this." [6]

But what of internal opponents of an existing political order? "We speak of people in Cyprus and Algeria as 'terrorists,' and our very choice of terms implies a moral judgment; but who, in fact, is the terrorist in Cyprus, Colonel Grivas, as perhaps 40 million English people think, or Colonel Harding, as perhaps 500 million Greeks, Africans and Indians think?" "As a Swiss commentator has pointed out, if the Algerians are 'terrorists,' so for the house of Hapsburg in the thirteenth century was William Tell." [7]

Barraclough finds the one residual sphere of practical morality for both historians and statesmen—and this is a point to which we shall return—in the ability to confront political reality on its own terms. To illustrate his concept, the Stevenson Professor chooses the controversy in an emergent German state between General von Gerlach and Prince Bismarck in the middle of the nineteenth century. Then, revolutionary France occupied the position Soviet Russia does today. In a debate of obvious contemporaneity, Gerlach charged Bismarck with failure to base his policy on opposition to the "evil spirit" of the Revolution in much the way that some contemporaries call for a holy war against Communism. He condemned "all political combinations as faulty, unsafe, and highly dangerous" when it came to courses of action in this profound moral struggle. Bismarck rejected Gerlach's approach, saying that to import such notions into politics was a surrender to "sympathies and antipathies." His ideal was "the habit of deciding independently of any feelings of antipathy to or preference for foreign states and their rulers." "The moral conception for which Gerlach stood

—a conception which many today unconsciously echo—implies an abstract, transcendent, ethical norm, an extraneous principle by which everything else is judged and which retains its imperative quality without reference to the fact whether or not it can be translated into political practice. For Bismarck, on the contrary, morality is not an abstract conception standing outside political reality, but stems from within it; it is concrete and immanent, and is expressed in the statesman's sense of moral responsibility for his actions." [8] This viewpoint frees the statesmen from the beckoning will-of-the-wisp of moral crusades against evil which eventuate so often in strident calls for preventive wars. In Bismarck's words: "A statesman cannot create anything himself; he must wait and listen until he hears the steps of God sounding through events and then leap up and grasp the hem of his garment." [9] On the eve of the Austro-Prussian War of 1866, he warned those who would punish Austria for its wickedness: "Austria was no more wrong in opposing our claims than we were in making them." [10] Barraclough posits this as a relevant morality for the West in the cold war.

Herbert Butterfield, the Cambridge historian and Master of Peterhouse, has analyzed international morality and the historical process in a series of important writings and his conclusions, though similar, are fundamentally different from Barraclough's. The most characteristic statement of his viewpoint appears in books like *Christianity, War and Diplomacy; Christianity and History* and *Christianity and European History*. Morality, in his view, is not one thing for the statesman and another thing for the rest of mankind. There is no such thing as a separate political ethic. Philosophers and poets, no less than decision-makers, must daily choose not between good and evil but between lesser evils or partial goods. The quality of the decision, fundamentally at least, is the same whether in politics or business, education or family life. Therefore Butterfield has argued: "I don't see why in politics the virtues which I associate with the Christian religion should be suspended: humility, charity, self-judgment, and acceptance of the problem Providence sets before one; also a disposition not to direct affairs as a sovereign will in the world, but to make one's action a form of co-operation with Providence." [11]

Professor Butterfield grounds his conception of international morality in three general propositions. First, morality, as he conceives it, derives ultimately from a "higher law" espoused alike by "lapsed Christians" and religious thinkers according to which nothing but human beings exist or matter. Second, morality must be sharply distinguished from every form of moralistic program and creed which, embodied in a crusade, would claim for its partial insights a more ultimate standing than they deserve. Third, an international order exists as the ultimately relevant objective standard against which national interests must be measured.

The first proposition prompts Professor Butterfield to insist that the social order requires men who would preserve themselves and their values to have "respect for the other man's personality, the other man's end. . . ."[12] In a word, men in the final analysis live in a moral order, however ambiguous its particular forms and expressions may be. Present-day thought has difficulty with this conception for, on the one hand, liberal philosophies which accept as their sole premise the "rights of man" run the risk of encouraging an unbridled egotism according to which man need obey the law only if he agrees with it. On the other hand, thinking which starts with the "duties of man" is likely to end by making him the slave of the state. That is why both man and the state must be subject to a transcendent moral and political order which prompts them to treat one another as more than means to an end. In this connection, "if in the Anglo-Saxon world there has been the necessary amount of the spirit of give-and-take, the disposition to compromise, respect for the other man's opinion and the reluctance to resort to desperation-policies,"[13] this may be due to our greater security, our longer political experience or our state of urbanity free from violence; but it may also be due to the survival of religious influences. We are members of a single Western civilization or cultural community which embraces the moral criteria of the Judaeo-Christian tradition. In some communities, the absence of "a higher law" or regulative principle makes for doctrinaire politics, and "those who have no religion are particularly liable to bring a religious fanaticism to problems of mundane organization which ought to be matters for transaction and negotiation. Lord Acton was probably right when he said that liberty is impossible except amongst people who have a sense that the whole political game is being played in a realm over which there rules a higher law." [14]

If the beginning of wisdom is the recognition that men live finally in some kind of a moral order, the next step is an awareness that the moral is not merely moralistic. Moral judgments can sometimes be used to conceal practical responsibilities from society and from oneself. "A careless librarian, who establishes no regular system for the checking of his books may be satisfied just to heap blame on the people whose delinquencies have resulted in gaps in his shelves." [15] His pious preachments against dishonesty and in favor of virtue can hardly excuse his lack of responsibility. Moreover, moral judgments may also spill over into Pharisaism, exemplified by the priggish moralizers Christ condemned in the Gospels. If there are obscurities in the Gospels, this text is not among them. Nothing is clearer than the distinction between those who claim to be and those who are righteous. We recall the parable of the Pharisee and the publican in the Gospel according to St. Luke.

The moral lesson to be drawn from this parable is not that some states are pharisaic and others truly righteous, but rather that all nations are strongly disposed to endow their particular national ethical systems with universal validity. Nations find themselves today in a situation not too dissimilar from that obtaining domestically within the United States prior to the Civil War. The sanctities of religion and science are invoked to show that one course of action, one nation's program, will execute a divine mandate. Nations go to war not in dispute over territorial boundaries but to make the world safe for democracy or to destroy human wickedness incarnated in evil men like Hitler and Mussolini. Wars of righteousness in which compromise and limited objectives are looked on as treason are today's counterpart of earlier historical wars of religion.

Professor Butterfield's diagnosis of the present crisis brings him to offer some practical alternatives. He finds that "once the aggressor is held in check, and once a balance of forces is achieved, the healing processes of time, and these alone, can solve our problem. . . ." [16] The core of his prescription for peace and mortality, therefore, is time and the absence of war and revolution. Any conflict that time and reason cannot solve will not be solved by war. He is persuaded that it is possible to live with ideological deadlocks and to discover a *modus vivendi,* as in the struggle between Catholicism and Protestantism, and Islam and Christianity. With patience and good luck, justice can eventually emerge. His critics ask whether this is not a counsel of perfection. How would this precept have applied to Hitler? Apparently, Butterfield believes that a balance of forces against Hitler sometime prior to 1939 might have prevented the conflict and allowed time to work its healing effect.

A more general alternative to wars of righteousness is a restoration of the international order. "On moral grounds, as well as on prudential calculations, national egotism requires to be checked, superseded and transcended." [17]

Partly this demands "every possible variation and extension of the art of putting oneself—and actually feeling oneself—in the other person's (or nation's) place." [18] It requires states to recognize themselves as imperfect parts of an imperfectly ethical world and to show a somewhat greater awareness of the moral complexities and disparities in the objective environment underlying the state behavior of others. Beyond this, statesmen must ask the question whether their policies are likely to produce the kind of international order in which their own values can survive. In this sense they transcend national self-interest at the point of the query, "Everything considered, what is best for the world?" Indeed "a state may fairly acquire virtue from the very fact that it contrives to make its self-interest harmonize with something that is good for the world in general." [19] A case in point may be the liquidation of large segments of the British Empire when morality and the necessity of reducing its overseas commitments converged in a common policy. In this same connection, the intrinsic logic of the Marshall Plan comes naturally to mind. In Mr. Butterfield's words: "Whether we are practising diplomacy, or conducting a war, or negotiating a peace treaty, our ultimate objective is the maintenance and the development of an international order. This is the purpose which transcends national egotism and puts the boundary to self-interest—the purpose to which all our immediate aims in foreign policy have reference." [20]

Two exceedingly able American diplomatists—former Secretary

of State Dean Acheson and onetime Director of the Policy Planning staff George F. Kennan—have each undertaken to define the place of morality and religion in international politics. Both share with historians like Barraclough and Butterfield a profound uneasiness over the prevailing trend toward national self-righteousness where every practical measure is cloaked in the garb of moral and political virtue. In Mr. Acheson's telling phrase: "To express collective indignation may bring the glow of moral principles vindicated without effort; but it is usually futile, and, more often than not, harmful." [21] We must be careful not to pose "as the schoolmistress of the Western hemisphere." [22] Both men are hesitant to "use the language of moral discourse," preferring instead to describe foreign policy in terms of purpose and effect. They are reluctant to introduce the distinctions of moral and immoral as descriptions of state behavior, because "the language of moral discourse—colored as it is apt to be at one end with fervor, and, at the other, with self-righteousness—is more likely to obscure than to clarify. . . ." [23] For this reason both men strike out against what they call "the moralistic-ideological" approach.

If I read them correctly, they mean by this the tendency of "finding in one theme both a central evil, which is thought to dominate our time, and also the clue to its eradication." [24] Such a theme oftentimes amounts to reducing moral principles to maxims which are easily corrupted into slogans. Such a theme I have already discussed in what has been said about "the dilemma of colonialism." According to Mr. Acheson, a moralistic approach to the colonial problem insists "that not only do communities which wish to break off existing political connections and become independent national states have a moral right to do so, but that a moral foreign policy on the part of the United States requires that we go to considerable lengths to help them, including the use of force. . . ." [25] This principle, whether we call it support of popular revolutionary movements or self-determination, was applied enthusiastically against our enemies in two world wars, particularly in the dismemberment of the Austro-Hungarian and Ottoman Empires. However, "as one looks back upon the results in Eastern Europe and the Middle East, one has more difficulty in seeing the moral or ideal achievement than in recognizing the immediate end, perhaps, irrevocable disaster." [26] The problem becomes most acute when we deal with states that are politically more intransigent and resistant. The cases of India in Kashmir, Hungary, and the Baltic states come quickly to mind. In cases such as these, policymakers ironically enough tend to shift the invocation of the principle in order to apply it boldly—perhaps in remission of failures elsewhere—to the problems of our friends. Mr. Acheson is brutally non-partisan in leveling this criticism at Senator Kennedy for his preachments directed toward the French. The single-factor approach, whether its object lies in Senator McCarthy's threat of Communists in government, or President Eisenhower's peril of Communist imperialism, or Senator Kennedy's end of colonialism partakes of an illusory simplicity. It carries within it, however, serious pitfalls and traps. If Communism is the sole threat, we run the risk of making dyed-in-the wool crusaders against Communism who historically have been demoniac figures like Hitler or Mussolini, or shadowy leaders like Franco, our staunchest co-workers in building resistance to Communist expansionism. The gravest peril lies in being driven to embrace allies because of what they oppose, not because of what they propose.

Under such circumstances, it would be better to adopt a strategic rather than a moralistic approach. The spirit of this approach is reflected in Bret Harte's "Tennessee's Partner." "In fact, he was a grave man, with a steady application to practical detail which was unpleasant in difficulty." [27] Lincoln was denounced for immorality alike by abolitionists and secessionists, but for Mr. Acheson, Lincoln's dedication to the supreme goal of preserving the Union remains the classic embodiment of the strategic approach. Many of our contemporaries appraising the "Great Emancipator" overlook his epic statement in the letter he wrote to Horace Greely on August 22, 1862:

> My paramount objective is to save the Union, and is not either to save or destroy slavery. If I could save the Union without freeing any slave, I would do it; and if I could save it by freeing all the slaves, I would do it; and if I could do it by freeing some and leaving others alone, I would also do that. What I do about slavery and the colored race, I do because I believe it helps to save this Union; and what I forebear, I forebear because I do not believe it would help to save the Union. I shall do less whenever I shall believe what I am doing hurts the cause, and I shall do more whenever I shall believe doing more will help the cause.

Any moral choice involves decisions in a complicated and ever-shifting field of action. The same course of action that under one set of circumstances may be moral, in another may be quite immoral. To sort out the moral elements in each successive crisis is the task of statesmanship, and simple moralism is more often an impediment than guide.

In more general philosophic terms, Mr. Kennan believes there are few if any absolutes in international politics. When one considers Kennan's viewpoint, one thinks of Lord Acton's counsel: "An absolute principle is as absurd as absolute power," or his advice: "When you perceive a truth, look for the balancing truth." Such a philosophy is singularly appropriate in foreign policy, for when our diplomats and statesmen are dealing with a foreign country their role is, at best, a marginal one. They can help or encourage existing or latent tendencies on foreign soil, but it is for those more intimately responsible for another country's affairs to realize them. Needless to say, this runs counter to certain basic American emotions. It is tempting to proclaim that this troubled world could be free of all conflict if only peoples everywhere would adopt the political institutions we have forged in the fire of national experience. "The Wilsonian thesis was . . . that, since the world was no longer safe for the American democracy, the American people were called upon to conduct a crusade to make the world safe for American democracy. In order to do this the principles of the American democracy would have to be made universal throughout the world." [28]

However, there is no absolutely best state for all peoples. We are reminded of de Tocqueville's words on the United States written in 1831: "The more I see of this country the more I admit myself penetrated with this truth: that there is nothing absolute in the theoretical value of political institutions, and that their efficiency depends almost always on the original circumstances and the social conditions of people to whom they are applied." The ways in which peoples move toward more enlightened forms of government constitute the most profound of the processes of national life. They stem from the bedrock of national character and existence; they have an organic growth. For example, Kennan, writing on the subject "When the Russians Rose Against the Czar," concludes by saying that if changes were to take place in the Soviet Union, Americans would do well "not to impede or embarrass the process by claiming it for our own and by attempting to see in it the repetition and vindication, in universal terms, of our own history. It is her own laws of development, not ours, that Russia must follow. The sooner we learn that there are many mansions in this house of nations, and many paths to the enrichment of human experience, the easier we will make it for other people to solve their problems, and for ourselves to understand our own." [29] In stressing this point it is barely possible that Mr. Kennan has neglected the corollary that notwithstanding endless variations there are minimum standards of justice and order that any polity must observe lest the fabric of mankind be threatened. It may be that some of the classical writers were more attuned to this problem than the children of our present relativist age. Classicists were ever in search of the attributes of the best state, however transcendent these might be.

Mr. Kennan and his school of policy planners has also resisted a too absolute conception of the possible goals and accomplishments of foreign policy. It is well to be ever aware of the limits as well as the purposes of foreign policy, the boundaries as well as the magnitudes. The statesman confronting the world is constrained, more often than not, to act within narrow limits. His choices are severely restricted and events pass swiftly beyond the realm of conscious choice. Often times he faces a moral predicament of an almost insoluble character. Such a predicament seems to be presented by World War II, for its roots are embedded fatefully and inextricably in the aftermath of World War I. France and England had been weakened far more deeply than they knew. Austria-Hungary had disappeared as a restraint on Germany. Russia was no longer a predictable and constructive force, for it had been seized by violent men who were implacably hostile to those capitalist societies to which political necessity might have united them as natural allies. Into this setting marched the one great united people in Central Europe, the Germans—"frustrated, impoverished, stung with defeat, uncertain in the breakdown of their traditional institutions." In the light of these facts it is all too easy to absolve Western statesmen of any responsibility and to regard them as "actors" in a tragedy beyond their making or repair." [30]

While the choices of Western statesmen were significantly and tragically narrowed by this tangled web of events and nothing approaching a complete solution was to be found, possibilities of making wiser and more effectual choices were never entirely eliminated. For example, it might have been possible to lend greater encouragement, support, and understanding to certain moderate forces within the Weimar Republic. A different attitude toward the defeated German people, "one less dominated by distaste, suspicion and social snobbery," might have strengthened the more liberal forces which were not totally lacking in Germany at that time. And once the struggle seemed inevitable the West might have deterred it—especially in 1936 at the time of the occupation of the Rhineland—by a firm show of strength, or later by a resolute military build-up that even tyrannies would have had to respect. At last, when war came, the allies could have made a decisive stand not for total victory but for more limited military and political objectives sometimes possible in war.

Finally, Kennan and Acheson, while admitting that individual and collective morality have something in common, are fearful of analogies that treat the two as more or less identical. "Generally speaking, morality . . . imposes upon those who exercise the powers of government a standard of conduct quite different from what might seem right to them as private citizens." [31] The moral rights and duties of the judge is not to do what he thinks right or, by his judicial action to recast society in terms more appropriate, say, to his vision of the justice of natural law. "It is our hope that the consciences of our judges will be guided, not by what they think is right, but what they believe the law requires them to decide, whether they like it or not." [32] Similarly, the pursuit of personal advantage or the service of special interests or groups, while commonly accepted in private life, has no legitimate place in public service. Indeed, a whole network of conflict-of-interest laws has been thrown up for government servants to guard them against vulnerability to private pressures.

Governments exist primarily to maintain order and justice within certain territorial boundaries and provide at the same time for the common defense. Neither the domestic nor international purposes of the state strictly coincide with Christian principles or the will of God. The function of the state is rather to protect man from himself—his greed, lust, and brutality. This is a worthy function, but one required less for Christian purposes than because men are less than Christian in conduct. The state being an agent and not a principal, a collectivity rather than an individual, is incapable of assuming the personal or subjective obligations that inhere in the concept of Christian justice. In Mr. Kennan's words: "Christian justice is a two way street, in that it implies an obligation of charity and humility and sacrifice on the dispenser of justice as well as on its object. The father's treatment of the prodigal son was founded on a Christian recognition of the relevance to this situation not just of the son's delinquency but also of the father's own sin and guilt. But our secular father, the state, is incapable of making any such recognition. It is always guiltless in its own eyes. Its justice, accordingly, remains—and must remain—less than Christian." [33] Relations among states are even more infected with this less than Christian quality. "Nowhere in Christ's teachings," Mr. Kennan argues, "was it suggested that mankind ought to be divided into political families . . . (of sovereign states), each a law unto itself, each recognizing no higher authority than its own national ego, each assuming its interest to be more worthy of service than any other with which it might come into conflict. . . . Before we could talk about a wholly Christian foreign policy, we would have to overcome this unlimited egoism of the sovereign national state and find a higher interest which all of us could recognize and serve."

Christian moralists and utopian rationalists interestingly enough are seized by the same illusion. It was comparatively simple for a brilliant essayist like Bertrand Russell in his exchanges in the *New Statesman* with Premier Khrushchev and Secretary Dulles last winter to point out contradictions. He noted that both believe in progress but both maintain that it will depend on adoption of their respective social systems even to the extent of preparing for nuclear war in defense of these goals. Yet nuclear war would mean mutual destruction and Lord Russell therefore called for full and free rational debate to establish the truth and bring a lessening in the acerbity of the East-West ideological struggle. At present both accuse the other's system of every kind of vice, claiming for their own every virtue. Lord Russell tended to argue that competing ideologies, like scientific theories, must be debated by appeal to fact and logic and modified when circumstances require.

However, a nation's political ideals are the cement by which a society is united and consolidated against the external world. Through them statesmen fuse the multifarious pressures that compose society into coherent lines of action. They are the means of concerting the national will; they represent everything about their people in a favorable light. Their function is not, as in science, to explain events but to assemble a vast miscellany of popular feelings and bring it to the point of action. It is illusory to imagine that such points of political doctrine can be judged and corrected by higher moral or rational standards or debated out of existence. The best we can hope is that if the people achieve a certain skepticism about the more absolute claims, their statesmen will reflect this when they come to the conference table and will fix more on the practical points in a settlement than scoring points in ideological war.

Mr. Kennan concludes: "All these reflections cause me to wince when I hear people confusing the possibilities and obligations of the state with the possibilities and obligations of the Christian individual. . . . I wince . . . when I hear it claimed that the foreign policy of our own government has already achieved so remarkable a state of innocence and purity of motive as to justify us in regarding it as a religious crusade and in giving it devotion and support in this quality." "To the extent that the Kingdom of God is to be realized at all on this earth, it is going to be realized in the human heart: in the struggle of the individual against the powers of darkness within himself, in his transcendence of instinctive self-will, . . . in his elevation of mind and spirit to that level of detachment and of compassionate identification with others which we know as Christian love. It is not to be realized in the workings of the state, with its imperfect justice, its pretense to moral infallibility, its purely external enemies, and its absurd claim to be a law and a purpose unto itself." [34]

Yet Kennan is constrained to urge that no one equate his viewpoint with a counsel of despair on the workings of sovereign states or an advocacy of quietism, passivity, or indifference for the Christian as he confronts the real world. The state "cannot assure the triumph of Christian love, but it can do things that affect the possibilities for its advancement." It can provide a decent human environment in which man can work out his destiny, and whether he succeeds in realizing this is singularly dependent on the individual's response to his responsibilities of citizenship and public duty. Mr. Kennan sees "no way in which we can absolve ourselves of our tiny individual share of responsibility for what the government does." That the state has immense possibilities for evil is all too plain from Nazi Germany, the Soviet Union, and Communist China, where the most appalling lines of cruelty have fostered "a real sickness of the human spirit . . . dreadfully adverse to . . . the Christian cause." However, the state also enjoys vast possibilities for good if the body politic be healthy, vital, and alert to international issues which may have significance from the Christian standpoint.

Mr. Kennan maintains that questions of method in foreign policy are generally the ones best suited to Christian concern as against questions of purpose which tend to be broadly determined by basic underlying forces. The latter involve such issues as a statesman's intent and all the excruciatingly complex relationships between a man's or government's aims and the consequences of action. In so far as methods go, "a government can pursue its purposes in a patient and conciliatory and understanding way, respecting the interests of others and infusing its behavior with a high standard of decency and honesty and humanity, or it can show itself petty, exacting, onerous, and self-righteous." Good purposes will be undermined by dubious methods "whereas sheer good manners will bring some measure of redemption to even the most ill-conceived and disastrous of undertakings." The Christian citizen, therefore, should focus his interest on a government's style and its methods of seeking its aim. "If we allow ourselves to copy our adversary' methods as a means of combatting him, we may have lost the battle before we start. . . ." In the cold war, "while Christian values may be, and often are, involved in the issues of our conflict with Soviet power, we cannot conclude that everything we want automatically reflects the purpose of God and everything they want—the purpose of the Devil. The pattern is complex, fuzzy and unstable. We must bear in mind all the things we do not know and cannot know. We must concede, I think, the possibility that there might be some areas of conflict involved in this cold war which a Divine Power could contemplate only with a sense of pity and disgust for both parties, and others in which . . . He might even consider us wrong."[35]

NOTES

1. John Maurice Clark, *Economic Institutions and Human Welfare* (New York: Alfred A. Knopf, 1957), pp. 35-36.
2. Geoffrey Barraclough, "History, Morals, and Politics," *International Affairs,* XXXIV, No. 1 (Jan. 1958), 1-15.
3. Quoted in *ibid.,* p. 4.
4. *Ibid.,* p. 6.
5. *Ibid.,* p. 9.
6. *Ibid.,* p. 10.
7. *Ibid.*
8. *Ibid.,* p. 14.
9. A. J. P. Taylor, *Bismarck, The Man and the Statesman* (New York: Knopf, 1955), p. 115.
10. *Ibid.,* p. 87.
11. Herbert Butterfield, "Morality and Historical Process in International Affairs," unpublished manuscript for June 12, 1956, meeting of Columbia University Seminar on Theory of International Politics, p. 1.
12. *Ibid.,* p. 2.
13. *Ibid.*
14. *Ibid.*
15. *Ibid.,* p. 3.
16. *Ibid.*
17. *Ibid.,* p. 10.
18. Professor Butterfield distinguishes between the moralist and the statesman in this way: "The moralist and the teacher, the prophet and the preacher, address themselves to the improvement of human nature itself. . . . The statesman is concerned to improve human conduct rather by the process of rectifying conditions." *Ibid.,* p. 8-9.
19. *Ibid.,* p. 10.
20. *Ibid.,* p. 11.
21. Dean Acheson, *Power and Diplomacy* (Cambridge, Massachusetts: Harvard University Press, 1958), p. 80.
22. *Ibid.*
23. *Ibid.,* p. 108.
24. Dean Acheson, "Morality, Moralism and Diplomacy," *The Yale Review,* XLVII, No. 4 (June 1958), 485.
25. *Ibid.,* p. 483.
26. *Ibid.*
27. Quoted in *ibid.,* p. 487.
28. Walter Lippmann, *Isolation and Alliances: An American Speaks to the British* (Boston: Little, Brown & Co., 1952), p. 22.

29. *New York Times Magazine,* March 10, 1957, p. 40.

30. George F. Kennan, *American Diplomacy, 1900-1950* (Chicago: University of Chicago Press, 1951), p. 78.

31. Acheson, "Morality, Moralism and Diplomacy," p. 489.

32. *Ibid.*

33. The following quotations are taken from an address by Mr. Kennan to the students and faculty of Princeton Theological Seminary in the winter of 1959, subsequently published as "Foreign Policy and Christian Conscience," *The Atlantic Monthly,* CCIII, No. 5 (May 1959), 44-49.

34. *Ibid.*

35. *Ibid.*

PART III

The Debate

8. Ethics in International Relations Today*

by Dean Acheson

THE DISCUSSION OF ETHICS OR MORALITY IN OUR RELATIONS WITH other states is a prolific cause of confusion. The righteous who seek to deduce foreign policy from ethical or moral principles are as misleading and misled as the modern Machiavellis who would conduct our foreign relations without regard to them.

Most of what we, and a good part of the noncommunist world, regard as ethical principles relates to conduct, the behavior of individuals toward one another. There is pretty general agreement that it is better to act straightforwardly, candidly, honorably, and courageously than duplicitously, conspiratorially, or treacherously. This is true of conduct toward friends and toward those who are ill-disposed to us. It is well that our government should give to foreigners as well as to our own people as clear an idea as possible of its intentions. To do so should inspire confidence and increase stability. One need not counsel perfection—for instance, to tell the the whole truth; but it ought not to be too much to advise telling nothing but the truth—advice which might usefully have been given to President Eisenhower before he began issuing statements about the U-2 aircraft shot down some years ago over the Soviet Union.

The French school of diplomacy, founded by Cardinal Richelieu, the dominant school for nearly three centuries, and probably still the best ever devised, was based, as François de Callieres stated, upon the principle that "open dealing is the basis of confidence" (a very different idea from President Wilson's ill-considered maxim,

* Address at Amherst College, December 9, 1964. By permission of Dean Acheson and through the courtesy of the Secretary of Amherst College.

"open covenants openly arrived at"). He adds, "The negotiator therefore must be a man of probity and one who loves truth; otherwise he will fail to inspire confidence." And again, "Deceit is the measure of the smallness of mind of him who uses it . . . a lie always leaves behind it a drop of poison . . . Menaces always do harm to negotiation . . ."

It does not detract from the purity of his morals that he supports them with worldly wisdom:

> The diplomatist must be . . . a good listener, courteous, and agreeable. He should not seek to gain a reputation as a wit, nor should he be so disputatious as to divulge secret information in order to clinch an argument. Above all the good negotiator must possess enough self control to resist the longing to speak before he has thought out what he wants to say . . . He should pay attention to women but never lose his heart . . . , possess the patience of a watch-maker . . . should not be given to drink . . . and be able to tell where, in any foreign country, the real sovereignty lies . . . Finally . . . a good cook is often an excellent conciliator.

For any of you who are contemplating a career in the Foreign Service, François de Callieres is as sound an adviser today as he was in 1716.

Without laboring the point further, I take it as clear that, where an important purpose of diplomacy is to further enduring good relations between states, the methods—the modes of conduct—by which relations between states are carried on must be designed to inspire trust and confidence. To achieve this result the conduct of diplomacy should conform to the same moral and ethical principles which inspire trust and confidence when followed by and between individuals.

The purpose of our own diplomacy, as of the French school, requires the inspiring of trust and confidence, for our governmental goal for many years has been to preserve and foster an environment in which free societies may exist and flourish. When we have said this, we had better stop and think before concluding that the policies which will advance us toward this goal can usefully be discussed or evaluated in terms of moral or ethical principles.

In the first place, a little reflection will convince us that the same conduct is not moral under all circumstances. Its moral propriety seems to depend, certainly in many cases, upon the relationship of those concerned with the conduct. For instance, parents have the moral right, indeed duty, to instill moral and religious ideas in their children and correct moral error. Ministers, priests, rabbis, and mullahs have much the same duties to their flocks, including that of correcting heresy, when they can make up their minds what it is.

But these same acts on the part of public officials—certainly in the United States—would be both wrong and a denial of the fundamental rights of the citizen. Indeed, even prayer prescribed and led by teachers in our public schools is condemned by our courts with the approval of some of our churches. The attempt of both governmental and religious bodies to censor literature, painting, sculpture, the theater, and the movies, under the aegis of those alliterative adjectives, lewd and lascivious, seems to me intolerable. Parents, if they are any good, can shield their children from whatever they choose. The rest of us had better take our chances with mortal sin, rather than to have policemen, trained to handle traffic and arrest criminals, become judges of what art we may see or read. And it is just as bad when the local watch and ward society or church body tries to do the same thing.

So, acts, moral in one human relationship, may become quite the reverse in another. Generally speaking, morality often imposes upon those who exercise the powers of government standards of conduct quite different from what might seem right to them as private citizens. For instance, the moral, and indeed the legal, duty of a judge in bringing to bear upon a party before him the coercive power of the state is not to do "what he thinks is right," or by his decision to mold the kind of society which seems to him to accord with divine will or high human aspiration. He has not been given this great power so that he might administer personal justice, even though his conscience be as clear as that of Harun al-Rashid or Henry the Second when they decided disputes by virtuous inspiration. Our courts are supposed to be courts of law; and whatever justice may be (I know of no satisfactory definition of it), it is to be achieved, as the phrase goes, "under law." It is our hope that the consciences of our judges will be guided, not by what they think is right, but what they believe the law requires them to decide, whether they like it or not.

So, too, what may be quite proper and moral for a private citizen—for instance, the pursuit of personal advantage, or the advantage of a group—often, and rightly, is condemned if done when he assumes legislative or executive office. This distinction is not always perceived and has gotten many people into trouble. Even a candidate for office cannot expect the same latitude given private individuals in exposing his ignorance and stupidity. November 3rd last made that rather clear.

Moreover, the vocabulary of morals and ethics is inadequate to discuss or test foreign policies of states. We are told that what is ethical is characterized by what is excellent in conduct and that excellence may be judged by what is right and proper, as against what is wrong, by existing standards. But when we look for standards we find that none exist. What passes for ethical standards for governmental policies in foreign affairs is a collection of moralisms, maxims, and slogans, which neither help nor guide, but only confuse, decision on such complicated matters as the multilateral nuclear force, a common grain price in Europe, policy in Southeast Asia, or exceptions and disparities under the Kennedy Round of tariff negotiations.

One of the most often invoked and delusive of these maxims is the so-called principle of self-determination. In the continuing dispute over Cyprus it has been invoked by nearly all parties to the struggle to support whatever they were temporarily seeking to achieve—by all Cypriots to justify revolt against British rule, by Archbishop Makarios to support an independent government for the whole island, by Greek Cypriots as foundation for enosis (union) with Greece, and by Turkish Cypriots for partition of the island and double enosis, union of one part with Greece and the other with Turkey.

Despite its approval by Woodrow Wilson, this maxim has a doubtful moral history. He used it against our enemies in the First World War to dismember the Austro-Hungarian and Ottoman Empires with results which hardly inspire enthusiasm today. After the Second World War the doctrine was invoked against our friends in the dissolution of their colonial connections. In all probability these connections would inevitably have been dissolved. But the results were immeasurably improved when considerations other than moralistic maxims were brought to bear on the process.

On the one occasion when the right of self-determination—then called secession—was invoked against our own government by the Confederate States of America, it was rejected with a good deal of bloodshed and moral fervor. Probably you agree that it was rightly rejected. You would doubtless also agree that the dialogue now in progress between the British and French speaking sections of Canada upon the problems of a common national life together would not be helped by conducting it in terms of the principle of self-determination.

Furthermore, this moralistic doctrine is not merely no help to wise policy decisions, it can be a positive menace to them. "Hitler's appeal to national self-determination in the Sudeten crisis in 1938," writes Henry Kissinger, "was an invocation of 'justice,' and thereby contributed to the indecisiveness of the resistance; it induced the Western powers to attempt to construct a 'truly' legitimate order by satisfying Germany's 'just' claims. Only after Hitler annexed Bohemia and Moravia was it clear that he was aiming for dominion, not legitimacy; only then did the contest become one of pure power."

Another set of moralisms and maxims crops up to bedevil discussion and decision about what is broadly called "foreign aid." A good deal of trouble comes from the anthropomorphic urge to regard nations as individuals and apply to our own national conduct vague maxims for individual conduct—for instance, the Golden Rule—even though in practice individuals rarely adopt it. The fact is that nations are not individuals; the cause and effect of their actions are wholly different; and what a government can and should do with the resources which it takes from its citizens must be governed by wholly different considerations from those which properly determine an individual's use of his own.

This does not mean that considerations of compassion have no place in governmental decisions. It does mean that the criteria are generally quite different and far more complicated. Some of these criteria will determine what funds can be made available; others will determine their allocation among uses always exceeding amounts available.

The overriding guide must be achievement of a major goal of policy—in this case, creating an environment in which free societies may flourish and undeveloped nations who want to work on their own development may find the means to do so. This is an exceedingly difficult matter for both aiding and aided governments. The criteria should be hard-headed in the extreme. Decisions are not helped by considering them in terms of sharing, brotherly love, and Golden Rule, or inducting our citizens into the Kingdom of Heaven.

But, you will say to me, at least one moral standard of right and wrong has been pretty well agreed to be applicable to foreign policy. Surely, the opinion of the world has condemned the use and threat of force by one state against another, as the United Nations Charter bears witness. Does this not give us firm ground on which to stand? Well, does it? Ever since the Charter was signed, those whose interests are opposed to ours have used force, or the threat of it, whenever it seemed to them advisable and safe—in Greece, Czechoslovakia, Palestine, Berlin, Korea, Indochina, and Hungary. Each side used it in regard to Suez.

Is it moral to deny ourselves the use of force in all circumstances, when our adversaries employ it, under handy excuses, whenever it seems useful to tip the scales of power against every value we think of as moral and as making life worth living? It seems to me not only a bad bargain, but a stupid one. I would almost say an immoral one. For the very conception of morality seems to me to involve a duty to preserve values outside the contour of our own skins, and at the expense of foregoing much that is desired and pleasant, including—it may be—our own fortunes and lives.

But, however that may be, those involved in the Cuban crisis of October, 1962, will remember the irrelevance of the supposed moral considerations brought out in the discussions. Judgment centered about the appraisal of dangers and risks, the weighing of the need for decisive and effective action against considerations of prudence; the need to do enough, against the consequences of doing too much. Moral talk did not bear on the problem. Nor did it bear upon the decision of those called upon to advise the President in 1949 whether and with what degree of urgency to press the attempt to produce a thermonuclear weapon. A respected colleague advised me that it would be better that our whole nation and people should perish rather than be party to a course so evil as producing that weapon. I told him that on the Day of Judgment his view might be confirmed and that he was free to go forth and preach the necessity for salvation. It was not, however, a view which I could entertain as a public servant.

What, then, is the sound approach to questions of foreign policy? I suggest that it is what we might call the strategic approach —to consider various courses of action from the point of view of their bearing upon major objectives. On August 22, 1862, President Lincoln wrote to Horace Greeley in response to the latter's question as to how the President viewed the question of slavery in relation to the war then in progress, "My paramount object in this struggle is to save the Union, and is not either to save or to destroy slavery. If I could save the Union without freeing any slave, I would do it; and if I could save it by freeing all the slaves, I would do it; and if I could do it by freeing some and leaving others alone, I would also do that. What I do about slavery and the colored race, I do because I believe it helps to save this Union: and what I forbear, I forbear because I do not believe it would help to save the Union. I shall do less whenever I shall believe what I am doing hurts the cause, and I shall do more whenever I shall believe doing more will help the cause."

This is what I mean by the strategic approach. If you object that is no different from saying that the end justifies the means, I must answer that in foreign affairs only the end can justify the means; that this is not to say that the end justifies any means, or that some ends can justify anything. The shifting "combinazioni," sought by the weak Italian city states of the Renaissance to plunder one another, not only failed to justify the means they used, but gave their diplomacy and its expounder, Niccolo Machiavelli, the bad name they have today.

The end sought by our foreign policy, the purpose for which we carry on relations with foreign states, is, as I have said, to preserve and foster an environment in which free societies may exist and flourish. Our policies and actions must be tested by whether they contribute to or detract from achievement of this end. They need no other justification or moral or ethical embellishment. To oppose powerful and brutal states which threaten the independence of others is not less admirable because it helps secure our own as well; nor is it less good to help others improve their lot because it is necessary to keep the free world free and to strengthen it.

In conducting our foreign affairs we can use any amount of intelligence, perseverance, nerve, and luck. But if we have an excess of moral or ethical enthusiasm or idealism, let us not try to find an outlet for it in the formulation of foreign policies. Rather in how we carry them out. In this country we have an unfortunate tendency to do fine and noble things in a thoroughly churlish way. Let us remember that often what we do may be less important than how we do it. "What one lives for may be uncertain," writes Lord Robert Cecil; "how one lives is not." We can be faulted far less in what we do, than in how we do it.

9. Morals and Power*

by John Foster Dulles

SINCE I HAVE BEEN SECRETARY OF STATE, I HAVE BEEN TO EUROPE, the Near East, and South Asia. Before that, in connection with negotiating the Japanese peace treaty, I had an excellent chance to get a firsthand look at our foreign representatives in Japan, Korea, and other parts of the Far East.

One of the things that most impressed me in these areas was the down-to-earth cooperation which existed between our civilian and military officials. The North Atlantic Treaty Organization is an outstanding example of large-scale military-civilian cooperative effort.

The current negotiations in embattled Korea are being carried on by General Harrison. And, to my way of thinking, he is doing an excellent job under very exacting conditions.

But behind General Harrison stands a team of Defense and State Department officials which, once again, testifies to the effectiveness of military and civilian cooperation.

I might mention that one of my first acts as Secretary of State was to invite the Joint Chiefs of Staff and their chairman to lunch with me at the State Department. They kindly responded and the five of us had an intimate exchange of views about the world situation and U.S. security. Ever since, we have cooperated with no single trace of friction. That, I am glad to say, is typical. Of course, there are often initial differences of opinion. But, by and large, our military and civilian officers both here in the United States and on duty overseas rise above differences when the chips

* U.S., *Department of State Bulletin,* Volume XXVIII, No. 731, June 29, 1953, pp. 895-897. Made before the National War College at Washington on June 16, 1953 (press release 321).

are down. In today's world, the chips are down almost everywhere.

It is teamwork between the military and civilian which has given us the necessary strength whenever and wherever we have needed it.

I should like to talk for a few minutes about power in a material sense, such as is represented by our splendid military establishment. What is the purpose of this power? Admiral Mahan is credited with one of the best answers to this question. It is that the role of power is to give moral ideas the time to take root. Where moral ideas already are well-rooted, there is little occasion for much military or police force. We see that illustrated in our own communities. Where the people accept the moral law and its great commandments, where they exercise self-control and self-discipline, then there is very little need for police power. Under these circumstances, it is sufficient to have a very modest force to take care of the small minority always found in every community which disregards the precepts of the moral law.

Where, however, there are many who do not accept moral principles, then that creates the need of force to protect those who do. That, unfortunately, is the case in the world community of today.

At the present time, there is no moral code which has worldwide acceptance. The principles upon which our society is based—the principles which we believe to be both humanitarian and just—are not accepted by governments which dominate more than one-third of mankind.

The result is that we have a world which is, for the most part, split between two huge combinations. On the one hand, there is the United States and its free-world associates. This is a voluntary alliance of free peoples working together in the recognition that without unity there could be catastrophe.

On the other hand, there is the totalitarian bloc led by the Soviet Union—an artificial, imposed unity which cannot be called an alliance in the sense that we use the word.

These huge concentrations are in conflict because each reflects differing aims, aspirations, and social, political, and economic philosophies. We must assume that they will continue to remain in basic conflict, in one way or another, until such time as the Communists so change their nature as to admit that those who wish to live by the moral law are free to do so without coercion by those who believe in enforced conformity to a materialistic standard.

This is one of the hard facts of international existence which we must accept. We cannot close our eyes to it. It will not go away simply because we hope that it will do so.

We must plan accordingly.

"KNOW YOUR ENEMY"

There is a sound military principle which we must take into consideration in our planning. It is "know your enemy."

What makes the Soviet Union—the fountainhead of world communism—act as it does? Why do the Soviets seek power and more power?

These complex questions are not simply answered. There are many forces which motivate the Soviet drive for power. Among these forces are these which I should like to mention: ideology, the historic imperialist urge, and the chronic insecurity complex which besets those who rule by force.

Take first the question of Communist ideology. Soviet theorists, as you know, refer to their ideology as Marxian-Leninist-Stalinism. Whose name will next be added remains to be seen.

Through the years, Communist ideology has taken a number of twists, turns, and shifts in emphasis. Upon occasion, it has almost seemed as if the ideology has been stood on its head to justify a policy which Soviet leaders have had to adopt to meet a given international or domestic crisis. Thus, in October 1939, the Soviet leaders proclaimed that Hitler was the peace lover and the British and French the aggressors.

There can be no question but that Soviet leaders use shifty tactics.

But the Soviet leaders have never departed from a certain basic thesis laid down by Marx. It is called "dialectical materialism."

It is important for us to remember that this Marxist principle continues to be basic to the Soviet credo despite any changes that have been made by Lenin and Stalin. Stalin's last published article, written shortly before his death, was based upon original Marxist assumptions when he predicted that the United States and its allies inevitably would split because of inner, economic contradictions.

The entire creed of Soviet communism is based upon this "dialectical materialism," the theory that there is no such thing as a moral law or spiritual truth; that all things are predetermined by the contradictory movements of matter; that so-called capitalism is historically fated to collapse; and that communism is the movement predestined to effect that collapse.

Now, let us look briefly at another of the springs of Soviet action, that of historical imperialism. This urge to expand is not something patented by the Communists of Soviet Russia. This urge has long been found with the "Great Russians" in the Eurasian heartland. It is a national urge, though it is clear that today communism has greatly intensified it.

The present Soviet Communist exertions in the Near East, Far East, and East Europe are a duplication of many past performances. Early in the 19th century Tsar Alexander, the most powerful ruler of his time, organized the so-called "Holy Alliance" in an effort to dominate the world.

Has the historic imperialist urge played a role in the Soviet drive for power? I think it is clear that it has.

The third and last influence which I will mention is that chronic sense of insecurity which pervades police-state rulers. Those who rule by force inevitably fear force. In a police state the rulers have a monopoly or near monopoly of weapons. But it is never possible to arm enough policemen to rule an unruly mass without in the process arming some who themselves may prove unruly. Also, the rulers of a police state greatly fear any weapons which they do not control, and they seek to extend their power to bring these weapons under control. They cannot imagine that armaments in the hands of others may be designed purely for internal security and self-defense. That is why the Soviet leaders have so consistently and so violently expressed their opposition to the North Atlantic Treaty Organization and fought the creation of a European Defense Community. To us their fears seem mere pretense. But perhaps they do have fear, because they do not understand that if force is in the hands of those who are governed by moral law, it will not be used as a means of aggression or to violate the principles of the moral law.

This picture which I have given of the international situation is not a pleasing one. It does not hold out the prospect of any quick change for the better or any early elimination of our need for power in order to permit moral principles to take root rather than be uprooted.

However, if we do maintain power, and if we do subject it to moral law and use it truly to enable moral principles to survive, and thrive, and spread in the world, we can have hope in the future. For we know that in the long run the fruits of a spiritual faith prevail over the fruits of materialism.

The great weakness of Soviet Communist doctrine is that it denies morality. That is its Achilles heel, of which we must take advantage. We can take advantage of it if—but only if—we ourselves accept the supremacy of moral law.

"RECAPTURING THE MOOD OF OUR FOREBEARS"

Our nation was founded by the men who believed that there was a Divine Creator who endowed men with unalienable rights. They believed, as George Washington put it in his farewell address, that religion and morality are the great pillars of human happiness and that morality cannot prevail in exclusion of religious principles.

Our Federal and State Constitutions, our laws and practices, reflect the belief that there is a Being superior to ourselves who has established His own laws which can be comprehended by all human beings and that human practices should seek conformity with those laws.

Seeking first the Kingdom of God and His righteousness, many material things were added to us. We developed here an area of spiritual, intellectual, and material richness, the like of which the world has never seen. What we did caught the imagination of men everywhere and became known everywhere as "the Great American experiment." Our free society became a menace to every despot because we showed how to meet the hunger of the people for greater opportunity and for greater dignity. The tide of despotism, which at that time ran high, was rolled back and we ourselves enjoyed security.

We need to recapture that mood.

Today some seem to feel that Americanism means being tough and "hard-boiled," doing nothing unless we are quite sure that it is to our immediate short-term advantage; boasting of our own merit and seeing in others only demerit.

That is a caricature of America. Our people have always been generous to help, out of their abundance, those who are the victims of misfortune. Our forebears have traditionally had what the

Declaration of Independence refers to as a decent respect for the opinion of mankind. They sought to practice the Golden Rule by doing to others as they would have others do unto them. Their conduct and example made our nation one that was respected and admired throughout the world.

So, in conclusion, I say to you who graduate from the National War College: Be proud of your association with U.S. power, which is indispensable in the world today; but remember that that power is worthy only as it is the shield behind which moral values are invigorated and spread their influence; and accept, as citizens, the obligation to preserve and enhance those moral values. They are the rich heritage that has been bequeathed us. It must be our ambition that future generations shall look back upon us, as we look back upon those who preceded us, with gratitude for the gift to our Republic of the qualities that make it noble, so that men call it blessed.

10. Old Myths and New Realities*

by J. William Fulbright

MR. PRESIDENT, THERE IS AN INEVITABLE DIVERGENCE, ATTRIBUTable to the imperfections of the human mind, between the world as it is and the world as men perceive it. As long as our perceptions are reasonably close to objective reality, it is possible for us to act upon our problems in a rational and appropriate manner. But when our perceptions fail to keep pace with events, when we refuse to believe something because it displeases or frightens us, or because it is simply startlingly unfamiliar, then the gap between fact and perception becomes a chasm, and action becomes irrelevant and irrational.

There has always—and inevitably—been some divergence between the realities of foreign policy and our ideas about it. This divergence has in certain respects been growing, rather than narrowing; and we are handicapped, accordingly, by policies based on old myths, rather than current realities. This divergence is, in my opinion, dangerous and unnecessary—dangerous, because it can reduce foreign policy to a fraudulent game of imagery and appearances; unnecessary, because it can be overcome by the determination of men in high office to dispel prevailing misconceptions by the candid dissemination of unpleasant, but inescapable, facts.

Before commenting on some of the specific areas where I believe our policies are at least partially based on cherished myths, rather than objective facts, I should like to suggest two possible reasons for the growing divergence between the realities and our perceptions of current world politics. The first is the radical change

* U.S., *Congressional Record,* 88th Congress, Second Session, Volume 110, Part 5 (March 25, 1964), pp. 6227-6232. (Exhibits 1 and 2 omitted.) (Reprinted by permission of Senator J. William Fulbright.)

in relations between and within the Communist and the free world; and the second is the tendency of too many of us to confuse means with end and, accordingly, to adhere to prevailing practices with a fervor befitting immutable principles.

Although it is too soon to render a definitive judgment, there is mounting evidence that events of recent years have wrought profound changes in the character of East-West relations. In the Cuban missile crisis of October 1962, the United States proved to the Soviet Union that a policy of aggression and adventure involved unacceptable risks. In the signing of the test ban treaty, each side in effect assured the other that it was prepared to forego, at least for the present, any bid for a decisive military or political breakthrough. These occurrences, it should be added, took place against the background of the clearly understood strategic superiority—but not supremacy—of the United States.

It seems reasonable, therefore, to suggest that the character of the cold war has, for the present, at least, been profoundly altered: by the drawing back of the Soviet Union from extremely aggressive policies; by the implicit repudiation by both sides of a policy of "total victory"; and by the establishment of an American strategic superiority which the Soviet Union appears to have tacitly accepted because it has been accompanied by assurances that it will be exercised by the United States with responsibility and restraint. These enormously important changes may come to be regarded by historians as the foremost achievements of the Kennedy administration in the field of foreign policy. Their effect has been to commit us to a foreign policy which can accurately—though perhaps not prudently—be defined as one of "peaceful coexistence."

Another of the results of the lowering of tensions between East and West is that each is now free to enjoy the luxury of accelerated strife and squabbling within its own domain. The ideological thunderbolts between Washington and Moscow which until a few years ago seemed a permanent part of our daily lives have become a pale shadow of their former selves. Now, instead, the United States waits in fascinated apprehension for the Olympian pronouncements that issue from Paris at 6-month intervals while the Russians respond to the crude epithets of Peiping with almost plain-tive rejoinders about "those who want to start a war against everybody."

These astonishing changes in the configuration of the postwar world have had an unsettling effect on both public and official opinion in the United States. One reason for this, I believe, lies in the fact that we are a people used to looking at the world, and indeed at ourselves, in moralistic rather than empirical terms. We are predisposed to regard any conflict as a clash between good and evil rather than as simply a clash between conflicting interests. We are inclined to confuse freedom and democracy, which we regard as moral principles, with the way in which they are practiced in America—with capitalism federalism, and the two-party system, which are not moral principles but simply the preferred and accepted practices of the American people. There is much cant in American moralism and not a little inconsistency. It resembles in some ways the religious faith of the many respectable people who, in Samuel Butler's words, "would be equally horrified to hear the Christian religion doubted or to see it practiced."

Our national vocabulary is full of "self-evident truths" not only about "life, liberty and happiness," but about a vast number of personal and public issues, including the cold war. It has become one of the "self-evident truths" of the postwar era that just as the President resides in Washington and the Pope in Rome, the Devil resides immutably in Moscow. We have come to regard the Kremlin as the permanent seat of his power and we have grown almost comfortable with a menace which, though unspeakably evil, has had the redeeming virtues of constance, predictability, and familiarity. Now the Devil has betrayed us by traveling abroad and, worse still, by dispersing himself, turning up now here, now there, and in many places at once, with a devilish disregard for the laboriously constructed frontiers of ideology.

We are confronted with a complex and fluid world situation and we are not adapting ourselves to it. We are clinging to old myths in the face of new realities and we are seeking to escape the contradictions by narrowing the permissible bounds of public discussion, by relegating an increasing number of ideas and viewpoints to a growing category of "unthinkable thoughts." I believe that this tendency can and should be reversed, that it is within our ability and unquestionably in our interests, to cut loose from established myths and to start thinking some "unthinkable thoughts" —about the cold war and East-West relations, about the underdeveloped countries and particularly those in Latin America, about the changing nature of the Chinese Communist threat in Asia and about the festering war in Vietnam.

The master myth of the cold war is that the Communist bloc is a monolith composed of governments which are not really governments at all but organized conspiracies, divided among themselves perhaps in certain matters of tactics, but all equally resolute and implacable in their determination to destroy the free world.

I believe that the Communist world is indeed hostile to the free world in its general and long-term intentions but that the existence of this animosity in principle is far less important for our foreign policy than the great variations in its intensity and character both in time and among the individual members of the Communist bloc. Only if we recognize these variations, ranging from China, which poses immediate threats to the free world to Poland and Yugoslavia, which pose none, can we hope to act effectively upon the bloc and to turn its internal differences to our own advantage of those bloc countries which wish to maximize their independence. It is the responsibility of our national leaders, both in the executive branch and in Congress, to acknowledge and act upon these realities, even at the cost of saying things which will not win immediate widespread enthusiasm.

For a start, we can acknowledge the fact that the Soviet Union, though still a most formidable adversary, has ceased to be totally and implacably hostile to the West. It has shown a new willingness to enter mutually advantageous arrangements with the West and, thus far at least, to honor them. It has, therefore, become possible to divert some of our energies from the prosecution of the cold war to the relaxation of the cold war and to deal with the Soviet Union, for certain purposes, as a normal state with normal and traditional interests.

If we are able to do these things effectively, we must distinguish between communism as an ideology and the power and policy of the Soviet state. It is not communism as a doctrine, or communism at it is practiced within the Soviet Union or within any other country, that threatens us. How the Soviet Union organizes its internal life, the gods and doctrines that it worships, are matters for the Soviet Union to determine. It is not Communist dogma as espoused within Russia but Communist imperialism that threatens us and other peoples of the non-Communist world. Insofar as a great nation mobilizes its power and resources for aggressive purposes, that nation, regardless of ideology, makes itself our enemy. Insofar as a nation is content to practice its doctrines within its own frontiers, that nation, however repugnant its ideology, is one with which we have no proper quarrel. We must deal with the Soviet Union as a great power, quite apart from differences of ideology. To the extent that the Soviet leaders abandon the global ambitions of Marxist ideology, in fact if not in words, it becomes possible for us to engage in normal relations with them, relations which probably cannot be close or trusting for many years to come but which can be gradually freed of the terror and the tensions of the cold war.

In our relations with the Russians, and indeed in our relations with all nations, we would do well to remember, and to act upon, the words of Pope John in the great Encyclical, *Pacem in Terris:*

> It must be borne in mind [said Pope John] that to proceed gradually is the law of life in all its expressions, therefore, in human institutions, too, it is not possible to renovate for the better except by working from within them, gradually. Violence has always achieved only destruction, not construction, the kindling of passions, not their pacification, the accumulation of hate and ruin, not the reconciliation of the contending parties. And it has reduced men and parties to the difficult task of rebuilding after sad experience, on the ruins of discord.

Important opportunities have been created for Western policy by the development of "polycentrism" in the Communist bloc. The Communist nations, as George Kennan has pointed out, are, like the Western nations, currently caught up in a crisis of indecision about their relations with countries outside their own ideological bloc. The choices open to the satellite states are limited but by no means insignificant. They can adhere slavishly to Soviet preferences or they can strike out on their own, within limits, to enter into mutually advantageous relations with the West.

Whether they do so, and to what extent, is to some extent at least within the power of the West to determine. If we persist in the view that all Communist regimes are equally hostile and equally threatening to the West, and that we can have no policy toward the captive nations except the eventual overthrow of their Communist regimes, then the West may enforce upon the Communist bloc a degree of unity which the Soviet Union has shown itself to be quite incapable of imposing—just as Stalin in the early postwar years frightened the West into a degree of unity that it almost certainly could not have attained by its own unaided efforts. If, on the other hand, we are willing to reexamine the view that all Communist regimes are alike in the threat which they pose for the West—a view which had a certain validity in Stalin's time—then we may be able to exert an important influence on the course of events within a divided Communist world.

We are to a great extent the victims, and the Soviets the beneficiaries, of our own ideological convictions, and of the curious contradictions which they involve. We consider it a form of subversion of the free world, for example, when the Russians enter trade relations or conclude a consular convention or establish airline connections with a free country in Asia, Africa, or Latin America—and to a certain extent we are right. On the other hand, when it is proposed that we adopt the same strategy in reverse—by extending commercial credits to Poland or Yugoslavia, or by exchanging Ambassadors with a Hungarian regime which has changed considerably in character since the revolution of 1956—then the same patriots who are so alarmed by Soviet activities in the free world charge our policymakers with "giving aid and comfort to the enemy," and with innumerable other categories of idiocy and immorality.

It is time that we resolved this contradiction and separated myth from reality. The myth is that every Communist state is an unmitigated evil and a relentless enemy of the free world; the reality is that some Communist regimes pose a threat to the free world while others pose little or none, and that if we will recognize these distinctions, we ourselves will be able to influence events in the Communist bloc in a way favorable to the security of the free world.

> It could well be argued [writes George Kennan] . . . [t]hat if the major Western Powers had full freedom of movement in devising

> their own policies, it would be within their power to determine whether the Chinese view, or the Soviet view, or perhaps a view more liberal than either would ultimately prevail within the Communist camp. (George Kennan, "Polycentrism and Western Policy," *Foreign Affairs,* January 1964, page 178.)

There are numerous areas in which we can seek to reduce the tensions of the cold war and to bring a degree of normalcy into our relations with the Soviet Union and other Communist countries —once we have resolved that it is safe and wise to do so. We have already taken important steps in this direction: the Antarctic and Austrian treaties and the nuclear test ban treaty, the broadening of East-West cultural and educational relations, and the expansion of trade.

On the basis of recent experience and present economic needs, there seems little likelihood of a spectacular increase in trade between Communist and Western countries, even if existing restrictions were to be relaxed. Free world trade with Communist countries has been increasing at a steady but unspectacular rate, and it seems unlikely to be greatly accelerated because of the limited ability of the Communist countries to pay for increased imports. A modest increase in East-West trade may nonetheless serve as a modest instrument of East-West détente—provided that we are able to overcome the myth that trade with Communist countries is a compact with the Devil and to recognize that, on the contrary, trade can serve as an effective and honorable means of advancing both peace and human welfare.

Whether we are able to make these philosophic adjustments or not, we cannot escape the fact that our efforts to devise a common Western trade policy are a palpable failure and that our allies are going to trade with the Communist bloc whether we like it or not. The world's major exporting nations are slowly but steadily increasing their trade with the Communist bloc and the bloc countries are showing themselves to be reliable customers. Since 1958 Western Europe has been increasing its exports to the East at the rate of about 7 per cent a year, which is nearly the same rate at which its overall world sales have been increasing.

West Germany—one of our close friends—is by far the leading Western nation in trade with the Sino-Soviet bloc. West German exports to bloc countries in 1962 were valued at $749.9 million.

Britain was in second place—although not a close second—with exports to Communist countries amounting to $393 million in 1962. France followed with exports worth $313.4 million, and the figure for the United States—consisting largely of surplus food sales to Poland under Public Law 480—stood far below at $125.1 million.

Our allies have made it plain that they propose to expand this trade, in non-strategic goods, wherever possible. West Germany, in the last 16 months has exchanged or agreed to exchange trade missions with every country in Eastern Europe except Albania. Britain has indicated that she will soon extend long-term credits to Communist countries, breaching the 5-year limit which the Western allies have hitherto observed. In the light of these facts, it is difficult to see what effect the tight American trade restrictions have other than to deny the United States a substantial share of a profitable market.

The inability of the United States to prevent its partners from trading extensively with the Communist bloc is one good reason for relaxing our own restrictions, but there is a better reason; the potential value of trade—a moderate volume of trade in nonstrategic items—as an instrument for reducing world tensions and strengthening the foundations of peace. I do not think that trade or the nuclear test ban, or any other prospective East-West accommodation, will lead to a grand reconciliation that will end the cold war and usher in the brotherhood of man. At the most, the cumulative effect of all the agreements that are likely to be attainable in the foreseeable future will be the alleviation of the extreme tensions and animosities that threaten the world with nuclear devastation and the gradual conversion of the struggle between communism and the free world into a safer and more tolerable international rivalry, one which may be with us for years and decades to come but which need not be so terrifying and so costly as to distract the nations of the world from the creative pursuits of civilized societies.

There is little in history to justify the expectation that we can either win the cold war or end it immediately and completely. These are favored myths, respectively, of the American right and of the American left. They are, I believe equal in their unreality and in their disregard for the feasibilities of history. We must disabuse ourselves of them and come to terms, at last, with the realities of a world in which neither good nor evil is absolute and in which those who move events and make history are those who have understood not how much but how little it is within our power to change.

Mr. President, in an address on February 18 at Bad Godesburg, the U.S. Ambassador to Germany, Mr. George McGhee, spoke eloquently and wisely about the character and prospects of relations between the Communist and the free worlds. I ask unanimous consent that Ambassador McGhee's address, "East-West Relations Today," be inserted in the Record at the end of my remarks.

The Presiding Officer (*Mr. Kennedy in the chair*). Without objection, it is so ordered.

Mr. Fulbright. Latin America is one of the areas of the world in which American policy is weakened by a growing divergency between old myths and new realities.

The crisis over the Panama Canal has been unnecessarily protracted for reasons of domestic politics and national pride and sensitivity on both sides—for reasons, that is, of only marginal relevance to the merits of the dispute. I think the Panamanians have unquestionably been more emotional about the dispute than has the United States. I also think that there is less reason for emotionalism on the part of the United States than on the part of Panama. It is important for us to remember that the issue over the canal is only one of a great many in which the United States is involved, and by no means the most important. For Panama, on the other hand, a small nation with a weak economy and an unstable government, the canal is the preeminent factor in the nation's economy and in its foreign relations. Surely in a confrontation so unequal, it is not unreasonable to expect the United States to go a little farther than halfway in the search for a fair settlement.

We Americans would do well, for a start, to divest ourselves of the silly notion that the issue with Panama is a test of our courage and resolve. I believe that the Cuban missile crisis of 1962, involving a confrontation with nuclear weapons and intercontinental missiles, was indeed a test of our courage, and we acquitted ourselves extremely well in that instance. I am unable to understand how a controversy with a small and poor country with virtually no military capacity, can possibly be regarded as a test of our bravery and will to defend our interests. It takes stubbornness but not courage to reject the entreaties of the weak. The real test in Panama is not of our valor but of our wisdom and judgment and common sense.

We would also do well to disabuse ourselves of the myth that there is something morally sacred about the treaty of 1903. The fact of the matter is that the treaty was concluded under circumstances that reflect little credit on the United States. It was made possible by Panama's separation from Colombia, which probably could not have occurred at that time without the dispatch of U.S. warships to prevent the landing of Colombian troops on the isthmus to put down the Panamanian rebellion. The United States not only intervened in Colombia's internal affairs but did so in violation of a treaty concluded in 1846 under which the United States had guaranteed Colombian sovereignty over the isthmus. President Theodore Roosevelt, as he boasted, "took Panama," and proceeded to negotiate the canal treaty with a compliant Panamanian regime. Panamanians contend that they were "shot gunned" into the treaty of 1903 as the price of U.S. protection against a possible effort by Colombia to recover the isthmus. The contention is not without substance.

It is not my purpose here to relate the events of 60 years ago but only to suggest that there is little basis for a posture of injured innocence and self-righteousness by either side and that we would do much better to resolve the issue on the basis of present realities rather than old myths.

The central reality is that the treaty of 1903 is in certain respects obsolete. The treaty has been revised only twice, in 1936 when the annual rental was raised from $250,000 to $430,000 and other modifications were made, and in 1955 when further changes were made, including an increase in the annual rental to $1.9 million, where it now stands. The canal, of course, contributes far more to the Panamanian economy in the form of wages paid to Panamanian workers and purchases made in Panama. The fact remains, nonetheless, that the annual rental of $1.9 million is a modest sum and should probably be increased. There are other issues, relating to hiring policies for Panamanian workers in the zone, the flying of flags, and other symbols of national pride and sovereignty. The basic problem about the treaty, however, is the exercise of American control over a part of the territory of Panama in this age of intense nationalist and anticolonialist feeling. Justly or not, the Panamanians feel that they are being treated as a colony, or a quasi-colony, of the United States, and this feeling is accentuated by the contrast between the standard of living of the Panamanians, with a per capita income of about $429 a year, and that of the Americans living in the Canal Zone—immediately adjacent to Panama, of course, and within it—with a per capita income of $4,228 a year. This is approximately 10 times greater. It is the profound social and economic alienation between Panama and the Canal Zone, and its impact on the national feeling of the Panamanians, that underlies the current crisis.

Under these circumstances, it seems to me entirely proper and necessary for the United States to take the initiative in proposing new arrangements that would redress some of Panama's grievances against the treaty as it now stands. I see no reason—certainly no reason of "weakness" or "dishonor" why the United States cannot put an end to the semantic debate over whether treaty revisions are to be "negotiated" or "discussed" by stating positively and clearly that it is prepared to negotiate revisions in the canal treaty and to submit such changes as are made to the Senate for its advice and consent.

I think it is necessary for the United States to do this even though a commitment to revise the treaty may be widely criticized at home. It is the responsibility of the President and his advisers, in situations of this sort, to exercise their own best judgment as to where the national interest lies even though this may necessitate unpopular decisions.

An agreement to "negotiate" revisions is not an agreement to negotiate any particular revision. It would leave us completely free to determine what revisions, and how many revisions, we would be willing to accept. If there is any doubt about this, one can find ample reassurance in the proceedings at Geneva, where several years of "negotiations" for "general and complete disarmament" still leave us with the greatest arsenal of weapons in the history of the world.

The problem of Cuba is more difficult than that of Panama, and far more heavily burdened with the deadweight of old myths and prohibitions against "unthinkable thoughts." I think the time is overdue for a candid re-evaluation of our Cuban policy even though it may also lead to distasteful conclusions.

There are and have been three options open to the United States with respect to Cuba: First, the removal of the Castro regime by invading and occupying the island; second, an effort to weaken and ultimately bring down the regime by a policy of political and economic boycott; and finally, acceptance of the Communist regime as a disagreeable reality and annoyance, but one which is not likely to be removed in the near future because of the unavailability of acceptable means of removing it.

The first option, invasion, has been tried in a half-hearted way and found wanting. It is generally acknowledged that the invasion and occupation of Cuba, besides violating our obligations as a member of the United Nations and of the Organization of American States, would have explosive consequences in Latin America and elsewhere and might precipitate a global nuclear war. I know of no responsible statesman who advocates this approach. It has been rejected by our Government and by public opinion and I think that, barring some grave provocation, it can be ruled out as a feasible policy for the United States.

The approach which we have adopted has been the second of those mentioned, an effort to weaken and eventually bring down the Castro regime by a policy of political and economic boycott. This policy has taken the form of extensive restrictions against trade with Cuba by United States citizens, of the exclusion of Cuba from the inter-American system and efforts to secure Latin American support in isolating Cuba politically and economically, and of diplomatic efforts, backed by certain trade and aid sanctions, to persuade other free world countries to maintain economic boycotts against Cuba.

This policy, it now seems clear, has been a failure, and there is no reason to believe that it will succeed in the future. Our efforts to persuade our allies to terminate their trade with Cuba have been generally rebuffed. The prevailing attitude was perhaps best expressed by a British manufacturer who, in response to American criticisms of the sale of British buses to Cuba, said: "If America has a surplus of wheat, we have a surplus of buses."

In cutting off military assistance to Great Britain, France, and Yugoslavia under the provisions of section 620 of the Foreign Assistance Act of 1963, the United States has wielded a stuffed club. The amounts of aid involved are infinitesimal: the chances of gaining compliance with our boycott policy are nil; and the annoyance of the countries concerned may be considerable. What we terminated with respect to Britain and France, in fact, can hardly be called aid; it was more of a sales promotion program under which British and French military leaders were brought to the United States to see—and to buy—advanced American weapons. Terminating this program was in itself of little importance; Britain and France do not need our assistance. But terminating the program as a sanction against their trade with Cuba can have no real effect other than to create an illusory image of "toughness" for the benefit of our own people.

Free world exports to Cuba have, on the whole, been declining over recent years, but overall imports have been rising since 1961.

Mr. President, I ask unanimous consent that there be inserted in the Record at the conclusion of my remarks two tables provided by the Department of State showing the trade of selected free world countries with Cuba from 1958 to 1963.

The Presiding Officer. Without objection, it is so ordered.

Mr. Fulbright. Mr. President, the figures shown in these tables provide little basis for expecting the early termination of free world trade with Cuba. The export table shows U.S. exports to Cuba in both 1962 and 1963 exceeding those of any other free world country. These American exports consisted almost entirely of ransom payments for the Bay of Pigs prisoners and should not be confused with normal trade.

There is an interesting feature to this table, which may not be well known. It is that the exports from Cuba to various allies of ours, particularly Japan, the United Kingdom, Morocco, and others, have been going up, and have been very substantial. This reflects, I believe, the importation from Cuba of sugar to a great extent, and also accounts for the accumulation by Cuba of substantial foreign aid as a result of the dramatic increase in the price of sugar during the past couple of years.

The exports from the free world to Cuba have been going up in similar instances, in the case of Japan, but generally speaking they have not been increasing. Of course, since 1958, when we accounted for more than half of Cuba's exports, they have gone down rather dramatically. In any case, the tables will speak for themselves.

I should like to make it very clear that I am not arguing against the desirability of an economic boycott against the Castro regime but against its feasibility. The effort has been made and all the fulminations we can utter about sanctions and retaliation against free world countries that trade with Cuba cannot long conceal the fact that the boycott policy is a failure.

The boycott policy has not failed because of any "weakness" or "timidity" on the part of our Government. This charge, so frequently heard, is one of the most pernicious myths to have been inflicted on the American people. The boycott policy has failed because the United States is not omnipotent and cannot be. The basic reality to be faced is that it is simply not within our power to compel our allies to cut off their trade with Cuba, unless we are prepared to take drastic sanctions against them, such as closing our own markets to any foreign company that does business in Cuba, as proposed by Mr. Nixon. We can do this, of course, but if we do, we ought first to be very sure, as apparently Mr. Nixon is, that the Cuban boycott is more important than good relations with our closest allies. In fact, even the most drastic sanctions are as likely to be rewarded with defiance as with compliance. For practical purposes, all we can do is to ask other countries to take the measures with respect to Cuba which we recommend. We have done so and in some areas, have been successful. In other areas, notably that of the economic boycott, we have asked for the full cooperation of other free world countries and it has been largely denied. It remains for us to decide whether we will respond with a sustained outburst of hollow and ill-tempered threats, all the while comforting ourselves with the myth that we can get anything we want if we only try hard enough—or, in this case, shout loud enough—or we can acknowledge the failure of our efforts and proceed, cooly and rationally, to re-examine the policies which we now pursue in relation to the interests they are intended to serve.

The prospects of bringing down the Castro regime by political and economic boycott have never been very good. Even if a general free world boycott were successfully applied against Cuba, it is unlikely that the Russians would refuse to carry the extra financial burden and thereby permit the only Communist regime in the Western Hemisphere to collapse. We are thus compelled to recognize that there is probably no way of bringing down the Castro regime by means of economic pressures unless we are prepared to impose a blockade against nonmilitary shipments from the Soviet Union. Exactly such a policy has been recommended by some of our more reckless politicians, but the preponderance of informed opinion is that a blockade against Soviet shipments of nonmilitary supplies to Cuba would be extravagantly dangerous, carrying the strong possibility of a confrontation that could explode into nuclear war.

Having ruled out military invasion and blockade, and recognizing the failure of the boycott policy, we are compelled to consider the third of the three options open to us with respect to Cuba: the acceptance of the continued existence of the Castro regime as a distasteful nuisance but not an intolerable danger so long as the nations of the hemisphere are prepared to meet their obligations of collective defense under the Rio Treaty.

In recent years we have become transfixed with Cuba, making it far more important in both our foreign relations and in our domestic life than its size and influence warrant. We have flattered a noisy but minor demagog by treating him as if he were a Napoleonic menace. Communist Cuba has been a disruptive and subversive influence in Venezuela and other countries of the hemisphere, and there is no doubt that both we and our Latin American partners would be better off if the Castro regime did not exist. But it is important to bear in mind that, despite their best efforts, the Cuban Communists have not succeeded in subverting the hemisphere and that in Venezuela, for example, where communism has made a major effort to gain power through terrorism, it has been repudiated by a people who in a free election have committed themselves to the course of liberal democracy. It is necessary to weigh the desirability of an objective against the feasibility of its attainment, and when we do this with respect to Cuba, I think we are bound to conclude that Castro is a nuisance but not a grave threat to the United States and that he cannot be gotten rid of except by means that are wholly disproportionate to the objective. Cuban communism does pose a grave threat to other Latin American countries, but this threat can be dealt with by prompt and vigorous use of the established procedures of the inter-American system against any act of aggression.

I think that we must abandon the myth that Cuban communism is a transitory menace that is going to collapse or disappear in the immediate future and face up to two basic realities about Cuba: first, that the Castro regime is not on the verge of collapse and is not likely to be overthrown by any policies which we are now pursuing or can reasonably undertake; and second, that the continued existence of the Castro regime, though inimical to our interests and policies, is not an insuperable obstacle to the attainment of our objectives, unless we make it so by permitting it to poison our politics at home and to divert us from more important tasks in the hemisphere.

The policy of the United States with respect to Latin America as a whole is predicated on the assumption that social revolution can be accomplished without violent upheaval. This is the guiding principle of the Alliance for Progress, and it may in time be vindicated. We are entitled to hope so, and it is wise and necessary for us to do all that we can to advance the prospects of peaceful and orderly reform.

At the same time, we must be under no illusions as to the extreme difficulty of uprooting long-established ruling oligarchies without disruptions involving lesser or greater degrees of violence. The historical odds are probably against the prospects of peaceful social revolution. There are places, of course, where it has occurred and others where it seems likely to occur. In Latin America, the chances for such basic change by peaceful means seem bright in Colombia, and Venezuela and certain other countries; in Mexico, many basic changes have been made by peaceful means, but these came in the wake of a violent revolution. In other Latin American countries, the power of ruling oligarchies is so solidly established and their ignorance so great that there seems little prospect of accomplishing economic growth or social reform by means short of the forcibly overthrow of established authorities.

I am not predicting violent revolutions in Latin America or elsewhere. Still less am I advocating them. I wish only to suggest that violent social revolutions are a possibility in countries where feudal oligarchies resist all meaningful change by peaceful means. We must not, in our preference for the democratic procedures envisioned by the Charter of Punta del Este, close our minds to the possibility that democratic procedures may fail in certain countries and that where democracy does fail violent social convulsions may occur.

We would do well, while continuing our efforts to promote peaceful change through the Alliance for Progress, to consider what our reactions might be in the event of the outbreak of genuine social revolution in one or more Latin American countries. Such a revolution did occur in Bolivia, and we accepted it calmly and sensibly. But what if a violent social revolution were to break out in one of the larger Latin American countries? Would we feel certain that it was Cuban or Soviet inspired? Would we wish to intervene on the side of established authority? Or would we be willing to tolerate or even support a revolution if it was seen to be not Communist but similar in nature to the Mexican revolution or the Nasser revolution in Egypt?

These are hypothetical questions and there is no readily available set of answers to them. But they are questions which we should be thinking about because they have to do with problems that could become real and urgent with great suddenness. We should be considering, for example, what groups in particular countries might conceivably lead revolutionary movements, and if we can identify them, we should be considering how we might communicate with them and influence them in such a way that their movements, if successful, will not pursue courses detrimental to our security and our interests.

The Far East is another area of the world in which American policy is handicapped by the divergence of old myths and new realities. Particularly with respect to China, an elaborate vocabulary of make-believe has become compulsory in both official and public discussion. We are committed, with respect to China and other areas in Asia, to inflexible policies of long standing from which we hesitate to depart because of the attribution to these policies of an aura of mystical sanctity. It may be that a thorough reevaluation of our Far Eastern policies would lead us to the conclusion that they are sound and wise, or at least that they represent the best available options. It may be, on the other hand, that reevaluation would point up the need for greater or lesser changes in our policies. The point is that, whatever the outcome of a rethinking of policy might be, we have been unwilling to undertake it because of the fear of many Government officials, undoubtedly well founded, that even the suggestion of new policies toward China or Vietnam would provoke a vehement public outcry.

I do not think the United States can or should, recognize Communist China, or acquiesce in its admission to the United Nations under present circumstances. It would be unwise to do so, because there is nothing to be gained by it so long as the Peiping regime maintains its attitude of implacable hostility toward the United States. I do not believe, however, that this state of affairs is necessarily permanent. As we have seen in our relations with Germany and Japan, hostility can give way in an astonishingly short time to close friendship, and, as we have seen in our relations with China, the reverse can occur with equal speed. It is not impossible that in time our relations with China will change again—if not to friendship, then perhaps to "competitive coexistence." It would therefore be extremely useful if we could introduce an element of flexibility, or, more precisely, of the capacity to be flexible, into our relations with Communist China.

We would do well, as former Assistant Secretary Hilsman has recommended, to maintain an "open door" to the possibility of improved relations with Communist China in the future. For a start, we must jar open our minds to certain realities about China, of which the foremost is that there really are not "two Chinas," but only one—mainland China: and that it is ruled by Communists, and is likely to remain so for the indefinite future. Once we accept this fact, it becomes possible to reflect on the conditions under which it might be possible for us to enter into relatively normal relations with mainland China. One condition, of course, must be the abandonment by the Chinese Communists, tacitly, if not explicitly, of their intention to conquer and incorporate Taiwan. This seems unlikely now; but far more surprising changes have occurred in politics and it is quite possible that a new generation of leaders in Peiping and Taipei may put a quiet end to the Chinese civil war, thus opening the possibility of entirely new patterns of international relations in the Far East.

Should such changes occur, they will open important opportunities for American policy; and it is to be hoped that we shall be able and willing to take advantage of them. It seems possible, for instance, that an atmosphere of reduced tensions in the Far East might make it possible to strengthen world peace by drawing mainland China into existing East-West agreements in such fields as disarmament, trade, and educational exchange.

These are long-range prospects, which may or may not materialize. In the immediate future, we are confronted with possible changes in the Far East resulting from recent French diplomacy.

French recognition of Communist China, although untimely and carried out in a way that can hardly be considered friendly to the United States, may nonetheless serve a constructive long-term purpose, by unfreezing a situation in which many countries, none more than the United States, are committed to inflexible policies by long-established commitments and the pressures of domestic public opinion. One way or another, the French initiative may help generate a new situation in which the United States, as well as other countries will find it possible to reevaluate its basic policies in the Far East.

The situation in Vietnam poses a far more pressing need for a reevaluation of American policy. Other than withdrawal, which I do not think can be realistically considered under present circumstances, three options are open to us in Vietnam: First, continuation of the antiguerrilla war within South Vietnam, along with renewed American efforts to increase the military effectiveness of the South Vietnamese Army and the political effectiveness of the South Vietnamese Government; second, an attempt to end the war, through negotiations for the neutralization of South Vietnam, or of both North and South Vietnam; and, finally, the expansion of the scale of the war, either by the direct commitment of large numbers of American troops or by equipping the South Vietnamese Army to attack North Vietnamese territory, possibly by means of commando-type operations from the sea or the air.

It is difficult to see how a negotiation, under present military circumstances, could lead to termination of the war under conditions that would preserve the freedom of South Vietnam. It is extremely difficult for a party to a negotiation to achieve by diplomacy objectives which it has conspicuously failed to win by warfare. The hard fact of the matter is that our bargaining position is at present a weak one; and until the equation of advantages between the two sides has been substantially altered in our favor, there can be little prospect of a negotiated settlement which would secure the independence of a non-Communist South Vietnam.

Recent initiatives by France, calling for the neutralization of Vietnam, have tended to confuse the situation, without altering it in any fundamental way. France could, perhaps, play a constructive mediating role if she were willing to consult and cooperate with the United States. For somewhat obscure reasons, however, France has chosen to take an independent initiative. This is puzzling to Americans, who recall that the United States contributed $11.2 billion to France's war in Indochina of a decade ago—which was 70 percent of the total cost of the conflict. Whatever its motivation, the problem posed by French intervention in southeast Asia is that while France may set off an unforseeable chain of events, she is neither a major military force nor a major economic force in the Far East, and is therefore unlikely to be able to control or greatly influence the events which her initiative may precipitate.

It seems clear that only two realistic options are open to us in Vietnam in the immediate future: the expansion of the conflict in one way or another, or a renewed effort to bolster the capacity of the South Vietnamese to prosecute the war successfully on its present scale. The matter calls for thorough examination by responsible officials in the executive branch; and until they have had an opportunity to evaluate the contingencies and feasibilities of the options open to us, it seems to me that we have no choice but to support the South Vietnamese Government and Army by the most effective means available. Whatever specific policy decisions are made, it should be clear to all concerned that the United States will continue to meet its obligations and fulfill its commitments with respect to Vietnam.

These, I believe, are some, although by no means all, of the issues of foreign policy in which it is essential to reevaluate long-standing ideas and commitments in the light of new and changing realities. In all the issues which I have discussed, American policy has to one degree or another been less effective than it might have been because of our national tendency to equate means with ends and therefore to attach a mythological sanctity to policies and practices which in themselves have no moral content or value except insofar as they contribute to the achievement of some valid national objective. I believe that we must try to overcome this excessive moralism, which binds us to old myths and blinds us to new realities and, worse still, leads us to regard new and unfamiliar ideas with fear and mistrust.

We must dare to think about "unthinkable" things. We must learn to explore all of the options and possibilities that confront us in a complex and rapidly changing world. We must learn to welcome rather than fear the voices of dissent and not to recoil in horror whenever some heretic suggests that Castro may survive or that Khrushchev is not as bad a fellow as Stalin was. We must overcome our susceptibility to "shock"—a word which I wish could be banned from our newspapers and magazines and especially from the Congressional Record.

If Congress and public opinion are unduly susceptible to "shock," the executive branch, and particularly the Department of State, is subject to the malady of chronic and excessive caution. An effective foreign policy is one which concerns itself more with innovation abroad than with conciliations at home. A creative foreign policy—as President Truman, for one, knew—is not necessarily one which wins immediate general approval. It is sometimes necessary for leaders to do unpleasant and unpopular things because, as Burke pointed out, the duty of the democratic politician to his constituents is not to comply with their every wish and preference but to give them the benefit of, and to be held responsible for, the exercise of his own best judgment.

We must dare to think about "unthinkable" things, because

when things become "unthinkable," thinking stops and action becomes mindless. If we are to act wisely and creatively upon the new realities of our time, we must think and talk about our problems with perfect freedom, remembering, as Woodrow Wilson said, that "The greatest freedom of speech is the greatest safety because, if a man is a fool, the best thing to do is to encourage him to advertise the fact by speaking."

11. Some Fundamentals of American Policy*

by Dean Rusk

I'M DELIGHTED TO HAVE THIS CHANCE TO PAY MY RESPECTS TO THE U.S. Council of the International Chamber of Commerce. You can be sure that we follow with the closest attention the attitudes of the International Chamber on our country's relations with the rest of the world. And we very deeply appreciate the stimulating and the constructive attention that you give to the complex problems of a somewhat turbulent scene.

I particularly would like to express my appreciation for the fact that you have given strong support to the International Cooperation Year. The headlines are not always encouraging in that respect. But it is tremendously important that, despite those headlines, as many of us as possible put our shoulders to the principal business of a peaceful world.

Some of you at this meeting have just returned from the International Chamber's 20th Congress in New Delhi. One of the unanimous conclusions in that Congress was that between government and private enterprise there should be confidence and readiness to cooperate with mutual recognition of each other's specific role and responsibility. This expresses very well, it seems to me, the attitude of the Johnson administration toward the relationship between the government and business. And it also describes, I think, the relationship between you and the Department of State—certainly the relationship which my colleagues and I hope to achieve.

* U.S., *Department of State Bulletin,* Volume LII, No. 1343, March 22, 1965, pp. 398-403. Address made before the U.S. Council of the International Chamber of Commerce at New York, N.Y., on Mar. 4 (press release 36, as-delivered text).

I have tried during these last 4 years to remind my colleagues all over the world that when Benjamin Franklin went abroad as the first distinguished diplomat of our colonial experience, working for our independence, while he was trying to obtain some arms and loans and other modern kinds of assistance, he was also given the most specific and direct instructions to promote the trade of the United States; and that it is the ambassador's job, and the job of everyone with him, to accept the notion that the expansion of American trading interests is a central function of diplomacy. And I have been encouraged to feel that, both on the business side and on the diplomatic side, we've been making some steady headway.

Tonight I shall speak briefly. I lived in New York long enough to know about commuter trains! But I shall also try to speak very simply.

OUR BASIC GOALS

In moments of crisis it is well for us to recall our deepest roots, our most elementary national interests, our most solemn duties, our loftiest aspirations. In the rush of daily events and the clamor of crises it is all too easy to lose sight of our central goal and the means by which we work our way toward it. The goals and our policies grow out of our interests as a nation and our basic commitment to the people—commitment to freedom and human dignity. The basic policies through which we work our way toward our goals have been developed during these postwar years under the leadership of four Presidents and with the active cooperation of the other leaders of both major parties. They have been, and they are, national policies.

I think you might be interested in knowing that in these past 4 years I have now had the privilege of sitting in on more than 200 executive sessions of committees of Congress. On no single occasion have the differences in those executive sessions turned on partisan lines. There have been differences, because many of these problems are extremely complex and many of the proposed answers are knife-edged, on-balance judgments, some of which reach beyond the competence of the mind of man. Of course there are differences. But not once have I seen those differences in a closed committee room fall on partisan lines, because those men, as all who have served this country in this postwar period in public office, have entered fully into the agony of the job in front of us and have tried to commit themselves to the service of the Nation as a whole.

But now that I have mentioned the word "goals," let me say that I suspect that some of you have already relaxed rather politely, in the thought: "Here we go again up into the clouds." You could not be more wrong. It may not be possible, of course, to use generalized ideas or propositions to cover our relations with 120 governments and authorities, with different interests and purposes, generating policies of their own, in a world scene so filled with contradictions. But the general ideas which are central to our policy have very concrete meaning. And I hope very much that all of you in this room can help us bring these general expressions of policy down to the grassroots, to the people that you deal with on a day-by-day basis.

For example, when we speak of "peace" and "a decent world order," we're talking about what happens to every home and every community across the Nation. When we talk about "the survival of the human race," we know that this means you, and your family, and your neighbor, and the rest like you in other countries. When a President of the United States finds himself facing some of the most exacting decisions in the history of man, he has sometimes been called a lonely man. Yes indeed he is, because he carries the final responsibility. But every President I have known in this postwar period also feels that he has 180 or 190 million Americans in that room with him who understand that we're not talking about general theories—we're talking about people and what happens to the people of the United States, right across the land.

THE RULE OF LAW

When we talk about "the rule of law," we are talking about the difference between rational behavior and the regime of the jungle. We know that law enlarges the area of freedom by making it possible to predict with greater confidence the behavior of others. We can be steadily encouraged by the growth of what we call "the common law of mankind"—not as a disembodied idea but as a summary of the arrangements by which we facilitate the most practical daily transactions in trade and transportation, in travel and the flow of news, in the elementary defenses against epidemic disease, in arrangements for the safety of life at sea and in the air, and in the widest range of intimate concerns of yours, which are supported by the more than 4,000 international agreements to which the United States is a party.

The rule of law is today of benefit to you in a hundred different ways, as you make your way around the world. The simple idea that agreements are to be kept is the special cement which holds us together, both in our domestic arrangements and in our international affairs, and one of the oldest notions of international law, it is a crucial necessity for the world of tomorrow. Should the central notion collapse, it would be more than a moral setback, important as that would be; the very structure of life would begin to collapse, and it would be difficult to find an answer to the question: "Where do we go from here?"

That is why it is no small matter for any nation to tear its agreements to shreds and give vent to the irritations and resentments of the day by retaliating through the destruction of agreements to which it is pledged.

So, too, with what the United Nations Charter calls "the suppression of acts of aggression or other breaches of the peace." Theory? In his final report as Chief of Staff of the Army in 1945, General George Marshall pointed out that the technique of war had put the United States "into the front line of world conflict," and that our homes and factories could not escape destructive bombardment in a third world war. General Marshall drew the inescapable conclusion when he said: "We are now concerned with the peace of the entire world." Most of us in this room are part of that generation which went to school and grew up in the period between the two wars, when the United States was not taking an active part in organizing the peace and at the same time was neglecting its defenses as a warning to those who might commit aggression.

But today we are committed, because we now can no longer draw the lessons from a great war and start again as we did in 1945 after so much cost, so much bloodshed. We shall not have that chance after World War III. We must draw those lessons before it begins and apply them before the war occurs, for, should it occur, there won't be much left for the mind of man to work upon for the reconstruction of civilization.

Surely we ought to know that today we can be secure only to the extent that the community of nations is secure—on land, at sea, in the air, and in the adjoining areas of space. And so our decision must be to do what we can to build the kind of world projected in the United Nations Charter, particularly in the preamble and articles 1 and 2—read it when you go home—a world of independent, national states, each with its own institutions, cooperating with other nations to further their mutual welfare, a peaceful world, a world increasingly responsive to the rule of law, a world in which all human beings enjoy their natural rights, regardless of nationality or creed or color, and a world in which all can share in the abundance which modern science and technology make possible.

If that goal is ever to be attained—and it is the most urgent, harshest necessity of our short-term existence—and, indeed, if freedom is to survive on this small planet, the first essential is to insure that there is an end to aggression—if possible, by preventing it, if not, by defeating it. And that, in essence, is the first purpose of the United Nations and must be one of the first purposes of the United States.

THE ISSUES IN SOUTHEAST ASIA

A clear understanding that it is imperative that aggression not be allowed to succeed produced the Truman Doctrine, a declaration of a general policy of assisting other free people who are defending themselves against external aggressions or threats. It produced our aid to Greece and Turkey and to Western Europe. It produced the Berlin airlift. It produced the North Atlantic Treaty and the other great defensive alliances of the free world. It produced the historic decision to repel the aggression against the Republic of Korea and the defensive military establishments of the free world. And it produced the decision to assist the peoples of Southeast Asia to preserve their independence.

Outright, large-scale, deliberate, massive aggressions carry with them suicidal risks to the aggressors. So the Communists in Southeast Asia have fallen back on aggression by the infiltration of arms and trained men across national frontiers. A clear and unequivocal recognition by the rest of the world that this is a form of aggression is long overdue. It is not a problem which will just go away, much as we should like to see it go away. It is not a problem in which others have no stake, for the very existence of more than a hundred small nations is engaged in the issues that exist at the present time in Southeast Asia.

And so I should like to talk to you very simply tonight about some of the central facts and policies about the situation in Southeast Asia. If it is repetitious in part, forgive me. Memories are short, and the simple things have to be said more than once.

South Viet-Nam is being subjected to an aggression from the North, an aggression which is organized and directed and supplied with key personnel and equipment by Hanoi. The hard core of the Viet Cong were trained in the North and have been reinforced by North Vietnamese from the North Vietnamese army. Anybody who any longer may be in doubt about it should take the time to get acquainted with the simple facts set forth in the white paper issued just last Sunday [February 27].[1]

From 1955 to 1959 South Viet-Nam made remarkable economic and social progress. That in itself may have encouraged Hanoi, with the backing of Peiping, to launch its increased guerrilla aggression in late 1959 and early 1960.

The Viet Cong rule and recruit largely by terror in the areas to which they have access. There is no indication that they have any major popular following. And so we believe that the pacification of South Viet-Nam would be relatively simple for the South Vietnamese themselves if the intervention from the North were brought to an end.

In Laos, also, North Viet-Nam has engaged in persistent aggression. And these acts have violated not only international law but pledges made by Hanoi and Peiping, among others, in 1954 and 1962.

Now we ourselves seek no bases or special position or rights in Southeast Asia. Our forces are there to help independent peoples resist aggressions. Our troops would come home tomorrow if the aggressors would go north—go back home, and stay at home.

The defeat of these aggressions is not only essential if Laos and South Viet-Nam are to remain independent; it is important to the security of Southeast Asia as a whole. You will recall that Thailand has already been proclaimed as the next target by Peiping. This is not something up in the clouds called the domino theory. You don't need that. Listen to the proclamation of militant, world revolution by Peiping, proclaimed with a harshness which has caused deep division within the Communist world itself, quite apart from the issues posed for the free world.

THE U.S. STAKE IN VIET-NAM

So what is our stake? What is our commitment in that situation? Can those of us in this room forget the lesson that we had in this issue of war and peace when it was only 10 years from the seizure of Manchuria to Pearl Harbor; about 2 years from the seizure of Czechoslovakia to the outbreak of World War II in Western Europe? Don't you remember the hopes expressed in those days: that perhaps the aggressor will be satisfied by this next bite, and perhaps he will be quiet? Remember that? You remember that we thought that we could put our Military Establishment on short rations and somehow we needn't concern ourselves with peace in the rest of the world. But we found that ambition and appetite fed upon success and the next bite generated the appetite for the following bite. And we learned that, by postponing the issue, we made the result more terrible, the holocaust more dreadful. We cannot forget that experience.

We have a course of aggression proclaimed in Peiping, very clear for all to see, and proclaimed with a militancy which says that their type of revolution must be supported by force and that much of the world is ripe for that kind of revolution. We have very specific commitments—the Manila Pact, ratified by the Senate by a vote of 82 to 1, a pact to which South Viet-Nam is a protocol state. We have the decision of President Eisenhower in 1954 to extend aid to South Viet-Nam, to assist it to recover from debilitating war and to maintain its security and its economic viability.[2] He said,

> The purpose of this offer is to assist the Government of Viet-Nam in developing and maintaining a strong, viable state, capable of resisting attempted subversion or aggression through miltary means.

The joint resolution of the Congress last August,[3] passed by a combined vote of 502 to 2, approved and supported "the determination of the President, as Commander in Chief, to take all necessary measures to repel any armed attack against the forces of the United States and to prevent further aggression." And it declared that "The United States regards as vital to its national interest and to world peace the maintenance of international peace and security in southeast Asia."

And some of you recall the very short statement by the President on the occasion of his signing that joint resolution:[4]

> To any armed attack upon our forces, we shall reply.
>
> To any in Southeast Asia who ask our help in defending their freedom, we shall give it.
>
> In that region there is nothing we covet, nothing we seek—no territory, no military position, no political ambition. Our one desire—our one determination—is that the people of Southeast Asia be left in peace to work out their own destinies in their own way.

We have tried to say over and over again that the key to peace in Southeast Asia is the readiness of all those in that area to live at peace and to leave their neighbors alone. I have not found that formulation mysterious, because I am quite sure that Hanoi knows exactly what it means.

Since the Geneva conference on Laos in 1962, the United States has been in active and continuous consultation with other governments about the danger created by aggression in Southeast Asia. It has been discussed in the United Nations, in the SEATO and NATO Councils, and on innumerable occasions directly with other governments through diplomatic channels. We have had direct discussions with almost every signatory of the agreements of 1954 and 1962. And at the moment, quoting from my press conference of last week,[5] because I want to emphasize one or two points here,

> What is still missing is any indication that Hanoi is prepared to stop doing what it is doing and what it knows it is doing against its neighbors. The absence of this crucial element affects the current discussion of "negotiation." Political channels have been and are open, and a considerable number of governments are actively interested in keeping them open to explore the possibilities of a peaceful solution. But a negotiation aimed at the acceptance

or the confirmation of aggression is not possible. And a negotiation which simply ends in bitterness and hostility merely adds to the danger.

Almost every successful negotiation in the postwar period has been preceded by some private contacts or indication that a negotiation might prove worthwhile. The missing piece is the lack of an indication that Hanoi is prepared to stop doing what it is doing, and what it knows that it is doing, to its neighbors. But the central object of American policy and action is peace in Southeast Asia and the safety of the independent states in that region. Many of the peoples in that area have been subjected to 25 years of turmoil and violence, and they are entitled to peace. As we ourselves indicated last week,[6] we'd much prefer to use our resources "as a part of an international effort to assist the economic and social development of the peoples of that area than to have them diverted into the harsh necessities of resisting aggression."

RESPONSIBILITY OF U.S. AS A GREAT POWER

May I comment very briefly on a few of the other problems in general—because there are difficulties in other parts of the world which are not just problems of confrontation between communism and the free world. There are a good many local disputes, difficulties, which cause all of us concern, perhaps a dozen or more of them at any one time boiling or simmering somewhere. They arise from disagreements over boundaries, or from racial or religious or tribal or national frictions, from the mischiefmaking of smalltime imperalists, and from dictators who turn to adventure abroad to cover up their failures at home. Some of these disputes had their origin even before our Republic was born. Others are relatively new. And many have grown out of the explosion of new states since the Second World War.

Most of these disputes are, therefore, what we would call "other people's business." That is, we usually don't have a part in their origin, or perhaps even a direct national interest in the details of the terms on which they are to be settled. But we can't turn our backs on them because so many of them come to the United Nations, where we have to take a position and give our help. Beyond that, we have a serious national interest in their settlement by peaceful means, for many of them drain away energies and resources that should be devoted to economic and social development. We have a practical interest in the most effective use of our economic aid, and we have a still broader interest in the orderly progress and political stability of the developing areas.

Moreover, disputes within the free world often afford the Communists opportunities in which they can cause more difficulties. And when a dispute erupts into a local war, there's always the possibility that the war will become a larger one—and, in the end, a confrontation between one or the other of the major Communist camps and the United States. And so we just can't ignore these local disputes without shirking our responsibilities as a great power and without increasing the danger to general peace and to our own national security.

We tend to get drawn in by pleas for support from the contesting parties. As a rule, each one wants us on its side, and on occasion both ask for us to help in finding some common ground.

All this doesn't mean that the United States goes around soliciting business as a peacemaker and policeman. Quite obviously we would prefer to have these matters solved somehow else, particularly when we value the lasting friendship of all the disputing parties. And so we are deeply gratified when local disputes can be handled peaceably through other channels: by direct negotiation, by assistance from the United Nations, through regional organizations, or through the mediation of some other nation.

But when all other efforts fail, we cannot safely stand aside and shrug, especially from those disputes which may erupt into war. We know that in many cases our immediate reward is likely to be disappointment and even resentment on the part of both or all of the parties in the dispute. But that is part of the burden of being a great power, committed to building a stable peace and a decent world order.

NOTES

1. For text, see "Aggression from the North: The Record of North Viet-Nam's Campaign to Conquer South Viet-Nam," BULLETIN of March 22, 1965, pp. 404-427.

2. For text of President Eisenhower's letter of Oct. 1, 1954, to President Ngo Dinh Diem, see BULLETIN of Nov. 15, 1954, p. 735.

3. For text, see *ibid.,* Aug. 24, 1964, p. 268.

4. For text, see *ibid.,* Aug. 31, 1964, p. 302.

5. *Ibid.,* Mar. 15, 1965, p. 362.

6. *Ibid.,* Mar. 15, 1965, p. 364.

PART IV

The Practice

12. A League for Peace*

by Woodrow Wilson

ON THE EIGHTEENTH OF DECEMBER LAST I ADDRESSED AN IDENTIC note to the governments of the nations now at war requesting them to state, more definitely than they had yet been stated by either group of belligerents, the terms upon which they would deem it possible to make peace. I spoke on behalf of humanity and of the rights of all neutral nations like our own, many of whose most vital interests the war puts in constant jeopardy. The Central Powers united in a reply which stated merely that they were ready to meet their antagonists in conference to discuss terms of peace. The Entente Powers have replied much more definitely and have stated, in general terms, indeed, but with sufficient definiteness to imply details, the arrangements, guarantees, and acts of reparation which they deem to be the indispensable conditions of a satisfactory settlement. We are that much nearer a definite discussion of the peace which shall end the present war. We are that much nearer the discussion of the international concert which must thereafter hold the world at peace.

In every discussion of the peace that must end this war it is taken for granted that that peace must be followed by some definite concert of power which will make it virtually impossible that any such catastrophe should ever overwhelm us again. Every lover of mankind, every sane and thoughtful man must take that for granted.

I have sought this opportunity to address you because I thought that I owed it to you, as the council associated with me in the final determination of our international obligations, to disclose to you without reserve the thought and purpose that have been taking form

* U.S., Congress, *Congressional Record,* 65th Congress, Second Session, Volume LIV, Part 2 (Washington: Government Printing Office, 1917), pp. 1741-1743. (Delivered before the United States Senate on January 22, 1917.)

in my mind in regard to the duty of our Government in the days to come when it will be necessary to lay afresh and upon a new plan the foundations of peace among the nations.

It is inconceivable that the people of the United States should play no part in that great enterprise. To take part in such a service will be the opportunity for which they have sought to prepare themselves by the very principles and purposes of their polity and the approved practices of their Government ever since the days when they set up a new nation in the high and honourable hope that it might in all that it was and did show mankind the way to liberty. They cannot in honour withhold the service to which they are now about to be challenged. They do not wish to withhold it. But they owe it to themselves and to the other nations of the world to state the conditions under which they will feel free to render it.

That service is nothing less than this, to add their authority and their power to the authority and force of other nations to guarantee peace and justice throughout the world. Such a settlement cannot now be long postponed. It is right that before it comes this Government should frankly formulate the conditions upon which it would feel justified in asking our people to approve its formal and solemn adherence to a League for Peace. I am here to attempt to state those conditions.

The present war must first be ended; but we owe it to candour and to a just regard for the opinion of mankind to say that, so far as our participation in guarantees of future peace is concerned, it makes a great deal of difference in what way and upon what terms it is ended. The treaties and agreements which bring it to an end must embody terms which will create a peace that is worth guaranteeing and preserving, a peace that will win the approval of mankind, not merely a peace that will serve the several interests and immediate aims of the nations engaged. We shall have no voice in determining what those terms shall be, but we shall, I feel sure, have a voice in determining whether they shall be made lasting or not by the guarantees of a universal covenant; and our judgment upon what is fundamental and essential as a condition precedent to permanency should be spoken now, not afterwards when it may be too late.

No covenant of cooperative peace that does not include the peoples of the New World can suffice to keep the future safe against war; and yet there is only one sort of peace that the peoples of America could join in guaranteeing. The elements of that peace must be elements that engage the confidence and satisfy the principles of the American governments, elements consistent with their political faith and the practical convictions which the peoples of America have once for all embraced and undertaken to defend.

I do not mean to say that any American government would throw any obstacle in the way of any terms of peace the governments now at war might agree upon, or seek to upset them when made, whatever they might be. I only take it for granted that mere terms of peace between the belligerents will not satisfy even the belligerents themselves. Mere agreements may not make peace secure. It will be absolutely necessary that force be created as a guarantor of the permanency of the settlement so much greater than the force of any nation now engaged or any alliance hitherto formed or projected that no nation, no probable combination of nations could face or withstand it. If the peace presently to be made is to endure, it must be a peace made secure by the organized major force of mankind.

The terms of the immediate peace agreed upon will determine whether it is a peace for which such a guarantee can be secured. The question upon which the whole future peace and policy of the world depends is this: Is the present war a struggle for a just and secure peace, or only for a new balance of power? If it be only a struggle for a new balance of power, who will guarantee, who can guarantee, the stable equilibrium of the new arrangement? Only a tranquil Europe can be a stable Europe. There must be, not a balance of power, but a community of power; not organized rivalries, but an organized common peace.

Fortunately we have received very explicit assurances on this point. The statesmen of both of the groups of nations now arrayed against one another have said, in terms that could not be misinterpreted, that it was no part of the purpose they had in mind to crush their antagonists. But the implications of these assurances may not be equally clear to all,—may not be the same on both sides of the water. I think it will be serviceable if I attempt to set forth what we understand them to be.

They imply, first of all, that it must be a peace without victory. It is not pleasant to say this. I beg that I may be permitted to put my own interpretation upon it and that it may be understood that no other interpretation was in my thought. I am seeking only to face realities and to face them without soft concealments. Victory would mean peace forced upon the loser, a victor's terms imposed upon the vanquished. It would be accepted in humiliation, under duress, at an intolerable sacrifice, and would leave a sting, a resentment, a bitter memory upon which terms of peace would rest, not permanently, but only as upon quicksand. Only a peace between equals can last. Only a peace the very principle of which is equality and a common participation in a common benefit. The right state of mind, the right feeling between nations, is as necessary for a lasting peace as is the just settlement of vexed questions of territory or of racial and national allegiance.

The equality of nations upon which peace must be founded if it is to last must be an equality of rights; the guarantees exchanged must neither recognize nor imply a difference between big nations and small, between those that are powerful and those that are weak. Right must be based upon the common strength, not upon the individual strength, of the nations upon whose concert peace will depend. Equality of territory or of resources there of course cannot be; nor any other sort of equality not gained in the ordinary peaceful and legitimate development of the peoples themselves. But no one asks or expects anything more than an equality of rights. Mankind is looking now for freedom of life, not for equiposes of power.

And there is a deeper thing involved than even equality of right among organized nations. No peace can last, or ought to last, which does not recognize and accept the principle that governments derive all their just powers from the consent of the governed, and that no right anywhere exists to hand peoples about from sovereignty to sovereignty as if they were property. I take it for granted, for instance, if I may venture upon a single example, that statesmen everywhere are agreed that there should be a united, independent, and autonomous Poland, and that henceforth inviolable security of life, of worship, and of industrial and social development should be guaranteed to all peoples who have lived hitherto, under the power of governments devoted to a faith and purpose hostile to their own.

I speak of this, not because of any desire to exalt an abstract political principle which has always been held very dear, by those who have sought to build up liberty in America, but for the same reason

I have spoken of other conditions of peace which seem to me clearly indispensable,—because I wish frankly to uncover realities. Any peace which does not recognize and accept this principle will inevitably be upset. It will not rest upon the affections or the convictions of mankind. The ferment of spirit of whole populations will fight subtly and constantly against it, and all the world will sympathize. The world can be at peace only if its life is stable, and there can be no stability where the will is in rebellion, where there is not tranquillity of spirit and a sense of justice, of freedom, and of right.

So far as practicable, moreover, every great people now struggling towards a full development of its resources and of its powers should be assured a direct outlet to the great highways of the sea. Where this cannot be done by the cession of territory, it can no doubt be done by the neutralization of direct rights of way under the general guarantee which will assure the peace itself. With a right comity of arrangement no nation need be shut away from free access to the open paths of the world's commerce.

And the paths of the seat must alike in law and in fact be free. The freedom of the seas is the *sine qua non* of peace, equality, and cooperation. No doubt a somewhat radical reconsideration of many of the rules of international practice hitherto thought to be established may be necessary in order to make the seas indeed free and common in practically all circumstances for the use of mankind, but the motive for such changes is convincing and compelling. There can be no trust or intimacy between the peoples of the world without them. The free, constant, unthreatened intercourse of nations is an essential part of the process of peace and of development. It need not be difficult either to define or to secure the freedom of the seas if the governments of the world sincerely desire to come to an agreement concerning it.

It is a problem closely connected with the limitation of naval armaments and the cooperation of the navies of the world in keeping the seas at once free and safe. And the question of limiting naval armaments opens the wider and perhaps more difficult question of the limitation of armies and of all programmes of military preparation. Difficult and delicate as these questions are, they must be faced with the utmost candour and decided in a spirit of real accommodation if peace is to come with healing in its wings, and come to stay. Peace cannot be had without concession and sacrifice. There can be no sense of safety and equality among the nations if great preponderating armaments are henceforth to continue here and there to be built up and maintained. The statesmen of the world must plan for peace and nations must adjust and accommodate their policy to it as they have planned for war and made ready for pitiless contest and rivalry. The question of armaments, whether on land or sea, is the most immediately and intensely practical question connected with the future fortunes of nations and of mankind.

I have spoken upon these great matters without reserve and with the utmost explicitness because it has seemed to me to be necessary if the world's yearning desire for peace was anywhere to find free voice and utterance. Perhaps I am the only person in high authority amongst all the peoples of the world who is at liberty to speak and hold nothing back. I am speaking as an individual, and yet I am speaking also, of course, as the responsible head of a great government, and I feel confident that I have said what the people of the United States would wish me to say. May I not add that I hope and believe that I am in effect speaking for liberals and friends of humanity in every nation and of every programme of liberty? I would fain believe that I am speaking for the silent mass of mankind everywhere who have as yet had no place or opportunity to speak their real hearts out concerning the death and ruin they see to have come already upon the persons and the homes they hold most dear.

And in holding out the expectation that the people and Government of the United States will join the other civilized nations of the world in guaranteeing the permanence of peace upon such terms as I have named, I speak with the greater boldness and confidence because it is clear to every man who can think that there is in this promise no breach in either our traditions or our policy as a nation, but a fulfillment, rather, of all that we have professed or striven for.

I am proposing, as it were, that the nations should with one accord adopt the doctrine of President Monroe as the doctrine of the world: that no nation should seek to extend its polity over any other nation or people, but that every people should be left free to determine its own policy, its own way of development, unhindered, unthreatened, unafraid, the little along with the great and powerful.

I am proposing that all nations henceforth avoid entangling alliances which would draw them into competitions of power, catch them in a net of intrigue and selfish rivalry, and disturb their own affairs with influences intruded from without. There is no entangling alliance in a concert of power. When all unite to act in the same sense and with the same purpose all act in the common interest and are free to live their own lives under a common protection.

I am proposing government by the consent of the governed; that freedom of the seas which in international conference after conference representatives of the United States have urged with the eloquence of those who are the convinced disciples of liberty; and that moderation of armaments which makes of armies and navies a power for order merely, not an instrument of aggression or of selfish violence.

These are American principles, American policies. We could stand for no others. And they are also the principles and policies of forward looking men and women everywhere, of every modern nation, of every enlightened community. They are the principles of mankind and must prevail.

13. Toward a Strategy of Peace*

by John F. Kennedy

"THERE ARE FEW EARTHLY THINGS MORE BEAUTIFUL THAN A UNIversity," wrote John Masefield, in his tribute to the English universities—and his words are equally true here. He did not refer to spires and towers, to campus greens and ivied walls. He admired the splendid beauty of the university, he said, because it was "a place where those who hate ignorance may strive to know, where those who perceive truth may strive to make others see."

I have therefore, chosen this time and this place to discuss a topic on which ignorance too often abounds and the truth is too rarely perceived—yet it is the most important topic on earth: world peace.

What kind of peace do I mean? What kind of peace do we seek? Not a *Pax Americana* enforced on the world by American weapons of war. Not the peace of the grave or the security of the slave. I am talking about genuine peace, the kind of peace that makes life on earth worth living, the kind that enables men and nations to grow and to hope and to build a better life for their children—not merely peace for Americans but peace for all men and women, not merely peace in our time but peace for all time.

I speak of peace because of the new face of war. Total war makes no sense in an age when great powers can maintain large and relatively invulnerable nuclear forces and refuse to surrender without resort to those forces. It makes no sense in an age when a single nuclear weapon contains almost 10 times the explosive force delivered by all of the Allied air forces in the Second World War.

* U.S., *Department of State Bulletin,* Vol. XLIX, No. 1253 (July 1, 1963), pp. 2-6. (Made at commencement exercises at The American University, Washington, D.C., on June 10. White House press release, as-delivered text.)

It makes no sense in an age when the deadly poisons produced by a nuclear exchange would be carried by the wind and water and soil and seed to the far corners of the globe and to generations yet unborn.

Today the expenditure of billions of dollars every year on weapons acquired for the purpose of making sure we never need to use them is essential to keeping the peace. But surely the acquisition of such idle stockpiles—which can only destroy and never create—is not the only, much less the most efficient, means of assuring peace.

I speak of peace, therefore, as the necessary rational end of rational men. I realize that the pursuit of peace is not as dramatic as the pursuit of war, and frequently the words of the pursuer fall on deaf ears. But we have no more urgent task.

Some say that it is useless to speak of world peace or world law or world disarmament—and that it will be useless until the leaders of the Soviet Union adopt a more enlightened attitude. I hope they do. I believe we can help them do it. But I also believe that we must reexamine our own attitude, as individuals and as a nation, for our attitude is as essential as theirs. And every graduate of this school, every thoughtful citizen who despairs of war and wishes to bring peace, should begin by looking inward—by examining his own attitude toward the possibilities of peace, toward the Soviet Union, toward the course of the cold war, and toward freedom and peace here at home.

THE POSSIBILITIES OF PEACE

First: Let us examine our attitude toward peace itself. Too many of us think it is impossible. Too many think it unreal. But that is a dangerous, defeatist belief. It leads to the conclusion that war is inevitable, that mankind is doomed, that we are gripped by forces we cannot control.

We need not accept that view. Our problems are manmade; therefore they can be solved by man. And man can be as big as we want. No problem of human destiny is beyond human beings. Man's reason and spirit have often solved the seemingly unsolvable, and we believe they can do it again.

I am not referring to the absolute, infinite concept of universal peace and good will of which some fantasies and fanatics dream. I do not deny the values of hopes and dreams, but we merely invite discouragement and incredulity by making that our only and immediate goal.

Let us focus instead on a more practical, more attainable peace, based not on a sudden revolution in human nature but on a gradual evolution in human institutions—on a series of concrete actions and effective agreements which are in the interest of all concerned. There is no single, simple key to this peace, no grand or magic formula to be adopted by one or two powers. Genuine peace must be the product of many nations, the sum of many acts. It must be dynamic, not static, changing to meet the challenge of each new generation. For peace is a process, a way of solving problems.

With such a peace there will still be quarrels and conflicting interests, as there are within families and nations. World peace, like community peace, does not require that each man love his neighbor; it requires only that they live together in mutual tolerance submitting their disputes to a just and peaceful settlement. And history teaches us that enmities between nations, as between individuals, do not last forever. However fixed our likes and dislikes may seem, the tide of time and events will often bring surprising changes in the relations between nations and neighbors.

So let us persevere. Peace need not be impracticable, and war need not be inevitable. By defining our goal more clearly, by making it seem more manageable and less remote, we can help all peoples to see it, to draw hope from it, and to move irresistibly toward it.

COMMON INTERESTS OF U.S. AND SOVIET UNION

Second: Let us reexamine our attitude toward the Soviet Union. It is discouraging to think that their leaders may actually believe what their propagandists write. It is discouraging to read a recent authoritative Soviet text on military strategy and find, on page after page, wholly baseless and incredible claims—such as the allegation that "American imperialist circles are preparing to unleash different types of wars . . . that there is a very real threat of a preventive war being unleashed by American imperialists against the Soviet Union . . . [and that] the political aims of the American imperialists are to enslave economically and politically the European and other capitalist countries . . . [and] to achieve world domination . . . by means of aggressive wars."

Truly as it was written long ago: "The wicked flee when no man pursueth." Yet it is sad to read these Soviet statements—to realize the extent of the gulf between us. But it is also a warning—a warning to the American people not to fall into the same trap as the Soviets, not to see only a distorted and desperate view of the other side, not to see conflict as inevitable, accommodation as impossible, and communication as nothing more than an exchange of threats. No government or social system is so evil that its people must be considered as lacking in virtue. As Americans we find communism profoundly repugnant as a negation of personal freedom and dignity. But we can still hail the Russian people for their many achievements—in science and space, in economic and industrial growth, in culture and in acts of courage.

Among the many traits the peoples of our two countries have in common, none is stronger than our mutual abhorrence of war. Almost unique among the major world powers, we have never been at war with each other. And no nation in the history of battle ever suffered more than the Soviet Union suffered in the course of the Second World War. At least 20 million lost their lives. Countless millions of homes and farms were burned or sacked. A third of the nation's territory, including nearly two-thirds of its industrial base, was turned into a wasteland—a loss equivalent to the devastation of this country east of Chicago.

Today, should total war ever break out again—no matter how—our two countries would become the primary targets. It is an ironical but accurate fact that the two strongest powers are the two in the most danger of devastation. All we have built, all we have worked for, would be destroyed in the first 24 hours. And even in the cold war, which brings burdens and dangers to so many countries—including this nation's closest allies—our two countries bear the heaviest burdens. For we are both devoting massive sums of money to weapons that could be better devoted to combating ignorance, poverty, and disease. We are both caught up in a vicious and dangerous cycle in which suspicion on one side breeds suspicion on the other and new weapons beget counter-weapons.

In short, both the United States and its allies, and the Soviet Union and its allies, have a mutually deep interest in a just and genuine peace and in halting the arms race. Agreements to this end are in the interests of the Soviet Union as well as ours, and even the most hostile nations can be relied upon to accept and keep those treaty obligations, and only those treaty obligations, which are in their own interest.

So let us not be blind to our differences, but let us also direct attention to our common interests and to the means by which those differences can be resolved. And if we cannot end now our differences, at least we can help make the world safe for diversity. For in the final analysis our most basic common link is that we all inhabit this planet. We all breathe the same air. We all cherish our children's future. And we are all mortal.

THE PURSUIT OF PEACE

Third: Let us reexamine our attitude toward the cold war, remembering that we are not engaged in a debate, seeking to pile up debating points. We are not here distributing blame or pointing the finger of judgment. We must deal with the world as it is and not as it might have been had the history of the last 18 years been different.

We must, therefore, persevere in the search for peace in the hope that constructive changes within the Communist bloc might bring within reach solutions which now seem beyond us. We must conduct our affairs in such a way that it becomes in the Communists' interest to agree on a genuine peace. Above all, while defending our own vital interests, nuclear powers must avert those confrontations which bring an adversary to a choice of either a humiliating retreat or a nuclear war. To adopt that kind of course in the nuclear age would be evidence only of the bankruptcy of our policy—or of a collective death wish for the world.

To secure these ends, America's weapons are nonprovocative, carefully controlled, designed to deter, and capable of selective use. Our military forces are committed to peace and disciplined in self-restraint. Our diplomats are instructed to avoid unnecessary irritants and purely rhetorical hostility.

For we can seek a relaxation of tensions without relaxing our guard. And, for our part, we do not need to use threats to prove that we are resolute. We do not need to jam foreign broadcasts out of fear our faith will be eroded. We are unwilling to impose our system on any unwilling people, but we are willing and able to engage in peaceful competition with any people on earth.

Meanwhile we seek to strengthen the United Nations, to help solve its financial problems, to make it a more effective instrument of peace, to develop it into a genuine world security system—a system capable of resolving disputes on the basis of law, of insuring the security of the large and the small, and of creating conditions under which arms can finally be abolished.

At the same time we seek to keep peace inside the non-Communist world, where many nations, all of them our friends, are divided over issues which weaken Western unity, which invite Communist intervention, or which threaten to erupt into war. Our efforts in West New Guinea, in the Congo, in the Middle East, and in the Indian subcontinent have been persistent and patient despite criticism from both sides. We have also tried to set an example for others—by seeking to adjust small but significant differences with our own closest neighbors in Mexico and in Canada.

Speaking of other nations, I wish to make one point clear. We are bound to many nations by alliances. Those alliances exist because our concern and theirs substantially overlap. Our commitment to defend Western Europe and West Berlin, for example, stands undiminished because of the identity of our vital interests. The United States will make no deal with the Soviet Union at the expense of other nations and other peoples, not merely because they are our partners but also because their interests and ours converge.

Our interests converge, however, not only in defending the frontiers of freedom but in pursuing the paths of peace. It is our hope—and the purpose of Allied policies—to convince the Soviet Union that she, too, should let each nation choose its own future, so long as that choice does not interfere with the choices of others. The Communist drive to impose their political and economic system on others is the primary cause of world tension today. For there can be no doubt that, if all nations could refrain from interfering in the self-determination of others, the peace would be much more assured.

This will require a new effort to achieve world law, a new context for world discussions. It will require increased understanding between the Soviets and ourselves. And increased understanding will require increased contact and communication. One step in this direction is the proposed arrangement for a direct line between Moscow and Washington, to avoid on each side the dangerous delays, misunderstandings, and misreadings of the other's actions which might occur at a time of crisis.

We have also been talking in Geneva about other first-step measures of arms control, designed to limit the intensity of the arms race and to reduce the risks of accidental war. Our primary long-range interest in Geneva, however, is general and complete disarmament, designed to take place by stages, permitting parallel political developments to build the new institutions of peace which would take the place of arms. The pursuit of disarmament has been an effort of this Government since the 1920's. It has been urgently sought by the past three administrations. And however dim the prospects may be today, we intend to continue this effort—to continue it in order that all countries, including our own, can better grasp what the problems and possibilities of disarmament are.

The one major area of these negotiations where the end is in sight, yet where a fresh start is badly needed, is in a treaty to outlaw nuclear tests. The conclusion of such a treaty—so near and yet so far—would check the spiraling arms race in one of its most dangerous areas. It would place the nuclear powers in a position to deal more effectively with one of the greatest hazards which man faces in 1963, the further spread of nuclear arms. It would increase our security; it would decrease the prospects of war. Surely this goal is sufficiently important to require our steady pursuit, yielding neither to the temptation to give up the whole effort nor the temptation to give up our insistence on vital and responsible safeguards.

I am taking this opportunity, therefore, to announce two important decisions in this regard.

First: Chairman Khrushchev, Prime Minister Macmillan, and I have agreed that high level discussions will shortly begin in Moscow looking toward early agreement on a comprehensive test ban treaty. Our hopes must be tempered with the caution of history, but with our hopes go the hopes of all mankind.

Second: To make clear our good faith and solemn convictions on the matter, I now declare that the United States does not propose to conduct nuclear tests in the atmosphere so long as other states do not do so. We will not be the first to resume. Such a declaration is no substitute for a formal binding treaty, but I hope it will help us achieve one. Nor would such a treaty be a substitute for disarmament, but I hope it will help us achieve it.

Therefore, as your President, performing my constitutional duty to "give to the Congress information of the state of the Union," I find it necessary to report that the future and the safety of our country and of our democracy are overwhelmingly involved in events far beyond our borders.

Armed defense of democratic existence is now being gallantly waged in four continents. If that defense fails, all the population and all the resources of Europe, Asia, Africa, and Australasia will be dominated by the conquerors. The total of those populations and their resources greatly exceeds the sum total of the population and resources of the whole of the Western Hemisphere—many times over.

In times like these it is immature—and incidentally untrue—for anybody to brag that an unprepared America, single-handed, and with one hand tied behind its back, can hold off the whole world.

No realistic American can expect from a dictator's peace international generosity, or return of true independence, or world disarmament, or freedom of expression, or freedom of religion—or even good business.

Such a peace would bring no security for us or for our neighbors. "Those who would give up essential liberty to purchase a little temporary safety deserve neither liberty nor safety."

As a Nation we may take pride in the fact that we are softhearted; but we cannot afford to be soft-headed.

We must always be wary of those who, with sounding brass and a tinkling cymbal, preach the "ism" of appeasement.

We must especially beware of that small group of selfish men who would clip the wings of the American eagle in order to feather their own nests.

I have recently pointed out how quickly the tempo of modern warfare could bring into our very midst the physical attack which we must expect if the dictator nations win this war.

There is much loose talk of our immunity from immediate and direct invasion from across the seas. Obviously, as long as the British Navy retains its power, no such danger exists. Even if there were no British Navy, it is not probable that any enemy would be stupid enough to attack us by landing troops in the United States from across thousands of miles of ocean, until it had acquired strategic bases from which to operate.

But we learn much from the lessons of the past years in Europe—particularly the lesson of Norway, whose essential seaports were captured by treachery and surprise built up over a series of years.

The first phase of the invasion of this hemisphere would not be the landing of regular troops. The necessary strategic points would be occupied by secret agents and their dupes, and great numbers of them are already here, and in Latin America.

As long as the aggressor nations maintain the offensive, they, not we, will choose the time and the place and the method of their attack.

That is why the future of all American republics is today in serious danger.

That is why this annual message to the Congress is unique in our history.

That is why every member of the executive branch of the Government and every Member of the Congress face great responsibility—and great accountability.

The need of the moment is that our actions and our policy should be devoted primarily—almost exclusively—to meeting this foreign peril. For all our domestic problems are now a part of the great emergency.

Just as our national policy in internal affairs has been based upon a decent respect for the rights and dignity of all our fellowmen within our gates, so our national policy in foreign affairs has been based on a decent respect for the rights and dignity of all nations, large and small. And the justice of morality must and will win in the end.

Our national policy is this:

First, by an impressive expression of the public will and without regard to partisanship, we are committed to all-inclusive national defense.

Second, by an impressive expression of the public will and without regard to partisanship, we are committed to full support of all those resolute peoples, everywhere, who are resisting aggression and are thereby keeping war away from our hemisphere. By this support, we express our determination that the democratic cause shall prevail, and we strengthen the defense and security of our own Nation.

Third, by an impressive expression of the public will and without regard to partisanship, we are committed to the proposition that principles of morality and considerations for our own security will never permit us to acquiesce in a peace dictated by aggressors and sponsored by appeasers. We know that enduring peace cannot be bought at the cost of other people's freedom.

In the recent national election there was no substantial difference between the two great parties in respect to that national policy. No issue was fought out on this line before the American electorate. Today it is abundantly evident that American citizens everywhere are demanding and supporting speedy and complete action in recognition of obvious danger.

Therefore, the immediate need is a swift and driving increase in our armament production.

Leaders of industry and labor have responded to our summons. Goals of speed have been set. In some cases these goals are being reached ahead of time; in some cases we are on schedule; in other cases there are slight but not serious delays; and in some cases—and I am sorry to say very important cases—we are all concerned by the slowness of the accomplishment of our plans.

The Army and Navy, however, have made substantial progress during the past year. Actual experience is improving and speeding up our methods of production with every passing day. And today's best is not good enough for tomorrow.

I am not satisfied with the progress thus far made. The men in charge of the program represent the best in training, ability, and patriotism. They are not satisfied with the progress thus far made. None of us will be satisfied until the job is done.

No matter whether the original goal was set too high or too low, our objective is quicker and better results.

To give two illustrations:

We are behind schedule in turning out finished airplanes; we are working day and night to solve the innumerable problems and to catch up.

We are ahead of schedule in building warships; but we are working to get even further ahead of schedule.

To change a whole nation from a basis of peacetime production of implements of peace to a basis of wartime production of implements of war is no small task. And the greatest difficulty comes at the beginning of the program, when new tools and plant facilities and new assembly lines and shipways must first be constructed before the actual matériel begins to flow steadily and speedily from them.

The Congress, of course, must rightly keep itself informed at all times of the progress of the program. However, there is certain information, as the Congress itself will readily recognize, which, in the interests of our own security and those of the nations we are supporting must of needs be kept in confidence.

New circumstances are constantly begetting new needs for our safety. I shall ask this Congress for greatly increased new appropriations and authorizations to carry on what we have begun.

I also ask this Congress for authority and for funds sufficient to manufacture additional munitions and war supplies of many kinds, to be turned over to those nations which are now in actual war with aggressor nations.

Our most useful and immediate role is to act as an arsenal for them as well as for ourselves. They do not need manpower. They do need billions of dollars' worth of the weapons of defense.

The time is near when they will not be able to pay for them in ready cash. We cannot, and will not, tell them they must surrender merely because of present inability to pay for the weapons which we know they must have.

I do not recommend that we make them a loan of dollars with which to pay for these weapons—a loan to be repaid in dollars.

I recommend that we make it possible for those nations to continue to obtain war materials in the United States, fitting their orders into our own program. Nearly all of their matériel would, if the time ever came, be useful for our own defense.

Taking counsel of expert military and naval authorities, considering what is best for our own security, we are free to decide how much should be kept here and how much should be sent abroad to our friends who, by their determined and heroic resistance, are giving us time in which to make ready our own defense.

For what we send abroad we shall be repaid, within a reasonable time following the close of hostilities, in similar materials or, at our option, in other goods of many kinds which they can produce and which we need.

Let us say to the democracies, "We Americans are vitally concerned in your defense of freedom. We are putting forth our energies, our resources, and our organizing powers to give you the strength to regain and maintain a free world. We shall send you, in ever-increasing numbers, ships, planes, tanks, guns. This is our purpose and our pledge."

In fulfillment of this purpose we will not be intimidated by the threats of dictators that they will regard as a breach of international law and as an act of war our aid to the democracies which dare to resist their aggression. Such aid is not an act of war, even if a dictator should unilaterally proclaim it so to be.

When the dictators are ready to make war upon us, they will not wait for an act of war on our part. They did not wait for Norway or Belgium or the Netherlands to commit an act of war.

Their only interest is in a new one-way international law, which lacks mutuality in its observance and, therefore, becomes an instrument of oppression.

The happiness of future generations of Americans may well depend upon how effective and how immediate we can make our aid felt. No one can tell the exact character of the emergency situations that we may be called upon to meet. The Nation's hands must not be tied when the Nation's life is in danger.

We must all prepare to make the sacrifices that the emergency—as serious as war itself—demands. Whatever stands in the way of speed and efficiency in defense preparations must give way to the national need.

A free nation has the right to expect full cooperation from all groups. A free nation has the right to look to the leaders of business, of labor, and of agriculture to take the lead in stimulating effort, not among other groups but within their own groups.

The best way of dealing with the few slackers or trouble makers in our midst is, first, to shame them by patriotic example; and if that fails, to use the sovereignty of government to save government.

As men do not live by bread alone, they do not fight by armaments alone. Those who man our defenses, and those behind them who build our defenses, must have the stamina and courage which come from an unshakable belief in the manner of life which they are defending. The mighty action which we are calling for cannot be based on a disregard of all things worth fighting for.

The Nation takes great satisfication and much strength from the things which have been done to make its people conscious of their individual stake in the preservation of democratic life in America. Those things have toughened the fiber of our people, have renewed their faith and strengthened their devotion to the institutions we make ready to protect.

Certainly this is no time to stop thinking about the social and economic problems which are the root cause of the social revolution which is today a supreme factor in the world.

There is nothing mysterious about the foundations of a healthy and strong democracy. The basic things expected by our people of their political and economic systems are simple. They are:

Equality of opportunity for youth and for others.

Jobs for those who can work.

Security for those who need it.

The ending of special privilege for the few.

The preservation of civil liberties for all.

The enjoyment of the fruits of scientific progress in a wider and constantly rising standard of living.

These are the simple and basic things that must never be lost sight of in the turmoil and unbelievable complexity of our modern world. The inner and abiding strength of our economic and political systems is dependent upon the degree to which they fulfill these expectations.

Many subjects connected with our social economy call for immediate improvement.

As examples:

We should bring more citizens under the coverage of old-age pensions and unemployment insurance.

We should widen the opportunities for adequate medical care.

We should plan a better system by which persons deserving or needing gainful employment may obtain it.

I have called for personal sacrifice. I am assured of the willingness of almost all Americans to respond to that call.

A part of the sacrifice means the payment of more money in taxes. In my Budget message I recommend that a greater portion of this great defense program be paid for from taxation than we are paying today. No person should try, or be allowed, to get rich out of this program; and the principle of tax payments in accordance with ability to pay should be constantly before our eyes to guide our legislation.

If the Congress maintains these principles, the voters, putting patriotism ahead of pocketbooks, will give you their applause.

In the future days, which we seek to make secure, we look forward to a world founded upon four essential human freedoms.

The first is freedom of speech and expression everywhere in the world.

The second is freedom of every person to worship God in his own way everywhere in the world.

The third is freedom from want, which, translated into world terms, means economic understandings which will secure to every nation a healthy peacetime life for its inhabitants everywhere in the world.

The fourth is freedom from fear—which, translated into world terms, means a world-wide reduction of armaments to such a point and in such a thorough fashion that no nation will be in a position to commit an act of physical aggression against any neighbor—anywhere in the world.

That is no vision of a distant millennium. It is a definite basis for a kind of world attainable in our own time and generation. That kind of world is the very antithesis of the so-called new order of tyranny which the dictators seek to create with the crash of a bomb.

To that new order we oppose the greater conception—the moral order. A good society is able to face schemes of world domination and foreign revolutions alike without fear.

Since the beginning of our American history we have been engaged in change—in a perpetual peaceful revolution—a revolution which goes on steadily, quietly adjusting itself to changing conditions—without the concentration camp or the quicklime in the ditch. The world order which we seek is the cooperation of free countries, working together in a friendly, civilized society.

This Nation has placed its destiny in the hands and heads and hearts of its millions of free men and women; and its faith in freedom under the guidance of God. Freedom means the supremacy of human rights everywhere. Our support goes to those who struggle to gain those rights or keep them. Our strength is in our unity of purpose.

To that high concept there can be no end save victory.

15. Pattern for Peace in Southeast Asia*

by Lyndon B. Johnson

LAST WEEK 17 NATIONS SENT THEIR VIEWS TO SOME TWO DOZEN countries having an interest in Southeast Asia. We are joining those 17 countries and stating our American policy tonight, which we believe will contribute toward peace in this area of the world.

I have come here to review once again with my own people the views of the American Government.

Tonight Americans and Asians are dying for a world where each people may choose its own path to change. This is the principle for which our ancestors fought in the valleys of Pennsylvania. It is a principle for which our sons fight tonight in the jungles of Viet-Nam.

Viet-Nam is far away from this quiet campus. We have no territory there, nor do we seek any. The war is dirty and brutal and difficult. And some 400 young men, born into an America that is bursting with opportunity and promise, have ended their lives on Viet-Nam's steaming soil.

Why must we take this painful road? Why must this nation hazard its ease, its interest, and its power for the sake of a people so far away?

We fight because we must fight if we are to live in a world where every country can shape its own destiny, and only in such a world will our own freedom be finally secure.

This kind of world will never be built by bombs or bullets. Yet the infirmities of man are such that force must often precede

* U.S., *Department of State Bulletin,* Vol. LII, No. 1346, April 26, 1965, pp. 606-610. Address made at Johns Hopkins University, Baltimore, Md., on April 7 (White House press release, as-delivered text).

reason and the waste of war, the works of peace. We wish that this were not so. But we must deal with the world as it is, if it is ever to be as we wish.

The world as it is in Asia is not a serene or peaceful place.

The first reality is that North Viet-Nam has attacked the independent nation of South Viet-Nam. Its object is total conquest. Of course, some of the people of South Viet-Nam are participating in attack on their own government. But trained men and supplies, orders and arms, flow in a constant stream from North to South.

This support is the heartbeat of the war.

And it is a war of unparalleled brutality. Simple farmers are the targets of assassination and kidnaping. Women and children are strangled in the night because their men are loyal to their government. And helpless villages are ravaged by sneak attacks. Large-scale raids are conducted on towns, and terror strikes in the heart of cities.

The confused nature of this conflict cannot mask the fact that it is the new face of an old enemy.

Over this war—and all Asia—is another reality: the deepening shadow of Communist China. The rulers in Hanoi are urged on by Peiping. This is a regime which has destroyed freedom in Tibet, which has attacked India, and has been condemned by the United Nations for aggression in Korea. It is a nation which is helping the forces of violence in almost every continent. The contest in Viet-Nam is part of a wider pattern of aggressive purposes.

WHY ARE WE IN SOUTH VIET-NAM?

Why are these realities our concern? Why are we in South Viet-Nam?

We are there because we have a promise to keep. Since 1954 every American President has offered support to the people of South Viet-Nam. We have helped to build, and we have helped to defend. Thus, over many years, we have made a national pledge to help South Viet-Nam defend its independence.

And I intend to keep that promise.

To dishonor that pledge, to abandon this small and brave nation to its enemies, and to the terror that must follow, would be an unforgivable wrong.

We are also there to strengthen world order. Around the globe, from Berlin to Thailand, are people whose well-being rests in part on the belief that they can count on us if they are attacked. To leave Viet-Nam to its fate would shake the confidence of all these people in the value of an American commitment and in the value of America's word. The result would be increased unrest and instability, and even wider war.

We are also there because there are great stakes in the balance. Let no one think for a moment that retreat from Viet-Nam would bring an end to conflict. The battle would be renewed in one country and then another. The central lesson of our time is that the appetite of aggression is never satisfied. To withdraw from one battlefield means only to prepare for the next. We must say in Southeast Asia—as we did in Europe—in the words of the Bible: "Hitherto shalt thou come, but no further."

There are those who say that all our effort there will be futile—that China's power is such that it is bound to dominate all Southeast Asia. But there is no end to that argument until all of the nations of Asia are swallowed up.

There are those who wonder why we have a responsibility there. Well, we have it there for the same reason that we have a responsibility for the defense of Europe. World War II was fought in both Europe and Asia, and when it ended we found ourselves with continued responsibility for the defense of freedom.

Our objective is the independence of South Viet-Nam and its freedom from attack. We want nothing for ourselves—only that the people of South Viet-Nam be allowed to guide their own country in their own way. We will do everything necessary to reach that objective, and we will do only what is absolutely necessary.

In recent months attacks on South Viet-Nam were stepped up. Thus it became necessary for us to increase our response and to make attacks by air. This is not a change of purpose. It is a change in what we believe that purpose requires.

We do this in order to slow down aggression.

We do this to increase the confidence of the brave people of South Viet-Nam who have bravely borne this brutal battle for so many years with so many casualties.

And we do this to convince the leaders of North Viet-Nam—and all who seek to share their conquest—of a simple fact:

We will not be defeated.

We will not grow tired.

We will not withdraw, either openly or under the cloak of a meaningless agreement.

We know that air attacks alone will not accomplish all of these purposes. But it is our best and prayerful judgment that they are a necessary part of the surest road to peace.

THE PATH OF PEACEFUL SETTLEMENT

We hope that peace will come swiftly. But that is in the hands of others besides ourselves. And we must be prepared for a long continued conflict. It will require patience as well as bravery—the will to endure as well as the will to resist.

I wish it were possible to convince others with words of what we now find it necessary to say with guns and planes: armed hostility is futile—our resorces are equal to any challenge—because we fight for values and we fight for principle, rather than territory or colonies, our patience and our determination are unending.

Once this is clear, then it should also be clear that the only path for reasonable men is the path of peaceful settlement. Such peace demands an independent South Viet-Nam—securely guaranteed and able to shape its own relationships to all others—free from outside interference—tied to no alliance—a military base for no other country.

These are the essentials of any final settlement.

We will never be second in the search for such a peaceful settlement in Viet-Nam.

There may be many ways to this kind of peace: in discussion or negotiation with the governments concerned; in large groups or in small ones; in the reaffirmation of old agreements or their strengthening with new ones.

We have stated this position over and over again 50 times and more to friend and foe alike. And we remain ready with this purpose for unconditional discussions.

And until that bright and necessary day of peace we will try to keep conflict from spreading. We have no desire to see thousands die in battle—Asians or Americans. We have no desire to devastate that which the people of North Viet-Nam have built with toil and sacrifice. We will use our power with restraint and with all the wisdom that we can command.

But we will use it.

A COOPERATIVE EFFORT FOR DEVELOPMENT

This war, like most wars, is filled with terrible irony. For what do the people of North Viet-Nam want? They want what their neighbors also desire—food for their hunger, health for their bodies, a chance to learn, progress for their country, and an end to the bondage of material misery. And they would find all these things far more readily in peaceful association with others than in the endless course of battle.

These countries of Southeast Asia are homes for millions of impoverished people. Each day these people rise at dawn and struggle through until the night to wrest existence from the soil. They are often wracked by diseases, plagued by hunger, and death comes at the early age of 40.

Stability and peace do not come easily in such a land. Neither independence nor human dignity will ever be won, though, by arms alone. It also requires the works of peace. The American people have helped generously in times past in these works, and now there must be a much more massive effort to improve the life of man in that conflict-torn corner of our world.

The first step is for the countries of Southeast Asia to associate themselves in a greatly expanded cooperative effort for development. We would hope that North Viet-Nam would take its place in the common effort just as soon as peaceful cooperation is possible.

The United Nations is already actively engaged in development in this area, and as far back as 1961 I conferred with our authorities in Viet-Nam in connection with their work there. And I would hope tonight that the Secretary-General of the United Nations could use the prestige of his great office and his deep knowledge of Asia to initiate, as soon as possible, with the countries of that area, a plan for cooperation in increased development.

For our part I will ask the Congress to join in a billion-dollar American investment in this effort as soon as it is underway. And I would hope that all other industrialized countries, including the

Soviet Union, will join in this effort to replace despair with hope and terror with progress.

The task is nothing less than to enrich the hopes and existence of more than a hundred million people. And there is much to be done.

The vast Mekong River can provide food and water and power on a scale to dwarf even our own TVA. The wonders of modern medicine can be spread through villages where thousands die every year from lack of care. Schools can be established to train people in the skills needed to manage the process of development. And these objectives, and more, are within the reach of a cooperative and determined effort.

I also intend to expand and speed up a program to make available our farm surpluses to assist in feeding and clothing the needy in Asia. We should not allow people to go hungry and wear rags while our own warehouses overflow with an abundance of wheat and corn and rice and cotton.

So I will very shortly name a special team of outstanding, patriotic, and distinguished Americans to inaugurate our participation in these programs. This team will be headed by Mr. Eugene Black, the very able former President of the World Bank.

THE DREAM OF OUR GENERATION

This will be a disorderly planet for a long time. In Asia, and elsewhere, the forces of the modern world are shaking old ways and uprooting ancient civilizations. There will be turbulence and struggle and even violence. Great social change—as we see in our own country—does not always come without conflict.

We must also expect that nations will on occasion be in dispute with us. It may be because we are rich, or powerful, or because we have made some mistakes, or because they honestly fear our intentions. However, no nation need ever fear that we desire their land, or to impose our will, or to dictate their institutions.

But we will always oppose the effort of one nation to conquer another nation.

We will do this because our own security is at stake.

But there is more to it than that. For our generation has a dream. It is a very old dream. But we have the power, and now we have the opportunity to make that dream come true.

For centuries nations have struggled among each other. But we dream of a world where disputes are settled by law and reason. And we will try to make it so.

For most of history men have hated and killed one another in battle. But we dream of an end to war. And we will try to make it so.

For all existence most men have lived in poverty, threatened by hunger. But we dream of a world where all are fed and charged with hope. And we will help to make it so.

The ordinary men and women of North Viet-Nam and South Viet-Nam, of China and India, of Russia and America, are brave people. They are filled with the same proportions of hate and fear, of love and hope. Most of them want the same things for themselves and their families. Most of them do not want their sons to ever die in battle, or to see their homes, or the homes of others, destroyed.

Well, this can be their world yet. Man now has the knowledge—always before denied—to make this planet serve the real needs of the people who live on it.

I know this will not be easy. I know how difficult it is for reason to guide passion, and love to master hate. The complexities of this world do not bow easily to pure and consistent answers.

But the simple truths are there just the same. We must all try to follow them as best we can.

POWER, WITNESS TO HUMAN FOLLY

We often say how impressive power is. But I do not find it impressive at all. The guns and the bombs, the rockets and the warships, are all symbols of human failure. They are necessary symbols. They protect what we cherish. But they are witness to human folly.

A dam built across a great river is impressive.

In the countryside where I was born, and where I live, I have seen the night illuminated, and the kitchen warmed, and the home heated, where once the cheerless night and the ceaseless cold held sway. And all this happened because electricity came to our area along the humming wires of the REA. Electrification of the countryside—yes, that, too, is impressive.

A rich harvest in a hungry land is impressive.

The sight of healthy children in a classroom is impressive.

These—not mighty arms—are the achievements which the

American nation believes to be impressive. And if we are steadfast, the time may come when all other nations will also find it so.

Every night before I turn out the lights to sleep I ask myself this question: Have I done everything that I can do to unite this country? Have I done everything I can to help unite the world, to try to bring peace and hope to all the peoples of the world? Have I done enough?

Ask yourselves that question in your homes—and in this hall tonight. Have we, each of us, all done all we can do? Have we done enough?

We may well be living in the time foretold many years ago when it was said: "I call heaven and earth to record this day against you, that I have set before you life and death, blessing and cursing: therefore choose life, that both thou and thy seed may live."

This generation of the world must choose: destroy or build, kill or aid, hate or understand. We can do all these things on a scale that has never been dreamed of before.

Well, we will choose life. And so doing, we will prevail over the enemies within man, and over the natural enemies of all mankind.

Conclusion

Conclusion

by David L. Larson

FOLLOWING WORLD WAR II THE LEADERSHIP OF THE FREE WORLD was thrust upon the United States in such a manner that it could no longer escape the concomitant responsibilities as it did following World War I. To avoid tragedies like those of the interwar period, order had to be created out of chaos. Some new or different means for meeting and accepting the responsibilities of world leadership were clearly needed.

This imperative was manifested as early as August 14, 1940, with the eighth principle of the Atlantic Charter which laid much of the conceptual basis for the postwar world:

> . . . They believe that all of the nations of the world, for realistic as well as spiritual reasons, must come to the abandonment of the use of force. Since no future peace can be maintained, if land, sea or air armaments continue to be employed by nations which threaten, or may threaten, aggression outside of their frontiers, they believe, pending the establishment of a wider and permanent system of general security, that the disarmament of such nations is essential. They will likewise aid and encourage all other practicable measures which will lighten for peace-loving peoples the crushing burden of armaments.
>
> (s) FRANKLIN D. ROOSEVELT
> (s) WINSTON S. CHURCHILL

The Atlantic Charter also symbolized the overdue transfer of world leadership from a gallant and historic friend to the United States. The inexorable press of events combined with a series of United Nations declarations and conferences to illustrate plainly the transfer of power, leadership, and responsibility to the United States. The United Nations system with its six quasi-political bodies sixteen functional agencies, and six ad hoc commissions was established largely through the support and assistance of the United States. The clearest evidence of this new role for the United States was its hosting of the Bretton Woods, Dumbarton Oaks, and San Francisco conferences, and the setting of the United Nations in New York.

Then the disillusionments of a rational international order began to impinge upon American idealism in such places as Greece, Turkey, Iran, Trieste, North Korea, mainland China and ultimately South Korea. The "Cold War" was on in a very real and unmistakable fashion. The misadventures of South Korea aroused and challenged the American people in a readily-understandable manner. However, with the Korean conflict came the realization that the United States could not have recourse to the ultimate weapon. This realization fully impressed the American and Soviet consciousness in October 1962, when the possibility of mutual destruction became all too real and hardly worth the "bones of a Cuban grenadier."

While the United States and the Soviet Union were ponderously maneuvering in a great international struggle for power, prestige, and prosperity, a sometimes quiet and subtle revolution was occurring under the aegis of the United Nations. Over fifty-seven new nation-states were admitted to the international community, with more to come.

For the most part, these newer nation-states were in the "pre-industrial and post-colonial" stages of economic, social, and political development, and required considerable patience and assistance. However, they were intent upon creating their own national identities, insofar as possible, apart from the Great Power struggles. This has thus far proved to be virtually impossible, as a practical matter of both external politics and internal economics. The necessity for seeking outside economic, technical, and social assistance inevitably forced these newer nations to come to one of the Great Powers, which created new or renewed old relationships.

The sensitivities of the newer nations to the diminution of their sovereignties has created strained and ambiguous relationships not only with the United States, but also with the Soviet Union, Communist China, France, and Great Britain. This was reflected in the Belgrade Conference of "neutral and non-aligned" nation-states in 1961 and again in the Cairo Conference of 1964. The most prevailing desire of these lesser developed nation-states is somehow to make the seemingly magical transformation to prosperous, industrial societies in the shortest possible time. This aspiration makes these nation-states susceptible to "get-rich-quick" schemes and their "follow-me-and-you-will-wear-diamonds" ideologies. To a struggling nation-state and its often despairing leadership, these schemes and ideologies are often hard to resist particularly when couched in the insidious doctrines of "peaceful coexistence."

Given this general situation, and the increasing frustrations of contending with the ambiguous content of "peaceful coexistence" as variously interpreted, espoused and practiced by Moscow, Belgrade, New Delhi, Peking, Cairo, and Djakarta, it would seem that the United States might try to recast its foreign policy. The substance would not vary greatly from contemporary practices, but the goals and procedures would. The essence of this new approach would be to proclaim a "thirty-year plan of international development." And in turn, the rationale of this "plan" would be development for the sake of development as an end in itself. This approach, of course, would be in distinct contrast to the present policies of using developmental assistance largely as a means to an end—the containment of Soviet, Chinese, and Cuban imperialism, and would seek to avoid making the assistance extended less subject to the vagaries of annual appropriations and stipulations.

If the United States is ever going to seize the initiative in this struggle against totalitarian imperialism, it must try to cast its policies in as positive and non-ideological a framework as possible. This would probably avoid much of the ideological stigma and sidestep some of the national sensitivities of the recipient nations.

One underlying assumption, in a "thirty-year plan of international development," is that real development in the broadest sense will take a considerable period of time. This approach ought to have a salutory effect upon the various schemes and ideologies. A second assumption is that "development for the sake of development as an end in itself" will eventually lead to economic, political, and social stability. A third assumption is that as societies become more pluralistic and diversified it is increasingly difficult to develop effective central planning and control, and that the exigencies of the polity and the economy will result in greater reliance upon democratic procedures and the market. A fourth assumption underlying this proposition is that the United States, Western Europe, Japan, and some of the more developed nation-states of the free world are uniquely suited and equipped to undertake such a plan in distinct contrast to Soviet Russia and Communist China. A fifth assumption in this approach is that all the more developed nation-states and the various international agencies would cooperate and coordinate their efforts. A sixth assumption is that this developmental assistance would cover the entire social spectrum and would be as objective and non-political as possible in order to be more acceptable and to retain the integrity of development as an end in itself.

Such an approach would do much to create an attitude of confidence and hope on the part of the less developed peoples of the world. It would also do much toward gaining the initiative for the United States. Undoubtedly it would also arouse greater enthusiasm for the United States as the responsible leader of the free world. That such a broad-scale, long-term approach would have some substantial subsidiary benefits for fuller employment, increased trade, and a growing involvement of the American people is not incidental. Also, it is not entirely inconceivable that such an approach might leap-frog or by-pass the more nationalistic or regional groupings that stand in the way of greater international cooperation.

Exactly how such a "thirty-year plan" should unfold and how it could be executed is extremely difficult to say, and undoubtedly would have to be worked out as it went along. However, it does seem that the essential leadership would have to be exercised by the President of the United States before the American people, before Congress, and before the world. That such a plan would require some additional sacrifices on the part of the American people is self-evident, but given the generosity and humanitarianism of the American people, a clearly defined goal within the national interest would probably call forth the necessary support. The support developed for the Marshall Plan and subsequent mutual assistance programs along with the Peace Corps and the various charitable organizations would seem to augur well for such a proposition.

As in 1940 and the subsequent years, it would seem that the American people and the people of the free world are at their finest when their ideals and values combine with their national interests. This seems to have been the case in the Atlantic Charter, and it may require a "Charter for International Development" to combine idealism and realism in a positive and constructive manner. This would seem to be a minimum requirement if Western Civilization and the other civilizations of the world are to survive, grow, and truly co-exist in a more rational international society.

Bibliography

Acheson, Dean. "Ethics in International Relations Today," Address at Amherst College (December 9, 1964).

Acheson, Dean. "Morality, Moralism and Diplomacy," *The Yale Review,* Vol. XLVII, No. 4 (Summer 1958).

Acheson, Dean. *Power and Diplomacy* (Cambridge: Harvard University Press, 1958).

Almond, Gabriel A. *The American People and Foreign Policy* (New York: Harcourt, Brace and Co., 1950).

Almond, Gabriel and Coleman, James S. *The Politics of Developing Areas* (Princeton, N.J.: Princeton University Press, 1960).

Aron, Raymond. *The Century of Total War* (Garden City, N.Y.: Doubleday and Co., 1954).

Barnett, Doak A. *Communist China and Asia, Challenge to American Foreign Policy* (New York: Harper and Brothers, 1960).

Barnet, Richard J. *Who Wants Disarmament?* (Boston: Beacon Press, 1963).

Bartlett, Ruhl J. *Policy and Power: Two Centuries of American Foreign Relations* (New York: Hill and Wang, 1963).

Beard, Charles A. with Smith, G. H. E. *The Idea of National Interest: An Analytical Study in American Foreign Policy* (New York: The Macmillan Company, 1934).

Beloff, Max. *Foreign Policy and the Democratic Process* (Baltimore: The Johns Hopkins Press, 1955).

Bemis, Samuel Flagg. *A Diplomatic History of the United States,* Fourth Edition (New York: Henry Holt and Company, 1955).

Bemis, Samuel Flagg. *American Foreign Policy and the Blessings of Liberty and Other Essays* (New Haven: Yale University Press, 1962).

Black, Eugene R. *The Diplomacy of Economic Development* (Cambridge: Harvard University Press, 1960).

Bloomfield, Lincoln P. *The United Nations and U.S. Foreign Policy* (Boston: Little, Brown & Co., 1960).

Brierly, James L. *The Law of Nations,* Sixth Edition (New York: Oxford University Press, 1962).

Brodie, Bernard. *Strategy in the Missile Age* (Princeton: Princeton University Press, 1959).

Brogan, Dennis W. *The American Problem* (London: Hamish Hamilton, 1944).
Brogan, Dennis W. and Verney, Douglas V. *Political Patterns in Today's World* (New York: Harcourt, Brace & World, 1963).
Brown, William A. and Redvers, Opie. *American Foreign Assistance* (Washington, D.C.: The Brookings Institution, 1953).
Bryce, James. *The American Commonwealth* (New York: Macmillan and Company, 1891).
Brzezinski, Zbigniew K. *Ideology and Power in Soviet Politics* (New York: Frederick A. Praeger, 1962).
Buchan, Alastair. *NATO in the 1960's,* Revised Edition (Frederick A. Praeger, 1963)
Cabot, John M. *Toward Our Common American Destiny* (Medford, Mass.: The Fletcher School of Law and Diplomacy, 1955).
Carleton William G. *The Revolution in American Foreign Policy,* Second Edition (New York: Random House, 1964).
Carr, Edward Hallett, *The Twenty Years' Crisis, 1919-1939: An Introduction to the Study of International Relations* (London: Macmillan & Co., Ltd., 1962).
Christiansen, Bjorn. *Attitudes towards Foreign Affairs as a Function of Personality* (Oslo: Oslo University Press, 1959).
Churchill, Winston S. *The Second World War,* Six Volumes (Boston: Houghton Mifflin Company, 1953).
Clark, Grenville and Sohn, Louis B. *World Peace Through World Law,* Second Edition (Cambridge, Mass.: Harvard University Press, 1960).
Claude, Inis L. *Power and International Relations* (New York: Random House, 1962).
Clausewitz, Karl von. *On War* (New York: Modern Library, 1943).
Commager, Henry Steele. *The American Mind,* (New Haven: Yale University Press, 1950).
Corbett, Percy E. *Morals, Law and Power in International Relations* (Los Angeles: John Randolph Haynes and Dora Haynes Foundation, 1956).
Crabb, Cecil V., Jr. *American Foreign Policy in the Nuclear Age,* Second Edition (New York: Harper & Row, 1965).
Dahl, Robert A. *Congress and Foreign Policy* (New York: Harcourt, Brace and Co., 1950).
de Jouvenal, Bertrand. *Sovereignty: An Inquiry into the Political Good* (Chicago: University of Chicago Press, 1957).
de Tocqueville, Alexis. *Democracy in America,* two volumes, original edition, 1834 (London: Oxford University Press, 1946).
Deutsch, Karl W. and others, *Political Community in the North Atlantic Area* (Princeton, N.J.: Princeton University Press, 1957).
DeVisscher, Charles. *Theory and Reality in Public International Law* (Princeton, N.J.: Princeton University Press, 1957).

Djilas, Milovan. *The New Class: An Analysis of the Communist System* (New York: Frederick A. Praeger, 1957).

Draper, Theodore. *Castro's Revolution* (New York: Frederick A. Praeger, 1962).

Earle, Edward Meade. *Nationalism and Internationalism* (New York: Columbia University Press, 1951).

Ebenstein, William (ed.). *Man and the State* (New York: Rinehart & Co., Inc., 1947).

Elliott, William Yandell (ed.). *The Political Economy of American Foreign Policy* (New York: Henry Holt and Company, 1955).

Fox, William T. R. *Theoretical Aspects of International Relations* (South Bend, Ind.: University of Notre Dame Press, 1959).

Frankel, Joseph. *The Making of Foreign Policy* (New York: Oxford University Press, 1963).

Fulbright, J. William. *Prospects for the West* (Cambridge: Harvard University Press, 1963).

Fulbright, J. William. *Old Myths and New Realities* (New York: Random House, 1964).

Garthoff, Raymond L. *Soviet Strategy in the Nuclear Age* (New York: Frederick A. Praeger, 1958).

Hahn, Walter F. and Neff, John C. (eds.). *American Strategy for the Nuclear Age* (Garden City, N.Y.: Doubleday & Company, Inc., 1960).

Halle, Louis J. *Civilization and Foreign Policy* (New York: Harper and Brothers, 1955).

Hallstein, Walter. *United Europe: Challenge and Opportunity* (Cambridge, Mass.: Harvard University Press, 1962).

Hamilton, Alexander; Madison, James; and Jay, John. *The Federalist Papers,* with introduction by Clinton Rossiter (New York: The New American Library, 1961).

Herz, John H. *Political Realism and Political Idealism* (Chicago, Ill.: University of Chicago Press, 1951).

Hirshman, Albert O. *The Strategy of Economic Development* (New Haven: Yale University Press, 1957).

Hoffmann, Stanley (ed.). *Contemporary Theory in International Relations* (Englewood Cliffs, N.J.: Prentice-Hall, Inc., 1960).

Hsieh, Alice L. *Communist China's Strategy in the Nuclear Era* (Englewood Cliffs, N.J.: Prentice-Hall, Inc., 1962).

Huntington, Samuel P. *The Common Defense* (New York: Columbia University Press, 1961).

Johnson, Howard C. and Niemeyer, Gerhart. "Collective Security—The Validity of an Ideal," *International Organization,* Vol. VIII, No. 1 (February, 1954).

Kahn, Herman. *On Thermonuclear War* (Princeton: Princeton University Press, 1960).

Kaplan, Morton A. *The Revolution in World Politics* (New York: John Wiley and Sons, 1962).

Kennan, George F. *American Diplomacy, 1900-1950* (Chicago: University of Chicago Press, 1951).

Kennan, George F. *Realities of American Foreign Policy* (Princeton: Princeton University Press, 1954).

Kennedy, John F. "Toward A Strategy of Peace," U.S., *Department of State Bulletin,* Volume XLIX, No. 1253 (July 1963).

Kindleberger, Charles P. *Economic Development* (New York: McGraw-Hill, 1958).

Kirk, Russell A. *The Conservative Mind* (Chicago: Henry A. Regnery, 1953).

Kissinger, Henry A. *Nuclear Weapons and Foreign Policy* (New York: Harper and Brothers, 1957).

Kohn, Hans. *American Nationalism: An Interpretive Essay* (New York: Macmillan Company, 1957).

Larson, David L. (ed.). *The "Cuban Crisis" of 1962: Selected Documents and Chronology* (Boston: Houghton Mifflin Co., 1963).

Larson, David L. "The Foreign Policy of the United States Toward Yugoslavia: 1943-1963," unpublished thesis, The Fletcher School of Law and Diplomacy, Tufts University, Medford, Massachusetts.

LeFever, Ernest W. *Ethics and United States Foreign Policy* (New York: Meriden Books, 1957).

Lerche, Charles O. et al. *Concepts of International Politics* (Englewood, N.J.: Prentice-Hall, Inc., 1963).

Lippmann, Walter. *Essays in the Public Philosophy* (Boston: Little, Brown and Company, 1955).

Lodge, George C. *Spearheads of Democracy* (New York: Harper and Row, 1962).

Machiavelli, Niccolo. *The Prince,* with introduction by Christian Gauss (New York: The New American Library, 1952).

Mackinder, Halford J. *Democratic Ideals and Reality* (Baltimore: Penguin Books, Inc., 1944).

Mackintosh, John M. *Strategy and Tactics of Soviet Foreign Policy* (New York: Oxford University Press, 1963).

MacKinnon, Donald MacKenzie. *Christian Faith and Communist Faith* (New York: St. Martin's Press, 1953).

Marshall, Charles B. *The Limits of Foreign Policy* (New York: Holt and Rinehart, 1954).

Martin, Lawrence W. *Neutralism and Nonalignment* (New York: Frederick A. Praeger, 1962).

Mikesell, Raymond F. *United States Economic Policy and International Relations* (New York: McGraw-Hill, 1952).

Millikan, Max F. and Blackmer, Donald. *The Emerging Nations* (Boston: Little, Brown & Co., 1961).

Morgenthau, Hans J. *In Defense of the National Interest: A Critical Examination of American Foreign Policy* (New York: Alfred A. Knopf, 1951).

Morgenthau, Hans J. *Politics Among Nations: The Struggle for Power and Peace* (New York: Alfred A. Knopf, 1961).

Nicolson, Harold. *Diplomacy* (New York: Oxford University Press, 1950).

Nicolson, Harold. *Peacemaking, 1919* (Boston: Houghton Mifflin Co., 1933).

Niebuhr, Reinhold. *Moral Man and Immoral Society: A Study in Ethics and Politics* (New York: Charles Scribner's Sons, 1960).

Niebuhr, Reinhold. *The Children of Light and the Children of Darkness* (New York: Charles Scribner's Sons, 1953).

Niebuhr, Reinhold. *The Irony of American History* (New York: Charles Scribner's Sons, 1954).

Osgood, Robert Endicott. *Ideals and Self-Interest in American Foreign Policy: The Great Transformation of the Twentieth Century* (Chicago: University of Chicago Press, 1953).

Padelford, Norman J. and Lincoln, George A. *The Dynamics of International Politics* (New York: The Macmillan Company, 1962).

Parrington, Vernon L. *Main Currents in American Thought* (New York: Harcourt, Brace & Co., 1958).

Parry, Ralph Barton. *Puritanism and Democracy* (New York: Harper & Row, 1964).

Perkins, Dexter. *The American Approach to Foreign Policy* (Cambridge: Harvard University Press, 1952).

Randall, Clarence B. *A Foreign Economic Policy for the United States* (Chicago: University of Chicago Press, 1954).

Rostow, Walt W. *Stages of Economic Growth* (London: Cambridge University Press, 1959).

Rostow, Walt W. *The United States in the World Arena* (New York: Harper and Brothers, 1960).

Rusk, Dean. "The Universal Appeal of the Declaration of Independence," *U.S. Department of State Bulletin,* Volume LI, No. 1308 (July 20, 1964), pp. 74-78.

Samuelson, Paul A. *Economics: An Introductory Analysis,* Fourth Edition (McGraw-Hill Book Co., Inc., 1958).

Schelling, Thomas C. *The Strategy of Conflict* (Cambridge, Mass.: Harvard University Press, 1960).

Schwarzenberger, Georg. *Power Politics: A Study of International Society* (New York: Frederick A. Praeger, Inc., 1951).

Silvert, Kalman H. (ed.). *Expectant Peoples: Nationalism and Development* (New York: Random House, 1963).

Sokolovskii, V. O. (ed.). *Soviet Military Strategy,* translated and introduced by Herbert S. Dinerstein, Leon Goure, and Thomas W. Wolfe (Englewood Cliffs, N.J.: Prentice-Hall, Inc., 1963).

Stone, Julius. *Legal Controls of International Conflict* (New York: Holt, Rinehart and Winston, 1954).

Stromberg, Roland N. *Collective Security and American Foreign Policy* (New York: Frederick A. Praeger, 1963).

Szulc, Tad. *The Winds of Revolution* (New York: Frederick A. Praeger, 1963).

Tannenbaum, Frank. *The American Tradition in Foreign Policy* (Norman, Okla.: University of Oklahoma Press, 1955).

Thompson, Kenneth W. *American Diplomacy and Emergent Patterns* (New York: New York University Press, 1963).

Thompson, Kenneth W. *Christian Ethics and the Dilemmas of Foreign Policy* (Durham, N.C.: The Duke University Press, 1959).

Thompson, Kenneth W. "Collective Security Re-examined," *The American Political Science Review,* Vol. XLVII, No. 3 (September 1953).

Thucydides, *The Peloponnesian War,* translated by Benjamin Jowett with introductions by Hanson Baldwin and Moses Hadas. (New York: Bantam Books, Inc., 1960).

Tucker, Robert C. *The Soviet Political Mind* (New York: Frederick A. Praeger, 1963).

U.S., Congress, Senate Committee on Foreign Relations. *United States Foreign Policy,* Study No. 10, "The Principal Ideological Conflicts, Variations Thereon, Their Manifestations, and Their Present and Potential Impact on the Foreign Policy of the United States," 86th Congress, Second Session (Washington: U.S. Government Printing Office, 1960).

Williams, John H. *Economic Stability in a Changing World* (New York: Oxford University Press, 1958).

Wilson, Woodrow. "Address by the President of the United States," U.S., Congress, *Congressional Record,* 65th Congress, Second Session, Volume 54, Part 2 (Washington, D.C.: Government Printing Office, 1917), pp. 1741-1743.

Westerfield, H. Bradford. *The Instruments of America's Foreign Policy* (New York: Thomas Y. Crowell Co., 1963).

Wolfers, Arnold. "Collective Security and the War in Korea," *The Yale Review,* Vol. XLIII, No. 4 (Fall, 1954).

Wolfers, Arnold. *Discord and Collaboration: Essays on International Politics* (Baltimore: Johns Hopkins Press, 1962).

Wright, Quincy. *A Study of War,* two volumes (Chicago: Chicago University Press, 1942).

Wriston, Henry M. *Diplomacy in a Democracy* (New York: Harper and Brothers, 1956).